Fire Borne

Anthroposophy in America

By Jean W. Yeager
JANUARY 15, 2023
ANTHROPOSOPHICAL PUBLICATIONS
Fremont, Michigan USA

Abgebrannt in der Silvesternacht 1922/23.

Copyright © 2022 by Jean W. Yeager©

All rights reserved.

No portion of this book may be reproduced in any form without written permission from the publisher or author, except as permitted by U.S. copyright law.

This publication is designed to provide accurate and authoritative information in regard to the subject matter covered. It is sold with the understanding that neither the author nor the publisher is engaged in rendering legal, investment, accounting or other professional services. While the publisher and author have used their best efforts in preparing this book, they make no representations or warranties with respect to the accuracy or completeness of the contents of this book and specifically disclaim any implied warranties of merchantability or fitness for a particular purpose. No warranty may be created or extended by sales representatives or written sales materials. The advice and strategies contained herein may not be suitable for your situation. You should consult with a professional when appropriate. Neither the publisher nor the author shall be liable for any loss of profit or any other commercial damages, including but not limited to special, incidental, consequential, personal, or other damages.

Cover Art by Hermann Linde

Cover design by James D. Stewart

Editor: James D. Stewart

ISBN: 978-1-948302-47-0 paper
   978-1-948302-48-7 eBook

First edition 2023
Anthroposophical Publications
Fremont, Michigan USA

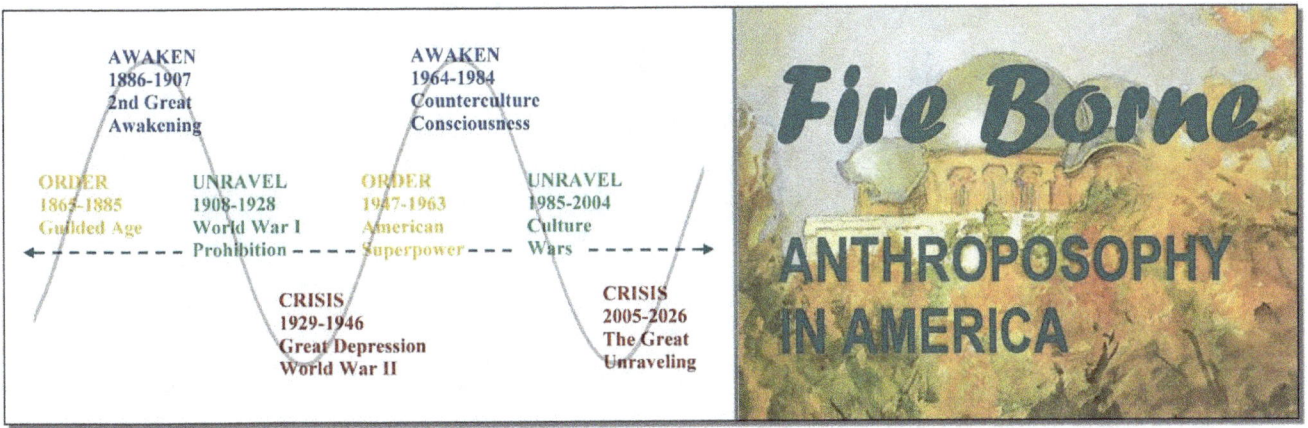

CULTURAL WAVE CHART © 2016 Jean W. Yeager[1]

FIRE BORNE INTRODUCTION

FIRE BORNE – On December 31, 1922-Jan 1, 1923, the two-domed Goetheanum building burned. It was as if the domes were gigantic spiritual pine or fir cones which, like actual cones when burned, broadcast their seeds. The fire which destroyed the domes did not stop the Anthroposophical Society but seemed to propel it worldwide. A spiritual wind bore the seeds of inspiration around the world. After the fire in 1923, the General Anthroposophical Society (G.A.S.) had to be re-founded, but already, anthroposophy was beginning to form in America and Steiner sent the "Verse for America." He was on the road starting country societies throughout Europe.

FIRE BORNE is the story of the biography of the Anthroposophical Society in America and related "daughter movements." What makes the book different is that this story is told within the context of American political, economic, cultural events as they evolved generation-by-generation from 1886-2026.

FIRE BORNE is structured on a series of cultural, generational cycles presented in the book *The Fourth Turning* by sociologists William Strauss and Neil Howe (Broadway Books, 1997) in which they establish their thesis of cultural and generational cycles which repeat throughout Western history.

The cultural cycles they present are:

1) A period of cultural STABILITY and harmony. Once this period of stability becomes "over ripe" it becomes culturally oppressive.

2) A period of AWAKENING through conscious, religious, economic, technologic, or political creativity, usually seen as a reaction to the oppressive nature of the stable culture.

3) A period of UNRAVELING of the stable culture in which counter-cultural elements appear and challenge authority in a variety of ways.

4) Finally, a CRISIS ensues in which many elements of the once stable culture are done away with or altered.

Once the culture is re-formed, then a period of STABILITY would ensue and start the process all over again.

I have illustrated this process in the CULTURAL WAVE FORM graphic below which repeats throughout this book.

---

[1] Dates / phases from THE FOURTH TURNING, William Strauss and Neil Howe, Broadway Books, 1997

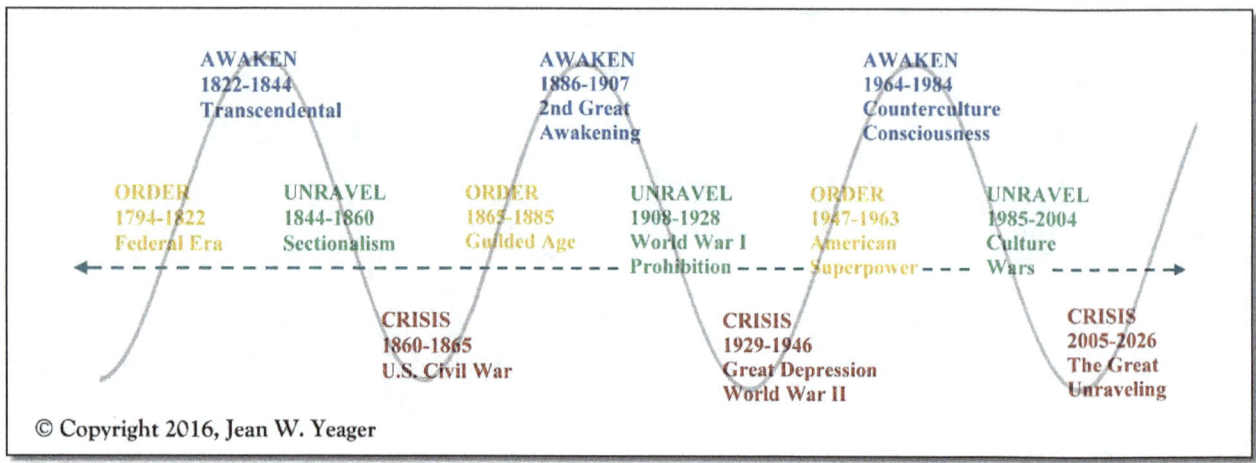

The Goetheanum building burned and the Anthroposophical Society was re-founded in a phase going from UNRAVELING just after WWI (1909-1928) into a CRISIS phase (1929-1946). Our era 1995-2004 has been an era of "Culture Wars" and UNRAVELING going into CRISIS, similar to the time when the Anthroposophical Society was re-founded.

Regardless of the "Culture Wars" and real Wars of his era, Steiner never saw anthroposophy separate from the world. At the conclusion of the 1924 re-founding of the Society – when it was born – he said:

> *"And so, my dear friends, bear out with you into the world your warm hearts in whose soil you have laid the Foundation Stone for the Anthroposophical Society, bear out with you your warm hearts in order to do work in the world that is strong in healing."*

So, FIRE BORNE has a role to remind the anthroposophical movement of the generational truth that the next phase to arrive may be as much of a period of stability and growth as you see happened between 1947-1963 when the Anthroposophical Society in America was:

"INSPIRED – KINDHEARTED – AND STRONG."

– Jean W. Yeager, 2022

FIRE BORNE CHAPTERS

CHAPTER 1 – 1886-1908 – (U.S.) "Second Great Awakening" PHASE: AWAKEN 7

U.S. GENERATION commonly called "The Lost Generation" experienced the Moral Landscape of: urban blight, massive immigration, unbridled drug use and drunkenness. Powerful religious, political and trade movements formed to combat these social ills and others such as child labor.

1908-1929 – "WWI / Prohibition" PHASE: UNRAVEL 11

U.S. GENERATION The Moral Landscape of "The G.I. Generation" was led by invention of "progress," significant rise in education, and women's suffrage but suffered in WWI's rapid technological change, chemical agriculture, widening class differences, and weak political leadership in a financial boom.

CHAPTER 2 – 1929-1946 – "Great Depression / WWII" PHASE: CRISIS 33

U.S.GENERATION the Moral Ecology of "The Silent Generation" is a Worldwide Crisis: the"Dust Bowl," the "Great Depression" an economic free fall, then Nazis and Fascists start World War II which ends with the U.S. A-Bomb attack on Japan. Anthroposophical thinking comes to the U.S. bringing a start to cultural renewal.

CHAPTER 3 – 1946-1964 "American Superpower" PHASE: ORDER (Stability) 60

U.S. GENERATION commonly called "The Baby Boomers" grow up in a Moral Ecology of suburbia, green lawns, shopping malls. Segregation by race and socially by gender, social class or sexual orientation is the norm. Corporations and "industry" won WWII and television has won the family life.

CHAPTER 4 – 1964-1984 "Counterculture Consciousness" PHASE: AWAKEN 87

U.S. GENERATION commonly called "The 13th Generation" rebel against the Moral Ecology of segregation, the Vietnam war, sexual restrictions, divorce, and abortion. They embrace risk and freedom over loyal corporatism, create a counterculture. Personal computing and personal technology originate in this era. It is a period of growth for many small spiritual groups.

CHAPTER 5 – 1985-2004 "Culture Wars" PHASE: UNRAVEL 103

U.S. GENERATION in which the Moral Landscape of the counterculture deepens and "old ways of doing things" come unraveled. The term "Cultural War" was coined in 1992 by then Presidential candidate Patrick Buchanan and describes the dramatic cultural and social unraveling which may continue through the 2020s. NGOs shift the terrain.

CHAPTER 6 – 2005-2026 "The Great Unraveling" PHASE: CRISIS 145

THIS IS A GENERATION IN A CRISIS MODE: The Moral Landscape is one in which the only thing that seems certain is change. The era starts with a Sub-Prime Mortgage melt-down which tumbles into nationwide bank failures and the Stock Market collapse. A quarter of a million people lose their jobs followed by a worldwide pandemic and hundreds of thousands of deaths. The Anthroposophical Society and "daughter movements" celebrate "Centennials Of Courage."

APPENDIX 171

HISTORICAL DOCUMENTS – The *Amicus Curiae* Court Brief filed by the Anthroposophical Society in the First Amendment Federal Lawsuit (2004). The Plaintiff failed to prove Anthroposophy is a religion for Establishment Clause purposes.

ADDITIONAL PUBLICATIONS

FIRE BORNE ADMINISTRATIVE COLLECTION

This is a compilation of By-Laws from 1933 to the Present. These show how the structure of the Society has changed over the years. As the General Council said in 1981 – "By-Laws provide the framework into which the Spiritually active life can unfold."

AKNIGHTS COLLECTION

An international task group formed at the 2000 Michael Conference to defend Anthroposophy, Waldorf Education, and Rudolf Steiner against internet hate attacks worldwide. This is a collection of documents and research gathered during that work for more than a decade. Other administrative documents and reports are included. This group was formed coincidentally with a comment Steiner made 4 April 1916 about such a "defensive" group arising around the year 2000.
https://wn.rudolfsteinerelib.org/Lectures/Dates/19160404p01.html

NOTES. Bibliography

ANTHROPOSOPHICAL PUBLICATIONS
https://AnthroposophicalPublications.org/

ABOUT THE AUTHOR Jean W. Yeager

38 Kendall Ave.
Rutland, VT
05701
jwyeager2@gmail.com
(802) 855-8877

Professional background site: https://www.the-three.com
Linkedin: https://www.linkedin.com/in/jeanyeager2/
bLog: https//www.threesimplequestions.blogspot.com

ACADEMIC/PROFESSIONAL

1970	– B.A. English, Colorado State University (CSU).
1971	– Post-grad studies Radio TV Film, CSU.
1972-1978	– Editor Regional Editions, *The United Methodist Reporter*, Dallas, TX. Established UMR book publishing division.
1978-1982	– The Stanford Agency, award winning copywriter / speechwriter.
1982-1989	– Jean W. Yeager creative services for companies and ad agencies across the U.S.
1989-1991	– Research, taught and consulted in Organizational Development at The Centre For Social Development, Emerson College, Sussex, U.K.
1991-1997	– Organization Development Consultant, Envision Associates, Spring Valley, NY.
1992-1994	– Managing Editor, *BIODYNAMICS* Journal
1993-1995	– Kimberton Waldorf School, Director of Development.
1996-2006	– Anthroposophical Society in America (ASiA), Administrative Director
1997-2002	– Biodynamic Association, Board member: Vice President 1998-2002, Marketing Committee 1998-2002
1997-2005	– Sunbridge College, Board Member: Board Secretary 2004
2007-2010	– Centre for Anthroposophy, taught Biography (Phase Development Theory) to Waldorf faculty around the country.
1998-2001	– Waldorf Teacher Development Association. Board Member
1998-Present:	Teaching in Maximum Security Prisons self-development programs: Introduction To Biography (Phases and Stages") and Six Subsidiary Exercises.
2005-2008	– Rudolf Steiner College, Board Chair
2013	– Camphill Ghent, Board Member.

FICTION / NON-FICTION

- 2020 – AGELESS AUTHORS, Winner Fiction, *"Old Pirates Of The Heart."*
- 2018 – AGELESS AUTHORS, Finalist Creative Non-Fiction, *"That Ol' Certainty"*, Story Category: "Dang! I Wish I Hadn't Done That!" https://www.agelessauthors.com/
- 2018 – RUTLAND READER, *"Never Too Late, AGELESS AUTHORS Open Reading"*, Phoenix Bookstore https://www.rutlandreader.com/its-never-too-late-ageless-authors-open-reading/

THEATRICAL

- Finalist 2022 Tennessee Williams One Act Competition, Tennessee Williams Festival, New Orleans; *Prisoner #101065 Book Report And Commentary By Nicolo Machiavelli.*
- Finalist, 2019 Las Vegas International Scriptwriting Competition, Category Western, *"How Santa Claus Came To Simpson's Bar"*
- Produced, 2018 *"Clothesline"*, 15th Annual One Act Play Festival, Dorset Players, Dorset, VT, 10:00

- Finalist, 2016 Tennessee Williams One Act Competition, Tennessee Williams Festival, New Orleans; *Christmas In The War Zone,* 25:00
- Produced, 2013 Theatre One "Slice Of Life" Festival, Middleboro, MA, *Dante In Jiffy Lube,* 10:00
- Produced, 2013 Lucky Penny Theatre, Napa Valley Playhouse, Napa CA, *How Santa Claus Came to Zone Whisky Alpha Romeo (W.A.R.),* 10:00
- Finalist, 2013 Collective NYC, Collective 10-Minute Festival, *How Santa Claus Came to Zone Whisky Alpha Romeo (W.A.R)*

BOOKS

2018 – THE KITE OF YOUR GENIUS LIFTS YOUR COMMUNITY - eBook
2015 –*TH3 SIMPLE QUESTIONS Slice Open Everyday Life* - 126 pg, 44 Chapters / Published by WestBow Press ISBN: 978-1-4908-7123-3
Based on bLog – www.threesimplequestions.blogspot.com

SOCIAL MEDIA

BLOGS

THREE SIMPLE QUESTIONS https://www.threesimplequestions.blogspot.com
200 – 1,000 / month readership
TIMELINEWONK – https://www.timelinewonk.blogspot.com
Timelines Of The Context Of Your Life - 69 / month readership
CALENDAR OF VIRTUES – https://www.calendarofvirtues.blogspot.com
110 / month readership

TWITTER

@THREESIMPLEQUEST – 931 followers
@TIMELINEWONK -

LIBRARIES COLLECTIONS

THE JEAN W. YEAGER COLLECTION - Duke University Libraries
John W. Hartman Center For Sales, Advertising Marketing History in the U.S.
https://library.duke.edu/rubenstein/findingaids/yeagerjean/

Advertising copy writer and artist who managed his own agency, Jean W. Yeager, Inc. based in Dallas, Tex. Later taught at several Waldorf Method institutions; director of the Anthroposophical Society in America. Collection spans the years 1959-2012 and includes correspondence, direct marketing printed materials, print advertisements and recordings of radio and television broadcast commercials and public service messages that document Yeager's career producing advertising primarily for companies based in Texas. Examples of Yeager's original art are also included. Formats include audio- and videocassettes, audio reels and 16mm films. Companies represented include 7-Eleven, Coca-Cola, Frito-Lay, Radio Shack, Republic Health Corporation, Schenley, Southland Corporation, and Sterling Optical. The collection also touches on Yeager's involvement with the Anthroposophical Society and related enterprises, including Waldorf Method schools such as the Kimberton Waldorf School in Detroit. Acquired as part of the John W. Hartman Center for Sales, Advertising & Marketing History.

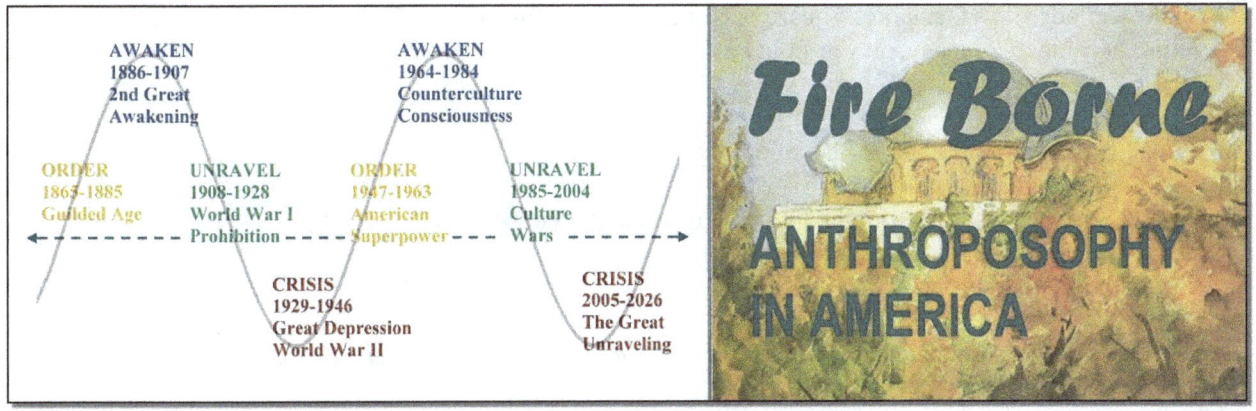

CULTURAL WAVE CHART © 2016 Jean W. Yeager[2]

1886-1908 – (U.S.) "Second Great Awakening"
PHASE: AWAKEN

U.S. GENERATION commonly called *"The Lost Generation"* experienced the Moral Landscape of urban blight, massive immigration, unbridled drug use and drunkenness. Powerful religious, political and trade movements formed to combat these social ills and others such as child labor.

Abbreviations:	RS Rudolf Steiner	ED Education	MED Medical	ASiA Anthroposophical Society in America
AG Agriculture	SM Spirit Matters	TF Threefold	SCI Science	GAS General Anthroposophical Society

All timeline entries are for U.S. events unless otherwise noted.

1886
– U.S. population in 1860 was 30 million and increased to 75 million by 1900.

END NOTE (1) – THE NATIONAL GRANGE – ORDER OF PATRONS OF HUSBANDRY *Encouraged farm families to band together and "… supported efforts by politicians to regulate rates charged by the railroads and grain warehouses. It claimed credit for the ideas of the* Cooperative Extension Service, Rural Free Delivery, *and the* Farm Credit System*."(Wikipedia)*

– Between 1820 and 1913 (WWI), nearly six million Germans (Lutheran or Catholic) immigrated; after 1865, nineteen-million Italians (Catholic), English (Presbyterian or Episcopalian). The previous large wave of Germans was following the German revolution of 1848, which came to be called "The 48ers."

– 1880s – Theosophical Society was founded in New York State in 1875 by Madame Blavatsky and Col. Olcott. Blavatsky maintained that she had been expressly "guided" to meet him (Col. Olcott). She herself later rejected Spiritualism, insisting she was never a Spiritualist. 'I have always known the reality of mediumistic phenomena, and defended that reality, that is all.' She supported Olcott in his efforts to interest Spiritualists and scientists to work together to establish the generally accepted recognition of the spiritual realities underlying the world as we have come to know it. It was this search for a mutually agreeable basis for Science and spiritualism to work together, which led to the founding of the "Theosophical Society." (*"Into The Heart's Land,"* Page 44)

– 20 million cattle were driven north from Texas and Kansas to board railway cars for processing plants in Nebraska, Iowa and Chicago.

---

[2] Dates / phases from THE FOURTH TURNING, William Strauss and Neil Howe, Broadway Books, 1997

– A bomb exploded in Haymarket Square, Chicago during a meeting of protesters against the McCormick Harvesting Machine Company. Seven police officers and four workers died and seventy police officers are wounded.

– American Federation of Labor (AFL) union organized.

– The Statue of Liberty, a gift from the French government, dedicated.

– Karl Marx publishes *Das Kapital*.

– Robert Louis Stevenson publishes *The Strange Case of Dr. Jekyll and Mr. Hyde*.

1887
– Edison / Swann electric lamps patented.

– U.S. Patent for telephone given to Alexander G. Bell.

1888
– Nikola Tesla, electric motor.

– Radio waves produced, Hertz.

– Eifel tower is built.

1889
– Benjamin Harrison inaugurated President.

1890
– With massive immigration, unemployment, farm failures, etc. and barrels of Corn Whisky and German beer making entrepreneurism, public drunkenness common. The reaction by religious "disciples" to this unambiguous moral degradation came on a massive basis and was known as "Social Gospel."

– Approximately 23,000 children worked in factories in thirteen southern states.

– Social Gospel preachers led huge rallies and tent revivals sharply attacking the Gilded Age's (1865-1885) drunkenness, plutocracy, wealth disparity, and sought to end child labor and dangerous factories.

– 40% of the population lived in poverty.

END NOTE (2) – SCHOOLING IN THE 1890s by URSULA K. LeGUIN
https://firebornecom.files.wordpress.com/2022/02/1890s-schooling-ursula-leguin.pdf
"Teaching from the first grade up centered on 'English,' not only because immigrants wanted their children fluent in it, but because literature – fiction, scientific works, history, poetry – was a major form of social currency. (Editor's note: with the very high level of immigration in the 1890s, it also explains why teaching English in public schools was an important part of being in America.) ..."

– Massive corn harvests continued and Corn Whiskey was made available at a very low price. Many asserted that drinking Corn Whiskey was a patriotic act which helped the farmers.

– REVOLUTIONARY NEW THINKING: "Scientific Management," developed by Frederick W. Taylor. His "time and motion" studies forever change manufacturing, bringing hourly wages, "piece goods" work, assembly line work and labor on the "shift" basis. This made "mass production" economic and kicked manufacturing in the U.S. into high gear. Eventually, when "scientific management" was applied to all factories, it meant that American life would transform from a farm / agricultural focus to an urban, industrial focus.

1891
RS – Germany – Rudolf Steiner awarded PhD in Natural Science from University of Rostock.

– U.S. Labor organizes and many trade unions form.

– Public Education Reform Movement tries to de-politicize education.

– "Muckraking" journalism takes on corporate monopolies, political machines and child labor.

1892
– The *"Populist Movement"* – the *People's Party* of agrarian populists reforms.

1893
– *Panic of 1893* – a serious depression produces political upheaval and the so-called *"War with the Wealthy."*

– Telegraph and telephone systems span the U.S.

– 150,000 United Mine Workers go on strike.

– Grover Cleveland inaugurated President.

– 1.7 million children under the age of 15 work in mills, mines and factories.

– **The Anti-Saloon League forms as a significant politically active group of Protestant churches which focuses on electing candidates who agreed with their agenda. They lobby for no taxation of churches and prohibition.** The influence of this movement still resounds in Protestant churches today.

WORLDWIDE PROHIBITION MOVEMENT
U.S. – Anti-Saloon League forms of all major denominations and becomes politically active. Lobbies for no taxation of churches and prohibition. Targets candidates for the first time.

END NOTE (3) – *ANTI-SALOON LEAGUE* ABOUT THIS WORLDWIDE SOCIAL / RELIGIOUS MOVEMENT

1894
RS – Germany – Steiner publishes *Philosophy Of Spiritual Activity*.

1897
– William McKinley inaugurated President.

1900
– Massive German immigration. Midwestern cities of St. Louis, Milwaukee, Cleveland, Chicago more than 40% German immigrants.

– Model "T" introduced by Henry Ford.

– First transmission of speech by radio waves.

END NOTE (4) – TIMELINE OF RUDOLF STEINER AGAINST ANTI-SEMITISM Starting in 1900, Rudolf Steiner spoke about the dangers of Anti-Semitism.

1901

– William McKinley assassinated – Theodore Roosevelt becomes President.

1902
RS – Germany – Steiner leads the Bruno Society.

– Germany – Steiner enters the Theosophical Society and becomes its leader in Germany. The spiritually "awakened" social conditions attract large crowds to lectures on *Karma* and *Reincarnation*.

– Theodore Roosevelt active in "Trust Busting."

1903
– First manned flight, the Wright Brothers. Countries around the world begin building aircraft for military purposes.

1904
– Radioactive substances research, Marie Curie.

1905
– Germany – *"Theory of Relativity,"* Albert Einstein

1906
– First AM radio program broadcast.

1907
– *Panic of 1907* financial collapse due to influence of railroad, steel, copper, sugar trusts.

COMBINED END NOTES CHAPTERS 1 & 2 on Page 20

---

9 March 1924

THE WORK OF THE SOCIETY
"Life, Nature, And The Cultivation Of Anthroposophy"

Members will have observed that in the public lectures which I give on behalf of the Anthroposophical Society I take every opportunity to refer to such points of knowledge or insight as our age has developed on the subject I am speaking of. I do so because Anthroposophy must not stand before the world like a sectarian belief, conceived in an arbitrary way. Anthroposophy must always bring to expression what it really is, namely the wider outlook on the world, the fuller conduct of life, for which our age is calling.
-- Rudolf Steiner
https://rudolfsteinerelib.org/Books/GA026/English/ASGB1963/GA026_c08.html

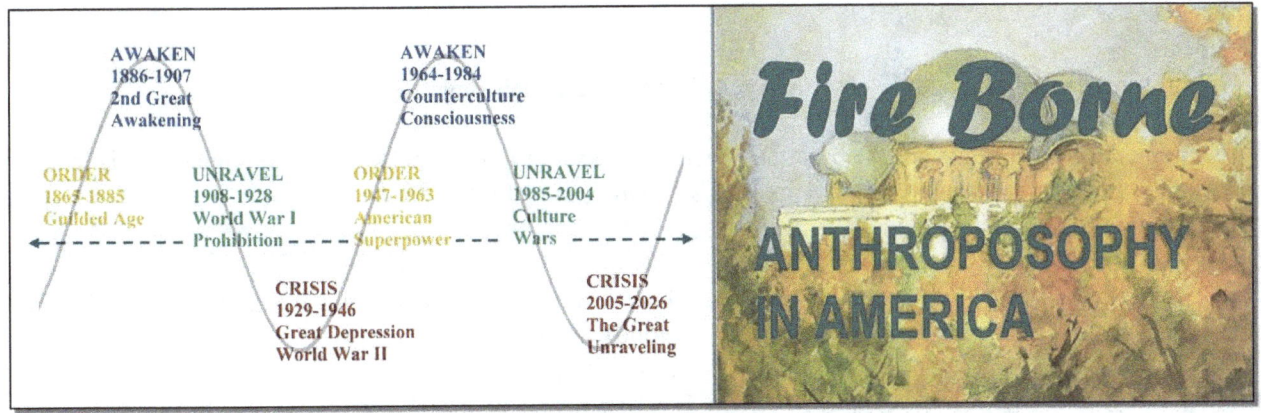
CULTURAL WAVE CHART © 2016 Jean W. Yeager

1908-1928 – "WWI / Prohibition"
PHASE: UNRAVEL

U.S. GENERATION The Moral Landscape of "The G.I. Generation" was led by invention of "progress," significant rise in education, and women's suffrage but suffered in WWI's rapid technological change, chemical agriculture, widening class differences, and weak political leadership in a financial boom.

Abbreviations:	RS Rudolf Steiner	ED Education	MED Medical	ASiA Anthroposophical Society in America
AG Agriculture	SM Spirit Matters	TF Threefold	SCI Science	GAS General Anthroposophical Society

All timeline entries are for U.S. events unless otherwise noted.

1908
– Ford assembly line revolutionizes auto manufacturing and transportation.

1909
– William Taft inaugurated President.

– Germany – Carl Bosch/Fritz Haber develop process to create synthetic ammonia, the key ingredient for fertilizer and bombs. This revolutionizes Industrial Agriculture and escalates German munitions production including poisonous gas.

– Germany drops one bomb a day on French civilians in Paris. U.S. press escalates outrage and anti-German sentiments. In response Germany leads a military parade singing *"Blood Will Drip From Our Knives."* German leaders declare they will target passenger ships with U-Boats (submarines).

1910
– 53% of all Americans live on farms.

– 10 million Europeans immigrate to America to flee WWI which causes 40% poverty.

– Immigrants include radicals and Communists.

– Two million children under age of 15 work in factories.

RS – Steiner publishes *"Occult Science: An Outline."*

1912
– U.S. Progressive Party slogan: *"Grassroots and Boots"* Jeremiah Beveridge.

RS – Steiner and Frau Smits speak about the spiritual forces that live in speaking and singing and this leads to considerations for a spiritual art of movement. *(Eurythmy Spring Valley, History)*

1913
RS – Steiner breaks from Theosophical Society and begins General Anthroposophical Society (GAS). His ideas went into an "unraveling" social / political situation following WWI.

END NOTE (5) – "LIVING IN A 'FOOL'S PARADISE' STEINER NEVER LET UP"

– Rudolf Steiner lays first *Foundation Stone*.

END NOTE (6) – "FOUNDATION STONE STUMBLING BLOCK FOR 'TOAD NATURES.'" – Rudolf Steiner

1914
– WWI starts. Europe in disarray. Mechanical tanks, airplanes, cheap ammonia for munitions of all types makes this war unlike any ever before seen in Europe. Death by asphyxiation from toxic gases was new and leaders were unprepared for the horror.

Photo Source – The Anthroposophical Publications website.

1915
– U.S. Eugenics Movement starts in New York by Madison Grant whose book *"The Passing of the Great Race"* lays scientific foundation for white supremacy. Grant's book becomes "official" Nazi scientific reference for Aryan supremacy. The basis for anti-immigration laws of "mentally deficient" people.

– Eurythmy has beginnings as a stage art in Dornach. *(Eurythmy Spring Valley, History)*

– Many U.S. states pass anti-German laws. Iowa bans speaking German.

1915-1920 – *Agricultural Industrialization* **using synthetic nitrogen fertilizer, monocropping, no rotation, and massive steam powered tractors.** >>>>

1916
– Second Ku Klux Klan is remodeled as a modern business system with recruiters.

1917
– U.S. Congress enacts *Espionage and Sedition Act* targeting foreigners. J. Edgar Hoover's FBI enforces with gusto.

Photo Source – Jean Yeager – My great-grandpa's steam tractor 1916.

RS TF – Germany – Steiner begins major *Threefold Social Order* speaking tour lecturing in factories to 1-2,000 workers at a time.

In this memorandum Steiner detailed his thoughts about "social life struggling to free itself from nationalism." What came to be called a "Threefold Commonwealth" the Memorandum, contained the key sentence:

> *"When human beings become free, so will the nations become free through them."*

END NOTE (7) – THE THREEFOLD MEMORANDUM

1917 – Rudolf Steiner publishes the *"Memorandum: An Appeal to the German People and the Cultural World"* which is signed by over 250 prominent people in Europe and circulated to leaders.

Over 80,000 copies of the *Memorandum* and text about the "Threefold Social Order" were sold.

END NOTE (8) – "THREEFOLD MEETS NATIONALISM – THE TRAJECTORY TOWARD THE GOETHEANUM FIRE"

EHRENFRIED PFEIFFER, then a student working in a factory, describes seeing Rudolf Steiner defending his ideas in audiences of Nationalists and Communists.

– Woodrow Wilson gives war message targeting "disloyalty" of German-Americans.

END NOTE (9) – THE KARMA OF UNTRUTHFULNESS – "Who Is paying for that opinion?"
RS TF – 1916-1917 – RS gives lecture series "THE KARMA OF UNTRUTHFULNESS" in which he describes the major international media technology and processes that creates a "fog of untruthfulness.." He says that the most crucial question of anything in the media is "who is paying for that opinion?" pg. 139.

1918
World War I ends. The end of combat meant that there was a huge stockpile of ammonia-based munitions which could be re-purposed as fertilizer. Worldwide government programs promoted the extensive use of these products which were seen to be the solution to worldwide food shortages.

END NOTE (10) – POSIONOUS CHEMICALS BANNED IN WAR BUT NOT AGRICULTURE

GAS – Switzerland – Anthroposophical world headquarters building, the Goetheanum, finished.

– U.S. 2 million job seeking soldiers return home. Starts post-war financial depression

ASiA – Discrimination against anthroposophists in the U.S. Intense anti-German sentiments led to anthroposophists in New York City being investigated by the Secret Service.

– Flu epidemic kills 500,000.

– Every state requires children to complete public elementary education.

– J. Edgar Hoover put in charge of "Radical Division" at Department of Justice. Creates "enemies file" of 200,000 individuals and organizations.

1919
TF – Steiner gives Threefold lectures at Waldorf-Astoria cigarette factory and Emil Molt asks him to lecture on education.

ED – First Waldorf/Steiner school founded in Stuttgart. *"The first school had twelve founding teachers who participated in a 14 day seminar with Rudolf Steiner exploring his anthroposophical ideas regarding the nature of man and education that focuses on developing character. They learned on-the-job while teaching their first classes, children and teachers learning together."* https://www.waldorf-100.org/en/waldorf-education/history/

– U.S. – 18th Amendment on Prohibition ratified banning production and consumption of alcohol.

– Labor strikes – 1.2 million workers of various unions strike.

– Severe financial depression in change from wartime to domestic economy in U.S. and Germany. 2-million U.S. soldiers return home.

– Terrorists bomb buildings in major cities. U.S. Attorney General says 5-million Communists plan government overthrow. This launches the *"Great Red Scare."*

1920
– U.S. Women's right to vote granted nationally after several decades of advancement in states.

– U.S. – Large newspaper publishing syndicates formed and published worldwide – THE HERALD TRIBUNE and NEW YORK TIMES. These two news sources dominated media because they owned newspapers in all the major cities in the U.S. and Europe. As radio gained influence in the 1920s these syndicates bought up major stations in major markets.

– U.S. – Syndicated newspaper columns began to emerge, gained readers and gained cultural influence around the world. Most popular were "Will Rogers Says," "Dear Abby" letters and comic strips. *"New York Day-By-Day"* by O.O. McIntyre appeared in 400 newspapers daily.

ASiA – END NOTE (11) – *"The Earliest Days Of Anthroposophy" In America* **– THE THREEFOLD COMMUNITY**
"... *a small band of anthroposophists – students of Rudolf Steiner – ran a rooming house, a laundry, a furniture-making shop, and a vegetarian restaurant near Carnegie Hall. Led by Ralph Courtney, members of the Threefold Commonwealth Group included Gladys Barnett (later Hahn), May Laird-Brown, Louise Bybee, and Charlotte Parker. Not the first association of anthroposophists in New York, the Threefold Group soon became the most active and lively in their efforts to put into practice the social ideals indicated in the writings and lectures of Rudolf Steiner."* "The Earliest Days of Anthroposophy" by Hilda Deighton (1890-1976) published in the *Winter 1984-85 Newsletter of the Society reported on this encounter with the Secret Service in 1918 – see End Note 11.*

END NOTE (12) – DIVERSITY IN THE ANTHROPOSOPHICAL SOCIETY 1900s-1920s *Anthroposophical Newsletter 1984-85.* "Although anti-German feeling was very strong, we continued to hold our meetings in New York. The (Carnegie Hall) studio was full of the precious German lecture cycles. One afternoon as Mr. Greene was teaching, three Secret Service men knocked on the door, took suitcases of lectures for examination, and coldly insisted that he go with them for questioning ..."

TF – Steiner founds "THE COMING DAY ASSOCIATION" as a shareholding corporation to "… engage in and directly support, independent, spiritual, cultural enterprises. … it was a landmark on the road to understanding the real role of the economy in a threefold social organism. … it became clear that … Coming Day had not succeeded in creating a new socioeconomic culture ... in the spring of 1923, Steiner resigned the administrative council of the association." *(In The Heart's Land,* pgs. 406-407)

RS TF – Steiner founds FUTURUM AG, the Swiss counterpart to the Coming Day. "The whole episode, however, sheds light on the dilemma in which Rudolf Steiner found himself – on more than one occasion … it was the initiative, the enthusiasm, the will to help that he especially valued. ... The Futurum itself was liquidated." In 1995, Christoph Lindenberg wrote later, "The seeds of the ideas and impulses have sprouted at last, after seventy-five years." *(In The Heart's Land,* pgs.408 -409)

RS MED – Europe – Steiner gives lectures to doctors which launch Anthroposophically-extended Medicine.

MED – Ehrenfried Pfeiffer studies with Steiner.

AG Steiner is approached by farmers who are beginning to see the negative effects of artificial nitrogen fertilizers on their farms, the cultural/economic pressure for more and cheaper food production to feed hungry citizens. When not on the road with lectures on Social Threefolding, Steiner begins initial research as background to the Agriculture research.

– U.S. – There were four (4) AM radio stations in the U.S. and only a handful around the world.

– U.S. – J. Edgar Hoover directs the largest mass arrests in U.S. history rounding up 10,000 "disloyalists," immigrants, subversives, liberals, suspected anarchists and Communists. Anyone who asked about someone arrested was also arrested.

END NOTE (13) – "VOELKISCHER BEOBACHER"
Germany – Steiner attacked by Adolf Hitler in the leading Germanic, Nationalistic, Anti-Semitic Nazi publication for his working with Jews including Zionists.

> **"Men of the State Or National Criminals?" by Adolf Hitler**
> "… And, who is behind this devilishness? The Jew! Friend of Doctor Rudolf Steiner, the friends of Simons (German Minister of Finance) …"
> In *Voelkischer Beobacher*, 15 March 1921

1921
RS Germany – Steiner asked to give esoteric insights to priests who found the Christian Community For Religious Renewal.

RS TF – Economics Course in which Steiner describes associative economics and Social Threefolding.

– U.S. – Radio station KYW, a 50,000 watt AM station a was launched in Chicago by Westinghouse Electronic and Manufacturing Co. and broadcast covered the entire Midwest from the Rocky Mountains to the Gulf of Mexico to the east coast.

MED AG – Ehrenfried Pfeiffer put in charge of testing Bio-dynamic preparations in the Bio-Chemical Lab at the Goetheanum with Ita Wegman, MD. End Note 14 describes the work.
END NOTE (14) – 1921 RESEARCHING BIOLOGICAL DYNAMIC FORCES

1922 –
– U.S. Congress passes *Dillingham Immigrations Restrictions Act*, a step in ending U.S. "Open Door" policy based on Eugenics propaganda to keep "drooling mentally defectives" from immigrating into the U.S.

– U.S. – AM radio bursts into culture. The number of stations went from 28 to 570.

RS TF – *RIOT AT STEINER'S MUNICH LECTURE* –
Proto-Nazis ("Brownshirts") physically attack Steiner in Munich at a Threefold lecture.
New York Times May 15, 1922 >>>>

> **RIOT AT MUNICH LECTURE.**
> Reactionaries Storm Platform When Steiner Discusses Theosophy.
> Copyright, 1923, by the New York Times Company.
> Special Cable to THE NEW YORK TIMES.
> BERLIN, May 16. — Munich enjoyed a riotous demonstration when Germany's high priest of Theosophy, Rudolf Steiner, delivered a lecture on "Vitalization of Thought," before an audience more than half composed of women. Organized reactionaries, Nationalists and anti-Semites attended the lecture in force, and toward the end the electric lights were switched off and pandemonium broke loose. Lighted firecrackers and stink bombs were thrown at the long haired Theosophist, and then Steiner's foes stormed the stage and free fight ensued until the police cleared the hall.
> Then the demonstrators marched to Railroad Station Square with the intention of hauling down the Republican colors. But these are now taken in at dark and secreted in safe places. The chagrined demonstrators therefore contented themselves with singing the imperialistic "Flag Song" around the flagless flagpoles.

– U.S. governmental incentives to "industrialize" agriculture has effect of boosting debt from purchasing large equipment and increasing costs.

– Germany – mirrors the industrialization of agriculture and increased artificial fertilizer.

GAS – Switzerland – **Anthroposophical world headquarters, the Goetheanum building is burned on New Year's Eve, 1922/23.** *"The fire made its murderous progress. First the two domes collapsed; then the walls were swallowed in flames. The big windows melting in the tremendous heat. ... Now nothing remained but two circles: one of fourteen columns, the other of twelve. They stood like flaming torches in the black night sky, a sight of both horror and beauty."* (A Student's Memories of Rudolf Steiner, Lisa Dreher Monges, JOURNAL FOR ANTHROPOSOPHY, Fall 2005, pgs. 100-101)
Photo Source– The Anthroposophical Society in America website.

1923 –
RS GAS – Many young Germans came into the Anthroposophical Society in Germany but "... found that the Anthroposophical Society was not the community they longed for. ... Rudolf Steiner knew what they longed for, and needed. But, the only way he could see to achieve this was to recommend the creation of a second, independent Society. ... In Stuttgart the Independent Anthroposophical Society was founded alongside the existing society." (*Into the Heart's Land*, pgs. 56-57)

RS GAS – In February, one thousand members met in a special Meeting of the German Anthroposophical Society in Stuttgart "It became increasingly clear that, for Steiner ... that both society and building would have to be rebuilt from the inside out." (*Into the Heart's Land*, pgs. 58.)
END NOTE (15) – "RUDOLF STEINER ON CULTIVATING ANTHROPOSOPHY THROUGH A SOCIETY?

RS GAS – END NOTE (16) – THE FOUNDATION STATUTE
CHRISTMAS FOUNDATION STONE MEETING – Re-founding of the General Anthroposophical Society (GAS) in Switzerland. The Executive Council of the Anthroposophical Society consisted of Albert Steffen, Marie Steiner, Elizabeth Vreede, Guenther Wachsmuth, Ita Wegman and Rudolf Steiner as President. At this meeting, Steiner gave the FOUNDATION STATUTE or By-Laws (the Swiss legal term is "Principles") for the General Anthroposophical Society. The School for Spiritual Science at the Goetheanum is the center of the Society, or the first sphere or Spiritual/Cultural sector of activity. Groups, Branches and individuals comprise the Membership of the Society, and may be located around the world. There is a third sphere or sector, the so-called "Daughter Movements" which are economic enterprises inspired by Anthroposophy (Waldorf education, Biodynamics, Medicine, the Arts, Publishing, etc.)

ASiA – U.S. Anthroposophical Society in America was founded in New York City with 172 members. Purchased a series of buildings before 211 Madison Ave. became the HQ. Threefold Farm was used for conferences. They operated informally as the number of Groups of the Society formed – SEE the 1927 NEWSLETTER in which groups in major cities are named. Group growth continued so that by 1933, the Anthroposophical Society in America incorporated in the State of New York.

The 1933 By-Laws subscribe the American Society to the Foundation Statute but, due to Swiss law, refer to it as the "Principles." The American Society incorporated as a Non-Profit Membership Organization and are published in CHAPTER 2 - 1929-1946 - End Notes Page 41 and are included in a separate publication ADMINISTRATIVE COLLECTION.

ASiA – END NOTE (17) – VIRGINIA SEASE HAD MUCH TO SAY ABOUT THE *"THREEFOLD (AMERICA) VERSE"* AND LEADERSHIP IN THE FUTURE.
"The United States of America received a great gift from Rudolf Steiner in 1923: the so called 'America Verse' given for the Foundation of the Threefold Group which was transmitted by a Swiss messenger directly from Rudolf Steiner to Ralph Courtney. Ralph Courtney met Rudolf Steiner in Paris in 1906 and later became a strong voice internationally for the Threefold Social Order. This verse was translated into English by Frederick

Heckel, a long-time editor of the Society's Newsletter." -Virginia Sease, Dornach, quoted in *BEING HUMAN* February 2020,

Threefold Verse	Dreifacher Vers
May our feeling penetrate	Dringe unser Fühlen
Into the center of our heart,	In unseres Herzens Mittelpunkt
And seek, in love, to unite itself	Und suche in Liebe sich zu vereinen
With the human beings seeking the same goal,	Mit den Menschen gleichen Zieles
With the spirit beings who, bearing grace,	Mit den Geistern die gnadevoll
Strengthening us from realms of light	Auf unser ernstlich herzliches Streben
And illuminating our love,	Aus Lichtregionen uns stärkend
Are gazing down upon	Und unsere Liebe erhellend
Our earnest, heart-felt striving.	Herunterschauen.
Translation by Frederick Heckel	*Rudolf Steiner*

ASHI – Anthroposophical Society in Hawaii formed. Lotti Ferreri was asked to write to Steiner about events and activities. (*Into The Heart's Land*, pg. 323)

1924
RS AG – END NOTE (18) – 1924 FOOD QUALITY DEGRADATION LEADS TO AGRICULTURE COURSE AND BIOLOGICAL THINKING
Steiner gives the *Agriculture Course* of principles of biological dynamic forces.
Ehrenfried Pfeiffer works in the laboratory on Biodynamic Preparations.

ED – Eurythmy training begins in Stuttgart, Germany. *(Eurythmy Spring Valley, History)*

– Switzerland – Research Circle of the Science Section of the Anthroposophical Society at the Goetheanum is formed to scientifically test bio-dynamic preparations. Pfeiffer organizes.

– U.S. Anti-Germanic laws pass in many states. Immigration laws do away with former "open door" policy.

– U.S. Eugenics Council advises Congress regarding Immigration Laws.

1925
AG Switzerland – Bio-Dynamic preparations continued testing by Science Section.

– GENEVA PROTOCOL FOR THE PROHIBITION OF THE USE IN WAR OF ASPHYXIATING, POISONOUS OR OTHER GASES, AND OF BACTERIOLOGICAL METHODS OF WARFARE was signed and agreed to by the combatant countries. There was one exclusion – ammonia and resulting nitrogenous compounds were specifically allowed to be used in agriculture. To policy makers, the application of chemicals in agriculture for fertilizer to increase crop yields seemed "scientific" and epitomized "progress."

END NOTE (19) – ORGANIC AGRICULTURE HISTORY

RS Switzerland – Rudolf Steiner dies in March. There is disagreement about the cause. After Steiner's death in April 1925, the individuals remaining on the Council could not see a way of working together or agree on how to continue the work left behind after Steiner's death. Tensions, hostility and the forming of factions and groups culminated in 1934-35. *(Anthroposophy Worldwide, No. 1-2, 2018, pg. 2)*

1926

– U.S. – liquid fuel rockets created and tested by Robert Goddard.

– U.S. – Anthroposophic Press started in New York.

– U.S. – Threefold Educational Foundation starts an anthroposophical community 30 miles northeast of New York City – includes schools, farms and businesses.

1927
END NOTE (20) – NEWSLETTER FOR MEMBERS VOL 1, NO 1

THE ANTHROPOSOPHICAL MOVEMENT IN AMERICA – LETTER FOR MEMBERS 1927 – VOL 1, NO 1

NEWS LETTER FOR MEMBERS

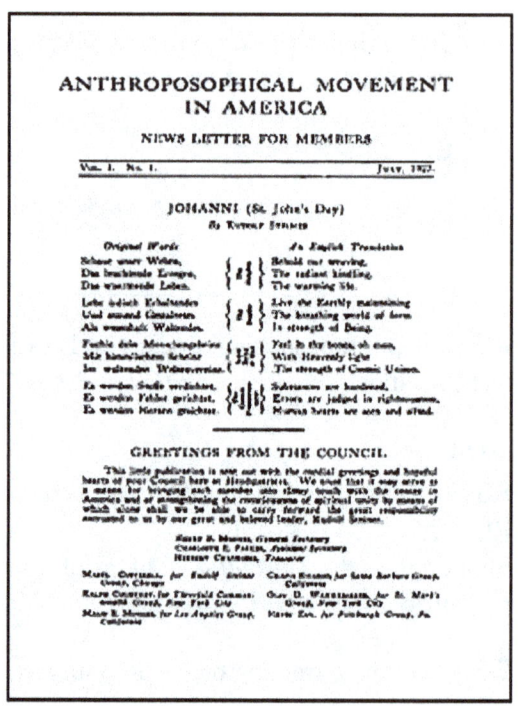

<SNIP> GREETINGS FROM THE COUNCIL This little publication is sent out with the cordial greetings and hopeful hearts of your Council here at Headquarters. We trust that it may serve as a means for bringing each member into closer touch with the center in America and of strengthening the consciousness of spiritual unity by means of which alone shall we be able to carry forward the great responsibility entrusted to us by our great and beloved leader, Rudolf Steiner. Henry B. Monges, General Secretary Charlotte E. Parker, Assistant Secretary Herbert Chaudiere, Treasurer Mabel Cotterell, for Rudolf Steiner Group, Chicago Ralph Courtney, for Threefold Commonwealth Group, New York City Maud B. Monges, for Los Angeles Group, California Gracia Ricardo, for Santa Barbara Group, California Olin D. Wannamaker, for St. Mark's Group, New York City Henri Zay, for Pittsburgh Group, Pa.

RUDOLF STEINER LIBRARY ONLINE COLLECTION
https://nyheritage.contentdm.oclc.org/digital/collection/nyrud/id/48/rec/14

1928
GAS Switzerland – Anthroposophical Society rebuilds Goetheanum with Steiner's organic concrete design.

– U.S. 27,000 movie theaters sold 100 million tickets a week. On any day, 1/6th of all Americans were at the "movies." Media syndicate companies began to produce "Newsreels" which were shipped (usually by bus freight) from small town theater to small town theater across the U.S. and the world. This created an additional audience of "viewers."

– U.S. – First intra-city transmission of television pictures and sound.

AG – Germany – Demeter Co-Operative formed to certify production standards used by Bio-Dynamic farms/gardens and allow use of the name – the first international agricultural certification and brand.

ED – U.S. – Rudolf Steiner School, New York City founded. (*Into The Heart's Land*, pg. 177)

– U.S. – Antibiotics, penicillin developed by Alexander Fleming.

NOTES:

Schooling in the 1890s Ursula K Le Guin, WORDS ARE MY MATTER, Small Beer Press, 2016, Page 68

1893 ANTI-SALOON LEAGUE https://en.wikipedia.org/wiki/Anti-Saloon_League

1900 TIMELINE RUDOLF STEINER ON ANTI-SEMITISM Rudolf Steiner on Anti-Semitism written for the Anthroposophical Society General Council, 1998, Jean Yeager

LIVING IN A FOOL'S PARADISE – MEETING RUDOLF STEINER, Sonia Tomara Clark and Jeannette Eaton, *Journal for Anthroposophy*, Number 75, Fall 2005, pg. 90

[THE MAN, RUDOLF STEINER, Andrei Belyi, *Journal for Anthroposophy*, Number 75, Fall 2005, pg. 72]

A Student's Memories of Rudolf Steiner, Lisa Dreher Monges, JOURNAL FOR ANTHROPOSOPHY, Fall 2005, pgs. 100-101

1920 EARLIEST DAYS – THREEFOLD COMMUNITY – https://threefold.org/our-foundation/history/

1918 POISONOUS CHEMICALS BANNED BUT NOT IN AGRICULTURE – "LORD NORTHBOURNE THE MAN WHO INVENTED ORGANIC FARMING, A BIOGRAPHY," John Paull, Journal Of Organic Systems, School of Land and Food, Tasmania, Australia, June 2014 pg. 32

THE KARMA OF UNTRUTHFULNESS, Rudolf Steiner, 1917-18, pg. 139

Into The Heart's Land, Henry Barnes, Steiner Books, 2013

Rudolf Steiner Library, https://rudolfsteinerlibrary.org/

Steiner Death Reported in 1935 – (Anthroposophy Worldwide, No. 1-2, 2018, pg. 2

1918 THREEFOLD MEETS NATIONALISM – Ehrenfried Pfeiffer, Personal Memorandum

CHAPTERS 1 & 2 END NOTES / LINK PAGES:

END NOTE (1) – PAGE 7 – 1886 – THE NATIONAL GRANGE – ORDER OF PATRONS OF HUSBANDRY
https://en.wikipedia.org/wiki/National_Grange_of_the_Order_of_Patrons_of_Husbandry

The Grange, officially named **The National Grange of the Order of Patrons of Husbandry**, is a social organization in the United States that encourages families to band together to promote the economic and political well-being of the community and agriculture. The Grange, founded after the Civil War in 1867, is the oldest American agricultural advocacy group with a national scope. The Grange actively lobbied state legislatures and Congress for political goals, such as the Granger Laws to lower rates charged by railroads, and rural free mail delivery by the Post Office.

In 2005, the Grange had a membership of 160,000, with organizations in 2,100 communities in 36 states. It is headquartered in Washington, D.C., in a building built by the organization in 1960. Many rural communities in the United States still have a Grange Hall and local Granges still serve as a center of rural life for many farming communities.

END NOTE (2) – PAGE 8 – 1890 – WHAT IT WAS LIKE – *SCHOOLING IN THE 1890's* by URSULA K. LeGUIN
https://firebornecom.files.wordpress.com/2022/02/1890s-schooling-ursula-leguin.pdf

Teaching from the first grade up centered on "English," not only because immigrants wanted their children fluent in it, but because literature – fiction, scientific works, history, poetry – was a major form of social currency. *(Editor's note: with the very high level of immigration in the 1890s, it also explains why teaching English in public schools was an important part of being in America.)*

To look at school books from 1892 or 1910 can be scary; the level of literacy and general cultural knowledge expected of a 10-year-old was rather awesome. Such texts, and lists of the novels kids were expected to read when compared to a nice girl in the 1960s, leads one to believe that Americans really wanted their children not only to be able to read, but to just do it, and not to fall asleep during it.

Literacy was not only the front door to any kind of individual economic advancement and class status, it was an important social activity. The shared experience of books was a genuine bond. A person reading seems to be cut off from everything around them, almost as much is the person shouting banalities into a cell phone as they ram their car into your car – that's the private aspect of reading. But there is a large public element, too, which consists in what you and others have read.

As people these days can maintain nonthreatening, unloaded, sociable conversation by talking about who murdered whom on the latest hit TV police procedural or Mafia show, so strangers on the train or coworkers on the job in the 1840s to talk perfectly unaffected together about the Old Curiosity Shop and whether poor Little Nell was going to cop it. Since public school education was strong on poetry and various literary classics, a lot of people would recognize and enjoy a reference to Tennyson, or Scott, or Shakespeare – shared properties, a social meeting ground. The man might be less likely to boast about falling asleep at *Schooling in the 1890s* Ursula K Le Guin, WORDS ARE MY MATTER, Small Beer Press, 2016, Page 68

END NOTE (3) – PAGE 9 – 1893 – ANTI-SALOON LEAGUE –
https://firebornecom.files.wordpress.com/2022/02/1893-anti_saloon-league.pdf
1893 ANTI-SALOON LEAGUE https://en.wikipedia.org/wiki/Anti-Saloon_League

The Anti-Saloon League was the leading organization lobbying for prohibition in the United States in the early 20th century. It was a key component of the Progressive Era, and was strongest in the South and rural North, drawing heavy support from pietistic Protestant ministers and their congregations, especially Methodists, Baptists, Disciples and Congregationalists. It concentrated on legislation, and cared about how legislators voted, not whether they drank or not. Founded as a state society in Oberlin, Ohio, in 1893, its influence spread rapidly. In 1895, it became a national organization and quickly rose to become the most powerful prohibition lobby in America, overshadowing the older Woman's Christian Temperance Union and the Prohibition Party. Its triumph was nationwide prohibition locked into the Constitution with passage of the 18th Amendment in 1920. It was decisively defeated when Prohibition was repealed in 1933.

END NOTE (4) – PAGE 9 – 1900 – TIMELINE OF RUDOLF STEINER AGAINST ANTI-SEMITISM
https://firebornecom.files.wordpress.com/2022/02/1900-steiner-and-anti-semitism.pdf

"Nothing will hasten humanity in its own downfall more than the propagation of ideals based on race, nation and blood." – Rudolf Steiner (1917)
- Beginning in the year 1900, Steiner spoke of the dangers of Anti-Semitism.
- Anthroposophy is opposed to Social Darwinism.
- Steiner's view of the future is one of a cosmopolitan striving for humanity and not one of nationalistic states based on race or blood. Steiner strongly advocated against both an "Aryan" state and a "Zionist" state.
- • 1897 Pre-dating Emil Zola, Steiner wrote in defense of Alfred Dreyfus, a Jewish French officer banished to "Devil's Island" for alleged treason.
- • 1899 (and 1904) Steiner lectured at the Social Democrat Worker's College in Berlin.
- 1901 Steiner wrote a series of articles for *"News Of The Association for the Prevention of Anti-Semitism."*
- 1919 Steiner warned against "Protocols of the Elders of Zion" on whose vile anti-Semitism "Mein Kampf" was drawn.
- 1919 Steiner founded the Threefold Social Order.
- A Dutch Commission on "Anthroposophy and the Question of Race" final report (April 2000) evaluated 89,000 pages of the collected works of Rudolf Steiner and determined there was no racial doctrine in Anthroposophy.
Rudolf Steiner on Anti-Semitism written for the Anthroposophical Society General Council, 1998, Jean Yeager

END NOTE (5) – PAGE 12 – 1913 – "LIVING IN A 'FOOL'S PARADISE' STEINER NEVER LET UP"
https://firebornecom.files.wordpress.com/2022/02/1908_1929.1-steiner-never-let-up.pdf

The years 1908-1928 in the schema of Howe and Strauss was called an era of "Unraveling."

"Living in a fool's paradise and enjoying a high level of prosperity, the peoples of Europe in the years preceding the first World War seemed to have no inkling of the destructive forces which such a conflict would unleash. Steiner was perhaps one of the few whose penetrating mind could read the future and embrace the magnitude of the danger hanging over the old continent. He was fully aware of the changes it might bring in its wake. Desperately he tried to warn his contemporaries of the follies of nationalistic adventures." [MEETING RUDOLF STEINER, Sonia Tomara Clark and Jeannette Eaton, *Journal for Anthroposophy*, Number 75, Fall 2005, pg. 90]

Over 150 men and women had gathered to work on the building the first Goetheanum building – a totally wooden structure. "Both by example and specific instructions, Steiner taught his amateur carvers. He teased them merrily with anecdotes, encouraged their efforts, paid no heed to their weariness and in the evening gathered them into the workshop to hear one of his profound and inspiring lectures." [IBID., pg. 91]

Steiner never let up on his lecture schedule throughout Europe even with war imminent: Vienna, Paris, Prague, Scandinavia and many German cities. The end of June, the Archduke Franz Ferdinand of Austria-Hungary was assassinated but several weeks passed before the war burst into flames.

When it did break out the young people at the Goetheanum were still united in their diversity. Russian Poet Andrei Bely wrote:

"The first reaction to the war: we must commit ourselves more emphatically to our common cause; all of us – Russians, Germans, Austrians, French, Poles – we are all brothers in misfortune, we are all victims of criminal politics; our 'politics' was devotion to the common cause, determination to continue building.

When Strauss the Bavarian was drafted and had to join the service as a medical aide, he noted down as many Russian words as possible so that he could help the wounded Russian prisoners. The motto that united us was 'Love, solidarity, Responsibility.'

We experienced our solidarity even more vividly during the days when panic broke out everywhere. The anticipation of an exodus, together with the Doctor, resembled something biblical. ... But, gradually calm returned: Swiss troops from all branches of the army were stationed in our vicinity, and when the border had been sealed with a mine barrier, the feeling of danger subsided. We continued carving on our building, aware that it could be destroyed at any moment by artillery shells." [THE MAN, RUDOLF STEINER, Andrei Belyi, *Journal for Anthroposophy*, Number 75, Fall 2005, pg. 72]

Marie Steiner was The Doctor's wife, secretary, confidante and companion on all his lecture tours. She was the one who maintained what could be described as his "usual" daily level of activity. She was the master of ceremonies for all meetings, scheduled all private visits, was custodian of all stenographs of talks.

"My impression: Steiner's home is always open: its effect is like that of a cell in a commune where no one places any value on comfort; every minute is already scheduled; and there are tasks, tasks, tasks, tasks. Here is somebody editing, there admission tickets for a lecture are being distributed; here books are being handed out. There correspondence is answered, and in between, something is corrected, or somebody receives help." [IBID, pg. 44 IBID pg]

Frau Steiner arranged for what must have been the "endlessly clattering typewriters" which the "the ladies of the office" used to put the words into form for publications. Stories about Fräulein Lehmann or Fräulein Hannah Mücke, workers in the library at the press, the *Philosophisch-Anthroposophischer Verlag*, are legend.

Steiner consulted individually with hundreds of people. "The number of consultation hours increased according to his capacity for absorption; the time it took to hold six consultations was used to hold twelve. If one went to Steiner's ... there was a long line of waiting people. When one left, there was the same line, the car parked in front of the house, the suitcases packed, but Steiner sat and listened, and how he listened!"

"Our last meeting went like this: a long line of person s ahead of me and behind me, the car was waiting. Steiner was scheduled to return to Dornach from Stuttgart. He greeted me and led me into the room. We sat down by a small desk.

Steiner was pale as death; it isn't easy to listen to such large numbers of people one after the other when each one comes with his most urgent problem.

His answers were always concrete and to the point, but they only unfolded their full nature in the course of years. All of this also passed before my mind during our last meeting. He turned his over tired face with the good-natured eagle nose in my direction and said with a smile difficult to describe. 'We do not have much time; try to say briefly everything you have on your mind.' The conversation of twenty minutes lives within me as if it had lasted many hours, not because I would have been able to say everything but because he replied to everything beyond any words. The answer grew out of the facts of the following years of my life."

This last conversation between Andrei Bely and Rudolf Steiner occurred in 1923. Following this Bely returned to Russia during an increasingly political climate which oppressed his literary activities. Bely was an opponent of Communism and his works continued to be suppressed during the years of Communism. Only his death in 1934 saved him from persecution and arrest.

END NOTE (6) – PAGE 12 – **1913 – "FOUNDATION STONE STUMBLING BLOCK FOR 'TOAD NATURES.'"**
https://firebornecom.files.wordpress.com/2022/02/1908_1929-1913-foundation-stumbling-block.pdf

The following is an original document provided by the Archive at the Goetheanum to the Anthroposophical Society in America in 1998. It is part of a collection of documents from the white supremacist, nationalist political party National Socialism (Nazis) that was forming itself in 1913. The Nazis viewed Spiritual Science, Rudolf Steiner and all Anthroposophically inspired groups as enemies which had nothing to do with the National Socialist idea of Volk.

The differences between the two groups intensified into conflict following the publishing of Steiner's "Threefold Memorandum" in 1917.

1913 FOUNDATION STONE STUMBLING BLOCK

The "Toad natures" Steiner warned about in 1913 when he laid the Foundation Stone eventually took over and the spiritual freedom, the "stumbling block" which Steiner predicted, eventually took over.

The following is an original document provided by the Archive at the Goetheanum to the Anthroposophical Society in America in 2000. (SEE NAZI DOCUMENTS in the next chapter.)

> "According to its historical development, the Anthroposophical Society is internationally oriented and even today continues to maintain close contacts to foreign freemasons, Jews and pacifists. The methods of teaching developed by its founder, Steiner, and followed in the anthroposophical schools still existing today follow an individualistic and human-oriented education, which has nothing in common with principles of National Socialistic education. As a result of its opposition to the National Socialistic idea of Volk (*Voelkische Gedanke*), the continued activity of the Anthroposophical Society imposes the danger of injuring the National Socialistic State. The organization is therefore to be dissolved on account of its subversive character and the danger it poses to the public."[2]

END NOTE (7) – PAGE 13 – 1917 – THREEFOLD MEMORANDUM
https://firebornecom.files.wordpress.com/2022/02/1908_1929.3-1917threefold-memorandum.pdf

Rudolf Steiner had a trajectory of his lectures and writings which were always responsive to questions which came to him.

His first phase of lectures were about the esoteric nature of the human being and man's relationship with the spiritual world. The split with the Theosophical Society and the formation of the Anthroposophical Society in 1913 roughly marks that phase.

World War One in 1914 through 1923 marks the second phase when there were huge social questions starting with the revolution in Germany and Russia (1918) and education of children (1919).

In 1917, Steiner wrote a Memorandum: "Appeal To The German People And The Cultural World" which was signed by over 250 well-known individuals including Hermann Hesse and Jakob Wasserman.

In this memorandum he detailed his thoughts about "social life struggling to free itself from nationalism," what came to be called a Threefold Commonwealth. the Memorandum, contained the key sentence:

"When human beings become free, so will the nations become free through them."

This Memorandum was circulated widely in Berlin and Vienna and a book which included the text of the Memorandum and additional materials sold over 80,000 copies.

Following the circulation of the Memorandum, Steiner went on an extensive speaking tour to thousands of citizens who were interested in what the future might bring. He was lecturing in some of the largest factories to audiences of 1,000-2,000 workers – in Daimler-Benz automotive works, Bosch Manufacturing and others. This lecture series caused a group of educators and others to take up his ideas and begin to organize a "free school" independent of government curriculum.

Steiner's three-folding Memorandum brought him into contact with individuals of significant influence in the Weimar Republic's government such as Walter Simons, Foreign Minister of the Weimar Republic (1920-1921) who was also close personal friend with General Helmuth von Moltke one of the leading generals during WWI who had long-time connections with Steiner. The idea of a spiritually inspired and radically new concept of a social order was a threat to nationalists. These were people who also took to the streets to demonstrate against a world view which they neither understood.

The following is an original document provided by the Archive at the Goetheanum to the Anthroposophical Society in America in 2000.

Documentary Material

1. Adolf Hitler about Rudolf Steiner and Three-folding

"In the course of the London affair, there gradually emerged such mysterious circumstances that it has become not only expedient but indeed necessary to look somewhat more closely at this Minister [Simons], the intimate friend of the Gnostic and Anthroposophist Rudolf Steiner, follower of Three-folding of the Social Organism and whatever all these Jewish methods of destroying the normal frame of mind of the people are called: to see whether that mindless face, as Lloyd George described it, is really just the result of a deficient intellect, or if it is the mask behind which something else is concealed... [*He continues with a protest against Simon's political activity, and particularly the movement to disarm the German people*] ... And who is the driving force behind all this devilishness? The Jew! Friend of Doctor Rudolf Steiner, the friends of Simons, the "mindless"..."

Adolf Hitler, Staatsmaenner oder Nationalverbrecher (Men of the State or National Criminals"), in: Voelkischer Beobachter, 35.Jg., 15. March 1921, S.2. (original German text)

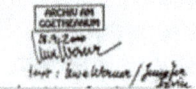

END NOTE (8) – PAGE 13 – 1918 – "THREEFOLD MEETS NATIONALISM – THE TRAJECTORY TOWARD THE GOETHEANUM FIRE"

https://firebornecom.files.wordpress.com/2022/02/2.3-threefold-meets-nationalismr2-1.pdf

THREEFOLD MEETS NATIONALISM A SPIRITUALITY WHICH WAS UNSETTLING

An eighteen year old Ehrenfried Pfeiffer who years later was to take Biodynamic agriculture to the U.S. recalled his first encounter with Steiner at one of the lectures at a labor union hall in Stuttgart:

```
"The Communists had assembled their agitators and speakers with the
Marxist dogma against the message of Rudolf Steiner of a new social
order. It was a hot day and Rudolf Steiner had to struggle to overcome
their resistance. Steiner was on the platform, perspiring profoundly.
The laborers sat at tables each with a glass of beer in front of him.
The Anthroposophists, a few of them, were in the balcony as silent
observers, because it was the laborers group meeting. I felt sorry for
the man on the platform and asked the waitress to put a bottle of seltzer
and a glass in front of him. He interrupted his speech and gulped it
down at once. I knew at that moment – the unknown little student and
laborer – it is my task to help this man whenever it is possible, to get
things done."

                                      Ehrenfried Pfeiffer, Personal Memorandum
```

– INTO THE HEART'S LAND – A Century of Rudolf Steiner's Work In North America, Henry Barnes, Steiner Books, 2005, pg. 232

END NOTE (9) – PAGE 13 – 1917 – "THE KARMA OF UNTRUTHFULNESS"

VOLUME 2, LECTURE 14 – 1 January 1917
"... the capacity is beginning to develop which will enable us to create a life of Imaginations – to develop thoughts that rise up freely – though so far this possibility is denied by materialists. However, it lies in the very nature of our age. that a life of Imagination must develop little by little. What is the counter-image of a life of Imagination? The counter-image of Imaginative life is fabrication, the creation of fabrications about reality and a corresponding thoughtlessness in alleging this or that. ... an inattentiveness to truth, to what is actual and real. The most wonderful thing with which mankind is presented in the fifth post-Atlantean period is the gradual ascent from mere one-sided intellectual life into Imaginative life, which is the first step into the spiritual world. This can err and become untruthfulness, the fabrication of untruths in relation to realities." (Karma of Untruthfulness, Vol.2, p. 7)

... so in our time, in the fifth post-Atlantean period, the art of printing books and everything that exists in the mercantile element serves these purposes. We have a foretaste of the terrible things to come in people's strong dependence on everything put out in the Press by mercantile groups by means of the medium of printing. The aims of these groups are anything but what they say they are in their newspapers. They want to make profits, or achieve certain things by doing business, and for this they possess the means by which they can disseminate views whose truthfulness is irrelevant but which serve the purpose of entering into some kinds of business. In the case of much of the printed matter distributed around the world today the right question to ask is not: What does this person mean? but: In whose service does this person stand? Who is paying for this or that opinion? This is often the crucial question these days. (*Karma of Untruthfulness, Vol.2*, pp. 180-181)

END NOTE (10) – PAGE 13 – 1918 – POSIONOUS CHEMICALS BANNED IN WAR BUT NOT AGRICULTURE
https://firebornecom.files.wordpress.com/2022/02/wwi-poisons-banned-but-not-ag.pdf

"The wartime chemistry of WWI (1914-1918) opened a Pandora's box of cheap nitrogenous compounds and poisonous gases (Charles, 2005). However, young men dying an ugly death from toxic gas seemed the antithesis of a heroic death and the perpetrators of this novel lethality seemed ungentlemanly. For the purposes of modern warfare, the box was more or less snapped shut by the Geneva Protocol for the Prohibition of the Use in War of Asphyxiating, Poisonous or other Gases, and of Bacteriological Methods of Warfare (von Eckardt & 42 others, 1925) – but not for agriculture. In the inter-war years, repurposing the chemistry of poisons and the output of the Haber-Bosch ammonia process of 'fixing' nitrogen, for application to the food chain, seemed, to many, and in particular to policy makers, to be 'scientific' and to epitomize 'progress' (Smil, 2001).

" LORD NORTHBOURNE THE MAN WHO INVENTED ORGANIC FARMING, A BIOGRAPHY, John Paull, Journal Of Organic Systems, School of Land and Food, Tasmania, Australia, June 2014 pg. 32

END NOTE (11) – PAGE 14 – 1920 – ABOUT THE EARLIEST DAYS OF ANTHROPOSOPHY IN AMERICA – THE THREEFOLD COMMUNITY
https://threefold.org/our-foundation/history/

"The first decades of the twentieth century were a time of social experimentation and spiritual exploration. In New York City in the 1920s, a small band of anthroposophists – students of Rudolf Steiner – ran a rooming house, a laundry, a furniture-making shop, and a vegetarian restaurant near Carnegie Hall. Led by Ralph Courtney, members of the Threefold Commonwealth Group included Gladys Barnett (later Hahn), May Laird-Brown, Louise Bybee, and Charlotte Parker. Not the first association of anthroposophists in New York, the Threefold Group soon became the most active and lively in their efforts to put into practice the social ideals indicated in the writings and lectures of Rudolf Steiner."

END NOTE (12) – PAGE 14 – DIVERSITY IN THE ANTHROPOSOPHICAL SOCIETY 1900s – 1920s Anthroposophical Newsletter 1984-85.
https://firebornecom.files.wordpress.com/2022/02/1900_1923-diversity-2.pdf

DIVERSITY IN THE ANTHROPOSOPHICAL SOCIETY IN AMERICA, 1900's through 1920's

A number of members of the Theosophical Society in the United States formed an Anthroposophical Society before the start of World War I.

As one can imagine, these members had a diverse array of background: European Jewish American, Polish Americans, Irish Americans and others.

We know that there was intense anti-German sentiment during World War I and that the Society in America was investigated by the Secret Service.

A recent (2001) request under the Freedom of Information Act (FOIA) did not reveal any documents about interviews conducted during World War I, we do have reports from early Society Newsletters: An article on "The Earliest Days of Anthroposophy" by Hilda Deighton (1890-1976) published in the Winter 1984-85 Newsletter of the Society reported on this encounter with the Secret Service in 1918:

"Although in 1918 anti-German feeling was very strong, we continued to hold our meetings in New York. The (Carnegie Hall) studio was full of the precious German lecture cycles. One afternoon as Mr. Greene was teaching, three Secret Service men knocked on the door, took suitcases of lectures for examination, and coldly insisted that he go with them for questioning. But, before the taxi reached police headquarters, they were so impressed with his perspicacity, candor and charm, that they asked him if he had ever seriously considered joining the United States Secret Service himself. Possessing, as he did, the best American traits, he saved the situation by the strength of his personality." (p. 33) (2)

END NOTE (13) – PAGE 15 – STEINER ATTACKED BY ADOLF HITLER IN LEADING VOLKISH PUBLICATION "VÖLKISCHER BEOBACHTER"

https://fireborncom.files.wordpress.com/2022/02/2.3-threefold-meets-nationalismr0.pdf

The following is an original document provided by the Archive at the Goetheanum to the Anthroposophical Society in America in 1998.

> **"Men of the State Or National Criminals?" by Adolf Hitler**
> *" ... And, who is behind this devilishness? The Jew! Friend of Doctor Rudolf Steiner, the friends of Simons (German Minister of Finance) ... "*
>
> In *Voelkischer Beobacher*,
> 15 March 1921

END NOTE (14) – PAGE 15 – 1921 – RESEARCHING BIOLOGICAL DYNAMIC FORCES
https://fireborncom.files.wordpress.com/2022/02/1921-researching-biological-dynamic-forces.pdf

Rudolf Steiner had a world view which did not exclude living physical and spiritual forces. He had anticipated the devastation which these powerful chemicals would have on the living organism of the soil. He wanted to demonstrate how it would be possible to work with spirit forces to heal the physical world after the devastation of chemical and corporate agriculture.

In 1921 Steiner established a Bio-Chemical Research Laboratory at the Goetheanum, the Anthroposophical world headquarters in Dornach, Switzerland.

To run the Bio-Chemical Research Laboratory Steiner put the young Ehrenfried Pfeiffer, only 22 years old at the time, in charge. Steiner mentored Pfeiffer's scientific education and personally designed his chemical scientific education. Steiner wanted Pfeiffer to have a rigorous study – "to overcome materialism" he said, "we must know its means and methods as well as we know our own."

Steiner focused the Bio-Chemical research on how to heal the devastation which he anticipated would come.

In 1922, two years before the questions and concern about the failing quality of chemical agricultural even arose, Steiner asked Pfeiffer, Ita Wegman and Guenther Wachsmuth to test what came to be known as the Biodynamic Compost Preparations the recipes which he had gained from spiritual insight.

Pfeiffer said that Steiner gave the group the recipes for the preparations without any sort of explanation, just "do this and then do that."

Test plots were made, and different plants grown using a planting calendar. The group made and applied the first batches of preparations and then adjusted them based on the results and Bio-Chemical analysis.

END NOTE (15) – PAGE 16 – 1923 – "CULTIVATING ANTHROPOSOPHY THROUGH A SOCIETY"
https://biographycache.files.wordpress.com/2022/01/rudolf-steiner-on-the-society.pdf

RUDOLF STEINER ON THE SOCIETY
(*From a "Letter to the Members," January 13, 1924.*)

In spiritual matters human life unfolds its essence in a mutual give and take. It is thus natural for those who wish to make Anthroposophy part of their lives to seek its cultivation through a society.

In all of these ways Anthroposophy generates a host of life tasks. Yet these tasks can only succeed in spreading to wider circles of humanity if their beginnings are fostered within a society ...

WHAT SHOULD BE IN STATUTES? A *description* of what it is that people would like to accomplish in a living and purely human relationship – such as the Anthroposophical Society.

Then should follow how they propose to carry out this cultivation within an independent school of spiritual science. We must not set up principles to which one is expected to subscribe. We should rather characterize a reality. Finally, it should be stated that whoever wants to add his efforts to what is being done at the Goetheanum may become a member.

As "statutes," then – which should be no "statutes" but rather the description of what arises from such a purely human and living relationship within a society – the following are proposed: (FOUNDATION STATUTE FOLLOWS)

END NOTE (16) – PAGE 16 – THE FOUNDATION STATUTE
https://www.goetheanum.org/en/members/foundation-statute-of-1923

The first "By-Laws" of the General Anthroposophical Society, this Foundation Statute is specifically referred to in the formal, legal By-Laws of the Anthroposophical Society in America as "Principles" due to Swiss law when they were drafted in 1933 and all subsequent versions.

Foundation Statute of the Anthroposophical Society of 1923

1. The Anthroposophical Society is to be an association of people whose will it is to nurture the life of the soul, both in the individual and in human society, on the basis of a true knowledge of the spiritual world.

2. The persons gathered at the Goetheanum in Dornach at Christmas, 1923, both the individuals and the groups represented, form the nucleus of the Society. They are convinced that there exists in our time a genuine science of the spiritual world, elaborated for years past, and in important particulars already published; and that the civilisation of today is lacking the cultivation of such a science. This cultivation

is to be the task of the Anthroposophical Society. It will endeavour to fulfil this task by making the anthroposophical spiritual science cultivated at the Goetheanum in Dornach the centre of its activities, together with all that results from this for brotherhood in human relationships and for the moral and religious as well as the artistic and cultural life. (1)

3. The persons gathered in Dornach as the nucleus of the Society recognise and endorse the view of the leadership at the Goetheanum (represented by the Vorstand [Executive Council] formed at the Foundation Meeting): 'Anthroposophy, as fostered at the Goetheanum, leads to results which can serve every human being as a stimulus to spiritual life, whatever his nation, social standing or religion. They can lead to a social life genuinely built on brotherly love. No special degree of academic learning is required to make them one's own and to found one's life upon them, but only an open-minded human nature. Research into these results, however, as well as competent evaluation of them, depends upon spiritual-scientific training, which is to be acquired step by step. These results are in their own way as exact as the results of genuine natural science. When they attain general recognition in the same way as these, they will bring about comparable progress in all spheres of life, not only in the spiritual but also in the practical realm.'

4. The Anthroposophical Society is in no sense a secret society but is entirely public. Anyone can become a member, without regard to nationality, social standing, religion, scientific or artistic conviction, who considers as justified the existence of an institution such as the Goetheanum in Dornach, in its capacity as a School of Spiritual Science. The Anthroposophical Society rejects any kind of sectarian activity. Party politics it considers not to be within its task.

5. The Anthroposophical Society sees the School of Spiritual Science in Dornach as a centre for its activity. The School will be composed of three classes. Members of the Society will be admitted to the School on their own application after a period of membership to be determined by the leadership at the Goetheanum. They enter in this way the First Class of the School of Spiritual Science. Admission to the Second or Third Classes (2) takes place when the person requesting this is deemed eligible by the leadership at the Goetheanum.

6. Every member of the Anthroposophical Society has the right to attend all lectures, performances and meetings arranged by the society, under conditions to be announced by the Vorstand.

7. The organising of the school of Spiritual Science is, to begin with, the responsibility of Rudolf Steiner, who will appoint his collaborators and his possible successor.

8. All publications of the Society shall be public, in the same sense as are those of other public societies. (3) The publications of the School of Spiritual Science will form no exception as regards this public character; however, the leadership of the School reserves the right to deny in advance the validity of any judgment on these publications which is not based on the same training from which they have been derived. Consequently, they will regard as justified no judgement which is not based on an appropriate preliminary training, as is also the common practice in the recognized scientific world. Thus, the publications of the School of Spiritual Science will bear the following note: 'Printed as manuscript for members of the School of Spiritual Science, Goetheanum, ... Class. No one is considered competent to judge the content, who has not acquired – through the School itself or in a manner recognized by the School as equivalent – the requisite preliminary knowledge. Other opinions will be disregarded, to the extent that the authors of such works will not enter into a discussion about them.'

9. The purpose of the Anthroposophical Society will be the furtherance of spiritual research; that of the School of Spiritual Science will be this research itself. A dogmatic stand in any field whatsoever is to be excluded from the Anthroposophical Society.

10. The Anthroposophical Society shall hold a regular General Meeting at the Goetheanum each year, at which time the Vorstand shall present a full report with accounting. The agenda for this meeting shall be communicated by the Vorstand to all members, together with the invitation, six weeks before the meeting. The Vorstand may call special meetings and fix the agenda for them. Invitations to such meetings shall be sent to members three weeks in advance. Motions proposed by individual members or groups of members shall be submitted one week before the General Meeting.

11. Members may join together in smaller or larger groups on any basis of locality or subject. The headquarters of the Anthroposophical Society is at the Goetheanum. From there the Vorstand shall bring to the attention of the members or groups of members what it considers to be the task of the Society. The Vorstand communicates with officials elected or appointed by the various groups. Admission of members will be the concern of the individual groups; the certificate of membership shall, however, be placed before the Vorstand in Dornach, and shall be signed by them out of their confidence in the officials of the groups. In general, every member should join a group. Only those for whom it is quite impossible to find entry to a group should apply directly to Dornach for membership.

12. Membership dues shall be fixed by the individual groups; each group shall, however, submit 15 Swiss Francs (4) for each of its members to the central leadership of the Society at the Goetheanum.

13. Each working group formulates its own statutes, but these must not be incompatible with the Statutes of the Anthroposophical Society.

14. The organ of the society is the weekly "Das Goetheanum," which for this purpose is provided with a supplement (5) containing the official communications of the Society. This enlarged edition of "Das Goetheanum" will be supplied to members of the Anthroposophical Society only.

15. The Founding Vorstand will be:

    President Dr. Rudolf Steiner
    Vice-President Albert Steffen
    Recorder Dr. Ita Wegman
    Members Marie Steiner
    Dr. Elisabeth Vreede
    Secretary and Treasurer Dr. Guenther Wachsmuth

(1) The Anthroposophical Society is in continuity with the Society founded in 1912. It would like, however, to create an independent point of departure, in keeping with the true spirit of the present time, for the objectives established at that time.

(2) These have not yet been established.

(3) The conditions under which one acquires training have also been made public, and their publication will be continued.

(4) At the General Meeting at Easter 1990 this was raised from 100 to 125 Swiss Francs, 300 Francs for those attached directly to Dornach.

(5) For English-speaking members, "Anthroposophy Worldwide" ten times a year contains translations of the supplement.
https://www.goetheanum.org/en/members/foundation-statute-of-1923

END NOTE(17) – PAGE 16 – 1924 – THE AMERICA VERSE AND LEADERSHIP IN THE FUTURE
https://anthroposophy.org/letter-from-virginia-sease/

VIRGINIA SEASE
Dornach, 24th February 2020

Dear Members and Friends of the Anthroposophical Society in America,

We may regard the current situation in regard to the future leadership in the United States as one necessitating deep reflection on the part of each citizen. Regardless of one's personal persuasion it is incumbent on each individual to cherish the hope that the right pathway into the immediate future and also beyond may be realized.

As members of the General Anthroposophical Society we are aware that at the end of the 4th Principle of the Society it states: "The Anthroposophical Society rejects any kind of sectarian activity. Party politics it considers not to be within its task." Bearing this in mind we may seek the right pathway through inner activity.

The United States of America received a great gift from Rudolf Steiner in 1923: the so called "America Verse" given for the Foundation of the Threefold Group which was transmitted by a Swiss messenger directly from Rudolf Steiner to Ralph Courtney. Ralph Courtney met Rudolf Steiner in Paris in 1906 and later became a strong voice internationally for the Threefold Social Order. This verse was translated into English by Frederick Heckel, a long-time editor of the Society's Newsletter.

Today many people work with this Verse privately and in groups and branches of the Anthroposophical Society in America. I would like to suggest that members and friends who are concerned about the destiny of America at this time, direct the thoughts which are within this Verse especially to the beings of the Third Hierarchy who may then be able to form this meditative effort into a positive direction. This Verse is actually both a meditation and a prayer.

From my perspective as an American citizen living now almost 36 years in Switzerland I experience frequently how people from many parts of the world while visiting the Goetheanum express their questions and concerns about my homeland.

These few words come with my grateful thoughts and my good wishes for everything which each person can inwardly contribute at this time.

With many warm greetings,

Virginia Sease, Ph.D.
Executive Council emerita
General Anthroposophical Society
Goetheanum
CH-4143 Dornach, Switzerland

END NOTE (17) – PAGE 16 – 1924 – FOOD QUALITY DEGRADATION LEADS TO AGRICULTURE COURSE

https://firebornecom.files.wordpress.com/2022/02/1922-food-quality-degredation-lead-to.pdf

By 1922-23 resistance to chemical agriculture accelerated when farmers, doctors, scientists and became very concerned about the degradation of seed stocks, soil quality, cultivated plants and animal health.

These concerns were drawn together by Count Carl von Keyserlingk who in June 1924 made his estate in England available for a course at which Steiner delivered a series of eight lectures called "The Agriculture Course" to a selected group of practical farmers, gardeners, doctors, scientists and student of anthroposophy. [THE ORIGINS OF THE ORGANIC MOVEMENT, pg. 69.]

Steiner was very ill [He died March 30, 1925.], he may have sensed just how gravely ill he was. The Agriculture Course is certainly one of his most esoteric.

And it was given after a super-human effort to promote Social Threefolding, an approach to heal the intra-war chaos in Europe which included speaking to thousands of workers in factories and industry leaders, and at the highest governmental levels. After being personally attacked by the Nazis, and having the Goetheanum burned, Steiner seemed anything but bitter.

As he said in his second Foundation Stone address only a few months before:

```
"Therefore, we shall have to be properly watchful and courageous in
holding our position! Perhaps the laying of the capstone will be only
the beginning of what we have to achieve for truth and by way of
standing up for truth." [The Foundation Stone page 46.]
```

Steiner was looking for a new beginning. He very much saw the Agriculture Course as perhaps one final opportunity to demonstrate spirit working into matter and so these lectures were some of the most esoteric he ever made.

Despite the esoteric basis of the lectures given in the Agriculture Course, many of the people who attended were clear that the methods and effects of the preparations were for all farmers, not just the Anthroposophists. [THE ORIGINS OF THE ORGANIC MOVEMENT, pg. 72.]

END NOTE (18) – PAGE 17 – 1924 – "THE AGRICULTURE COURSE" BIOLOGICAL THINKING
https://firebornecom.files.wordpress.com/2022/02/1924-introducing-biological-thinking.pdf

1924 INTRODUCING BIOLOGICAL THINKING

Ehrenfried Pfeiffer believe that anyone who adopted biodynamic practices would develop a perspective, a way of thinking and even observing biological processes that was different from the more materialistic chemical farmer – it was what Pfeiffer came to call "biological thinking."

Steiner said this about the course:

```
"It shows that it is possible for Anthroposophy to work with both the
most highly spiritual side and from the most practical. In actuality
we are only working in the right way when these two sides are woven
together in complete harmony. When we work Anthroposophy it is all
too easy to make the mistake of not letting things on the spiritual
side breakthrough into practical life, of having them remain as some
kind of theory or mere faith in words – not even faith in the thought
content, but faith in words. We fail to grasp the fact that spiritual
things can really enter into immediate, practical life. Just take an
example the fact that nobody understands the essence of manuring
anymore.1
```

SPIRITUAL FOUNDATIONS OF AGRICULTURE, Rudolf Steiner, pg. 9

END NOTE (19) – PAGE 17 – 1925 – ORGANIC AGRICULTURE HISTORY
https://firebornecom.files.wordpress.com/2022/02/1925-geneva-protocols-banned-substances-but-not-ag.pdf

GENEVA PROTOCOLS (1925) BANNED SUBSTANCES BUT NOT FOR AG USE

"The wartime chemistry of WWI (1914-1918) opened a Pandora's box of cheap nitrogenous compounds and poisonous gases (Charles, 2005). However, young men dying an ugly death from toxic gas seemed the antithesis of a heroic death and the perpetrators of this novel lethality seemed ungentlemanly. For the purposes of modern warfare, the box was more or less snapped shut by the Geneva Protocol for the Prohibition of the Use in War of Asphyxiating, Poisonous or other Gases, and of Bacteriological Methods of Warfare (von Eckardt & 42 others, 1925) – but not for agriculture. In the inter-war years, repurposing the chemistry of poisons and the output of the Haber-Bosch ammonia process of 'fixing' nitrogen, for application to the food chain, seemed, to many, and in particular to policy makers, to be 'scientific' and to epitomize 'progress' (Smil, 2001)."

LORD NORTHBOURNE THE MAN WHO INVENTED ORGANIC FARMING, A BIOGRAPHY, John Paull, Journal Of Organic Systems, School of Land and Food, Tasmania, Australia, June 2014 pg. 32

END NOTE (20) – PAGE 18 – 1927 – NEWSLETTER FOR MEMBERS VOL 1, NO 1

THE ANTHROPOSOPHICAL MOVEMENT IN AMERICA
– LETTER FOR MEMBERS 1927 –
VOL 1, NO 1

NEWS LETTER FOR MEMBERS

<SNIP> GREETINGS FROM THE COUNCIL This little publication is sent out with the cordial greetings and hopeful hearts of your Council here at Headquarters. We trust that it may serve as a means for bringing each member into closer touch with the center in America and of strengthening the consciousness of spiritual unity by means of which alone shall we be able to carry forward the great responsibility entrusted to us by our great and beloved leader, Rudolf Steiner.

Henry B. Monges, General Secretary	Ralph Courtney, 3fold Commonwealth, New York City
Charlotte E. Parker, Assistant Secretary	Maud B. Monges, Los Angeles Grp, California
Herbert Chaudiere, Treasurer	Gracia Ricardo, Santa Barbara Grp, California
Mabel Cotterell, for Rudolf Steiner Group, Chicago	Olin D. Wannamaker, St. Mark's Grp, New York City

Henri Zay, for Pittsburgh Group, Pa.

https://nyheritage.contentdm.oclc.org/digital/collection/nyrud/id/48/rec/14

VII. THE WORK IN THE SOCIETY   *2 March 1924*

The truths of Nature, experienced with free and open mind, lead us already toward the truths of the Spirit. When we fill ourselves with the beauty, greatness and majesty of Nature, it grows in us to a fountain of true feeling for the Spirit. And when we open our heart to the silent gesture of Nature revealing her eternal innocence beyond all good and evil, our eyes are opened presently to the spiritual world, from whence – into the dumb gesture – the living Word rings forth, revealing good and evil.

https://rudolfsteinerelib.org/Books/GA026/English/ASGB1963/GA026_c07.html

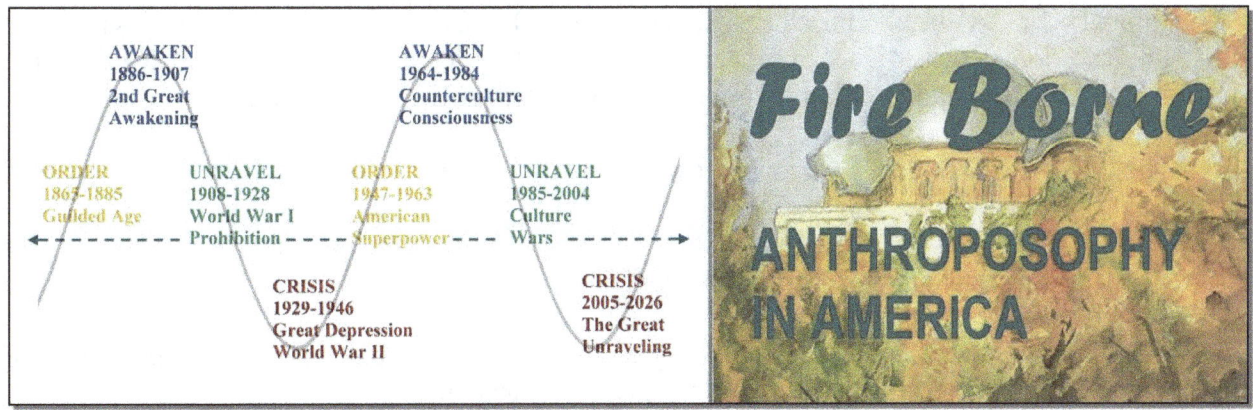

CULTURAL WAVE CHART © 2016 Jean W. Yeager[3]

1929-1946 – "Great Depression / WWII"
PHASE: CRISIS

U.S.GENERATION the Moral Ecology of *"The Silent Generation"* **is a Worldwide Crisis: the "Dust Bowl, the "Great Depression" an economic free fall, then Nazis and Fascists start World War II which ends with the U.S. A-Bomb attack on Japan. Anthroposophical thinking comes to the U.S. bringing a start to cultural renewal.**

| Abbreviations: | RS Rudolf Steiner | ED Education | MED Medical | ASiA Anthroposophical Society in America |
| AG Agriculture | SM Spirit Matters | TF Threefold | SCI Science | GAS General Anthroposophical Society |

All timeline entries are for U.S. events unless otherwise noted.

1929
– OCTOBER 24 STOCK MARKET CRASH causes worldwide depression.

– 60% citizens have income less than $2,000, enough for the basics.

ED – Rudolf Steiner School in New York City chartered.

1930s
– Surge of food co-ops during financial depression.

– Mexico – Rev. Coughlin broadcasts anti-Semitic programs from an A.M. station in Mexico and is eventually jailed.

1931
– First regularly scheduled television broadcast.

MED – Weleda established in New York to distribute medicines and body care products. (*Into The Heart's Land*, pg. 166)

1932

---

[3] Dates / phases from THE FOURTH TURNING, William Strauss and Neil Howe, Broadway Books, 1997

AG – Holland – 1932-1936 Ehrenfried Pfeiffer converts 500 acres at Loverdale Farm to Bio-dynamic. This demonstration farm is visited by many non-chemical agriculture pioneers. Lord Northbourne consults with Pfeiffer and invites him to give keynote lectures at U.K. conference.

– RUN ON BANKS. U.S. banks are locally owned. A "run on banks" is a rush to withdraw deposits that causes banks to collapse.

– More than 10% unemployment, 13-million people out of work.

– WWI Veterans "Bonus Army" demand Congress pay them the "bonus" they were promised for fighting in WWI. They are attacked by the Army, two veterans killed.

– 3,000 workers march on Ford Motor's Rouge Plant seeking jobs. Police fire with a machine gun and kill four who they claim are Communists. 30,000 people attend the funeral in Detroit.

– Franklin Roosevelt runs for President promising a "New Deal." Later he says he was trying to stop an outright revolution.

1933
– *Agricultural Adjustment Act* – farmers paid not to grow certain crops.

AG – **Ehrenfried Pfeiffer lectures at summer conference at Threefold Farm, NY.**

– 67,000 homeless children living "rough" on the streets in New York City.

– European anthroposophists flee Germany to the U.S. and South America.

AG – Pfeiffer sets up a temporary Bio-Chemical Research Laboratory at Threefold Farm in New York.

– Steiner books banned in Germany.

GAS – General Anthroposophical Society (G.A.S.) Leadership Council, in a private meeting, unanimously renounces National Socialism – Nazis. Leaders do not publicly renounce the Nazis for fear of retribution.

https://go.elib.com/elzly

1933 – Ehrenfried Pfeiffer lectures at Anthroposophical Summer conference at Threefold Farm, NY. *"Dr. Rudolf Steiner's Biologic Dynamic Agricultural Methods Practically Applied To Farming"*

AG Germany – Bio-dynamic farmers adopt "peaceful and passive resistance" to the Nazis. *(See Hitler on the Demeter newsletter cover.)*

ASiA – Anthroposophical Society in America legally incorporated in New York State as a Membership Organization. By-Laws are the legal frame on which an organization does its work in the world. The Society changed its structure many times over the years. Note how these by-laws link this "Branch" to the General Anthroposophical Society (GAS) at the same time Fascists are seeking to eradicate spiritual thinking. See End Note 2 and actual Nazi documents.

END NOTE (1) – 1933 BY-LAWS OF THE ANTHROPOSOPHICAL SOCIETY IN AMERICA

– Germany – Gestapo agents go house to house in some areas to collect anthroposophical books and burn them in the streets.

– Germany – Nazis send anthroposophists to concentration camps.
VIKTOR ULLMANN, composer, an anthroposophist, produces his *"Emperor of Atlantis"* opera in Theresienstadt concentration camp. The performance is about the redemption of "the emperor" (Hitler) through art. Guards are outraged. Ullmann and his family are killed in Auschwitz. *(1998 – Ullmann Honored At Ceremony At Asia Headquarters At The Rudolf Steiner House In Ann Arbor, MI.)*
https://firebornecom.files.wordpress.com/2022/02/1998-diversity-viktor-ullman-1.pdf

1934
– U.S. "DUST BOWL" largest man-made disaster caused by a world view of "Industrial Agriculture": overuse of ammonia fertilizer, herbicides, introduction of heavy farm equipment and elimination of farm practices that were once designed to conserve soil fertility. Millions of acres were literally blown away in dust storms. One farmer turned his plow upside down on his barn so he could plow his farm as it was blown into the next state.

END NOTE (2). – "ANTHROPOSOPHY AT THE TIME OF NAZI GERMANY" *THE ACTUAL NAZI DOCUMENTS FROM THE ARCHIV AM GOETHEANUM >>>>.*
These include the official documents which give the reasons the National Socialist State were afraid of the world view of Anthroposophical Spiritual Science and anthroposophists, the formal documents used to ban the Anthroposophical Society and Waldorf education.

GAS – BREAK UP OF THE ANTHROPOSOPHICAL SOCIETY
– "During the Annual General Meeting of 14 March 1934 for which 1,820 members came together in the still unfinished Goetheanum, a group of members supported by the remaining members of the Executive Council moved that Ita Wegman and Elizabeth Vreede be excluded from the Executive Council and divested of all duties ... The movers also demanded the exclusion of various leading members from Great Britain, the Netherlands

and Germany, as well as the exclusion of the British and Dutch Anthroposophical Societies and other groups that had come together in an association of independent Anthroposophical groups." *(Anthroposophy Worldwide, No. 1-2, 2018, pg. 2)*

ANTHROPOSOPHICAL WORLD VIEW BANNED BY THE NAZIS:
"... every undertaking and activity of anthroposophy necessarily arises out of the Anthroposophical world view. The anthroposophical worldview is in its most important points directly opposed to National Socialism. Therefore, schools which are built out of the anthroposophical worldview and led by anthroposophists mean danger to true German education."
Jakob Wilhelm Hauer, Professor of Religion at the University of Tübingen and member of the Secret Service of the S.S.

<<<< *1935 – NAZIS BAN Anthroposophical Society and Waldorf schools based on world view of human freedom and racial diversity as opposed to "Blood And Soil."*

– Roosevelt wins U.S. Presidential election.

– American Eugenics Association documentary film argues it is "foolishly sentimental to keep retarded, or "deficient" people alive." Eugenics is adopted by the Nazis who exterminate all people seen as "deficient."

– Germany – Jesse Owens, a black athlete, wins four gold medals in track events at Berlin Olympics.

ASiA – The Board of Directors of the Anthroposophical Society in America issued a NEW CONSTITUTION 10/18/35 changing the way in which the Society could transact business. This was a significant change from the original by-laws of 1933. (will be in the Administrative Collection)

1936
TF – Rudolf Steiner Foundation (RSF) incorporated as the Treasury for the Anthroposophical Society in America and practiced Threefolding principles. The foundation remains small for nearly 50 years. (*Into The Heart's Land*, pg. 409.) www.rsfsocialfinance.org

1937
– U.S. government estimates 500,000 workers took part in sit-down strikes Sept 1936 through May 1937.

– Jet engine designed by Frank Whittle and Hans von Ohain.

– DDT formulated as toxic insecticide for military use. Shortly DDT is sold for commercial agricultural and even household use.

<<<< **As shown in *National Geographic* magazine photos, all immigrants who arrive to the U.S. at Ellis Island in New York are routinely "dusted" (or 'de-loused') with DDT.**
PHOTO SOURCE: National Geographic Magazine Archive.

1938
– U.S. Disney's *Snow White and the Seven Dwarfs* top movie.

AG – Ehrenfried Pfeiffer's book *"Bio-Dynamic Farming and Gardening"* based on his direct work with Rudolf Steiner, his laboratory experiments with the bio-dynamic preparations and four-year conversion of Loverdale farm in Holland is published. In this book Pfeiffer articulates Rudolf Steiner's practical method for working with active biological dynamic forces. The book is translated into eight languages and encourages "biological thinking."

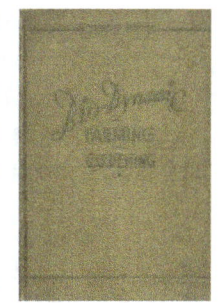

AG – Pfeiffer comes to the U.S. and starts Bio-dynamic Farming and Gardening Association in New York state. *(Into The Heart's Land,* pg. 209)

– 40% of American farms electrified. REA (Rural Electrical Association) active.

AG – Pfeiffer sets up Bio-Chemical research laboratory at Threefold Center in New York. J.I. Rodale funds his early experiments in organics and nutrition. Pfeiffer begins formulating biodynamic compost preparations.

> **THE START OF POLLUTION AND GLOBAL WARMING**
> **1938** – Thomas Midgley, a General Motors (GM) chemist, creates "ethyl" gasoline by adding lead for high powered engines that is a major pollutant. GM knows vaporized lead is toxic.
> Midgley also formulated chloro-fluorocarbons (CFCs) for refrigeration which caused "greenhouse gas" and led to global warming.

MED – Pfeiffer's Bio-Chemical Lab develops medical "sensitive crystallization" method for blood tests for tuberculosis and cancer which is used at Hahnemann Hospital in Philadelphia.

– Nobel Prize to Ernest O. Lawrence for cyclotron, essential for nuclear reactions.

– Albert Steffen Group founded in Pittsburgh, PA.

1939
– WORLD WAR II BEGINS IN EUROPE – German armies invade Poland. Two days later, Great Britain and France declare war.

– U.S.-*"The World Of Tomorrow,"* the World's Fair in New York City attended by 44 million Americans, roughly 30% of the population, who had endured the Great Depression. They were hungry for a "modern" future with high powered cars and electric refrigeration.

MED – Camphill Village formed in Scotland. The founding men are held in an internment camp so it is the women of the community who operate the village. (*Into The Heart's Land,* pg. 389)
https://www.camphillscotland.org.uk/the-camphill-movement/founding-values/

"By the start of World War II, 34 Waldorf schools had been founded – in Germany, Switzerland, Holland, England, Norway, Sweden, Hungary, Austria, and in the USA." https://www.waldorf-100.org/en/waldorf-education/history/

MED – Pfeiffer awarded honorary degree of Doctor of Medicine from Hannemann Medical College in Philadelphia for research into Sensitive Crystallization, a diagnostic process originated at the Goetheanum and refined by Pfeiffer.

AG U.K. – Lord Northbourne invites Pfeiffer to England to give the keynote talk at the *Betteshanger Summer School and Conference on Bio-Dynamic Farming* at Northbourne's estate in Kent, 1-9 July 1939. Pfeiffer's keynote lecture is *"The Farm as a Biological Organism"*

END NOTE (3) – AN "ORGANIC ARMY" RALLIED AROUND A SPIRITUAL SCIENTIFIC TRUTH – "FARM AS ORGANISM" AND LAUNCHED "ORGANIC AGRICULTURE" WORLDWIDE

> **FROM STEINER'S "FARM ORGANISM" TO "ORGANIC" AGRICULTURE**
>
> **1939** – Ehrenfried Pfeiffer gives lectures based on the Ag Course at Britain's first BD conference at estate of Lord Northbourne in Kent. The concept of "farm organism" is translated into the term "organics" by Lord Northbourne.

– U.K. Lord Northbourne publishes "organic manifesto *Look To The Land*" in which he coins the term "organic."

ED AG – U.S. – Alarik and Mable Pew Myrin found Kimberton Farms Waldorf school in Pennsylvania. Their original idea was to set up a boarding school as a place to receive students from Michael Hall school outside London when they fled the "blitz." That did not happen. FOLLOW THIS LINK TO READ ABOUT THE HISTORY OF KIMBERTON FARM SCHOOL: https://www.kimberton.org/about/kws-history/

ED – Kimberton Waldorf School, Phoenixville, PA founded. (*Into The Heart's Land,* pg. 179)

– Myrin invites Pfeiffer to Kimberton to start the *"Pennsylvania Project,"* a biodynamic research and education center. The project was not sustainable.

1940
– 23% of Americans live on farms, down from 30% in 1920.

– *The Smith Act* required all aliens to be fingerprinted. The act was the first to condone "guilt by association."

1941
– Roosevelt addresses 77th Congress and appeals for *Four Essential Freedoms*: Freedom of Speech, Freedom of Religion, Freedom from Want and Freedom from Fear.

– *Lend Lease Bill #1776* signed into law. Provided $50 billion in arms, services and supplies for our allies in Europe who were nearly bankrupt at the time.

– Roosevelt freezes all German and Italian assets, all assets of countries already invaded or occupied, and all assets of the Japanese. Prohibits shipments to Japan.

BD – Pfeiffer starts *Bio-dynamic Journal* at headquarters in Chester, NY. He writes under three different pen names for many of the newly created organic newsletters.

– PEARL HARBOR BOMBED. U.S. enters war.

1942
– U.S. – National Association of Evangelicals formed.

ED – High Mowing Waldorf School, Wilton NH founded. (*Into The Heart's Land*, pg. 179)
https://www.highmowing.org/about/history

– *Executive Order #9066* allows military to move 112,000 Japanese-Americans into concentration camps.

ASiA – ADMINISTRATIVE COLLECTION Amendments which reflect the growing membership and Groups and Branches of the Society, and expanding Board of Directors. The role of the Rudolf Steiner Foundation is also evolving. (to be published separately)

ASiA – END NOTE (4) – INVESTIGATION BY THE OFFICE OF SECRET SERVICE (O.S.S.), HONOLULU
DIVERSITY – Documents gathered under the Freedom of Information Act (FOIA) in 1997 reveals history of FBI investigation of the Anthroposophical Society Hawaii in 1942-43.

– Tokyo bombed. Pacific war battles of Coral Sea and Midway.

1943
END NOTE (5) – THE WHITE ROSE – GERMANY Nazis crush a student resistance movement called "The White Rose." Some members are executed. One member who survives SS Prison is Traute Lefrenze (Page). After the war she comes to the U.S. to study medicine. Eventually Dr. Page becomes Co-General Secretary of the Anthroposophical Society in America.

INDEX OF EDUCATION AS AN ART 1940-1978
https://go.elib.com/hReFl

While WWII was underway, Waldorf (Steiner) Education was growing – New York City School, 1927, Kimberton Waldorf School 1939, High Mowing School 1942. This is an index to the Journal which started in 1940.

– Race riots in Detroit based on false rumors. Only integrated neighborhoods untouched.

– Los Angeles *Zoot Suit* riots between white military and Mexican *pachucos*. Police just watch.

– Billy Graham starts Chicago radio ministry and revival meetings.

– **U.K. Sir Albert Howard** *"An Agricultural Testament"* published by Rodale Press advocates "the law of return" a central concept to organic agriculture to build and maintain soil fertility.

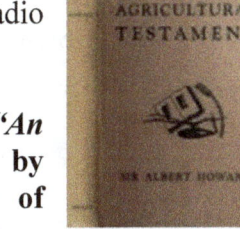

1944
– D-DAY IN EUROPE – June 6. At least 156,000 allied soldiers landed on Normandy beaches or were parachuted behind German lines.

– U.S. Interstate Highway System bill proposed by FDR, as conceptualized by General Motors, envisions a massive highway system and powerful autos.

1945
– WORLD WAR II IN EUROPE ENDS when Germany surrenders (May 7).

– ATOMIC BOMBINGS. Hiroshima, Aug 6. Nagasaki, Aug. 9.

FIRE BORNE 1929-1946

– U.S. – "Green Revolution" – tons of surplus synthetic ammonia and nitrate fertilizers and biocides are "dumped" onto civilian market by military Surplus Property Board.

<<<< *Rodale Organic Gardening Magazine* – **Pfeiffer contracts with J.I. Rodale to write articles.**

– 4 hours per week of network television broadcasting. 7,000 television sets in American households.

– Calculation by Electronic Numerical Integrator and Computer (ENIAC).

NOTES:

Rudolf Steiner Foundation (RSF) incorporated as the Treasury for the Anthroposophical Society in America and practiced Threefolding principles. The foundation remains small for nearly 50 years. (*Into The Heart's Land*, pg. 409.) https://rsfsocialfinance.org/

High Mowing Waldorf School, Wilton NH founded. (*Into The Heart's Land*, pg. 179) https://www.highmowing.org/about/history

Freedom of Information Act (FOIA) in 1997 reveals history of FBI investigation of the Anthroposophical Society Hawaii in 1942-43.

Into The Heart's Land, Henry Barnes, Steiner Books, 2013

Rudolf Steiner Library, https://rudolfsteinerlibrary.org/

END NOTES / LINK PAGES:

THE ADMINISTRATIVE COLLECTION OF THE **BY-LAWS OF THE ANTHROPOSOPHICAL SOCIETY IN AMERICA**

First edition 2023, Anthroposophical Publications, Fremont, Michigan USA

ASA BYLAWS LINK LIST
Chapter 2 – 1929-1946
1933 ASA BYLAWS
The by-laws reflect the fact that the Society is legally formed as a NON-PROFIT MEMBERSHIP ORGANIZATION in New York State. RUDOLF STEINER FOUNDATION designated as the financial "arm" of the Society.
1935 ASA BYLAWS
Reflect a significant change in focus from members to groups and changes the way in which the Council was created.
1952 ASA BYLAWS AMENDMENTS THROUGH 1942
Chapter 3 – 1946-1964
1953 ASA AMENDMENT TO BYLAWS
1954 – ABSTRACT ARTICLE 17 – TRUSTEE FOUNDATION RUDOLF STEINER FOUNDATION
1954 – ASA PROPOSED APPROVED BYLAWS
1957 AMENDMENT ARTICLE 17 MEMBER APPROVAL FORM
1963 ASA BYLAWS AMENDMENT GEOGRAPHICAL REGIONS OF THE SOCIETY
1964 ASA BYLAWS
1964 AS MEMORANDUM RE: BYLAW CHANGES
Chapter 4 – 1965-1984
1981_1 REGIONALIZATION A BRIEF SUMMARY OF THE HISTORY
1981_2 REGIONALIZATION PROPOSED BYLAWS
1981_3 ASA BYLAWS
Chapter 5 – 1985-2004
1990 ASA BYLAWS
1995 ASA BYLAWS
In 1997, following proper legal protocol, the NON-PROFIT MEMBERSHIP ORGANIZATIONAL New York state legal form was laid down and the Society was re-chartered in New York State as a CORPORATE NON-PROFIT. Membership involvement in major changes altered.
Chapter 6 – 2005-2026
2010 ASA BYLAWS – A very significant shift at this time.

END NOTE (1) – PAGE 35 – 1**933 BY-LAWS OF THE ANTHROPOSOPHICAL SOCIETY IN AMERICA**
https://fireborncom.files.wordpress.com/2022/09/1933-by-laws-of-anthroposopohical-society.pdf
By-Laws and other legal documents that reveal a "behind the scenes" activity which affects the Society's "biography" extends throughout this book beginning with these first by-laws of 1933. By-laws are the "rules of the road" which pertain to legal, financial, and local/national and international relationships. The 1933 By-Laws subscribe the American Society to the Foundation Statute but, due to Swiss law, refer to it as the "Principles."

ANTHROPOSOPHICAL SOCIETY IN AMERICA, INC.

Adopted 1933(?). Amended and replaced by new By-Laws in 1954 (H Barnes)

BY-LAWS

1. **NAME** The name of the Society shall be the Anthroposophical Society in America, Inc.

2. **ADHERENCE TO GENERAL ANTHROPOSOPHICAL SOCIETY** The Society herewith affirms its adherence to and acceptance of the *Principles of the General Anthroposophical Society whose center and main office are at the Goetheanum, Dornach, Switzerland. A copy of the same is attached hereto as part of these By-Laws.

3. **MEMBERSHIP** (a) Anyone subscribing to the above Principles may apply for membership in the Anthroposophical Society in America, Inc.

    (b) Whereas it is not obligatory, members of the Society are requested to become, where possible, members of officially constituted Working Groups.

    (c) Any seven members may, by agreement, form themselves into and apply for recognition as an officially constituted Working Group within the Society. These Groups shall govern themselves as they may elect, provided their rules and regulations conform to these By-Laws.

    (d) The number of members who may belong to a Group is not limited.

    (e) A member may hold membership in one or more Groups, provided the dues are paid in each Group.

    (f) Non-group members may, if they wish, associate themselves with the General Secretary and, in conjunction with him, form a single Working Group for the purposes of these By-Laws.

4. **ORGANIZATION** The conduct of the affairs of the Society shall be in the hands of:
    (a) An Administrative Body comprising three officers: a President or General Secretary, a Secretary and a Treasurer. These same shall also be the Board of Directors and the Officers of the Society as a Corporation.

    (b) An Initiative Council advising the General Secretary and Board of Directors.

    (c) A General Meeting or Assembly of all members.

5. **ADMINISTRATIVE BODY** (a) This Body, comprising the Officers and Board of Directors of the Society, shall conduct its affairs in accordance with the advice given by the Initiative Council.

    (b) Meetings of the Administrative Body may be held upon seven days' notice in writing or at any time by unanimous consent.

*Article 2. The Statutes of the General Anthroposophical Society given by Dr. Steiner to the General Meeting of the Christmas Conference of 1923/24. Later, the word "principles" was substituted for "statutes" because when the Anthroposophical Society was incorporated under the Swiss law governing membership associations, it was found necessary to have other legal statutes also. In order to avoid confusion, the original Statutes were called Principles. The American Society derives its legal Statutes from its Certificate of Incorporation under the law of the State of New York governing membership corporations. This Certificate establishes the Society's legal right to receive gifts and legacies. Our present Statutes are not involved.

-2-

(c) A quorum of the Administrative Body shall be two of its members.

6. ELECTION OF OFFICERS (a) Whenever an election of a President or General Secretary is to be held, the Secretary shall send, on or before the 15th of December of the year preceding this election, a letter to the Heads of officially constituted Working Groups inviting nominations from the Groups for this office. If two-thirds of the Group Heads nominate the same candidate in the first instance, this candidate is to be considered elected. If such a contingency does not occur, then copies of all nominations thus received shall be forwarded to all Group Heads with a request that each Group now make its final choice of nominated candidates within the following thirty days. Should a two-thirds majority of Group Heads be in agreement in their final choice, the candidate on whom they are thus agreed shall be deemed to be elected

(b) But if there is no such agreement, the results of the last vote and a request for a new ballot shall be sent out for reply within two weeks. In the event that there is still no two-thirds majority agreement in these last returns, this process shall be continued until a two-thirds agreement is reached. Pending such agreement, the existing General Secretary or, in his absence, the Secretary, shall act as General Secretary.

[handwritten in margin: Paragraph (b) has been changed in April 1947. see page 5 for correct reading]

[handwritten: see pg. 5]

(c) Once elected, the General Secretary shall continue in office for three years from the current Annual Meeting or until such time as a majority of the officially constituted Working Groups may signify in writing their desire for a new election.

(d) The offices of Secretary and Treasurer shall be subject to annual election or re-election. Immediately after the election of a General Secretary and thereafter on or before the 15th day of February of each year, the General Secretary shall send his nominations for those offices to all Group Heads, who shall be asked within two weeks to signify their approval or disapproval and, in the latter case, the General Secretary shall make new nominations. Such correspondence between the General Secretary and the Group Heads shall be continued in this sense until a majority of the latter and the General Secretary are in agreement as to those who are to occupy the offices in question.

7. INITIATIVE COUNCIL (a) There shall be no voting in the proceedings of the Initiative Council except as a device for obtaining expressions of opinion.

(b) The General Secretary shall act as Chairman of its meetings. In his absence, a chairman shall be selected by those present.

(c) The Secretary and the Treasurer of the Society shall be additional members of the Initiative Council ex officio, as well as visiting Group Heads or other properly accredited visiting Group members.

(d) The General Secretary or other members of the Initiative Council may invite others to sit temporarily at its meetings for the purpose of giving special advice unless objections are raised to any such invitations by seven or more of its members.

(e) A quorum of the Initiative Council shall be a majority of its selected members.

(f) Notices of all meetings of the Initiative Council shall be mailed seven days in advance.

8. GENERAL MEETINGS AND CHOICE OF INITIATIVE COUNCIL MEMBERS

   (a) General Meetings of Members may be held during the year either at the Easter Season for the purpose of selecting the members of the Initiative Council from those nominated, and of discussing any and all questions of importance to the well-being and work of the Society.

   (c) Written notice of such meetings shall be sent out to all members at least thirty days in advance.

   (d) The General Secretary shall act as Chairman of the General Annual Meeting or, in his absence, the Secretary, or the Treasurer.

   (e) At the General Annual Meeting the General Secretary shall, after having received suggestions from Groups and individual members, present his nominations of at least 12 members who shall sit upon and constitute the Initiative Council of the Society until the next General Annual Meeting. These nominations may be added to or changed by the General Secretary at the Meeting until at least 12 nominations are approved by a majority of members present

9. DUTIES OF OFFICERS OF THE SOCIETY (a) The President, besides presiding at all meetings of the members and of the Administrative Body or Board of Directors, shall sign or countersign, as may be necessary, all such bills, notes, cheques, contracts and other instruments as may pertain to the ordinary course of the Society's business, and shall sign all contracts, deeds, orders, liens, licenses and other instruments of a special nature. He may also, in the absence or disability of the Treasurer, endorse cheques, drafts and other negotiable instruments for deposit or collection. He shall have such usual powers of supervision and amendment as may pertain to the office of President and perform all such other duties as are incident to his office or are properly required of him by the Board of Directors. The President, as General Secretary, shall have charge of all correspondence of the Society, including the correspondence between this Society and the General Anthroposophical Society at Dornach, Switzerland. He shall supervise and sign membership applications as well as letters recognizing new Working Groups to be formed within the Society.

   (b) The Secretary shall issue notices for all meetings of members and Directors, shall keep the Minutes, shall have charge of the Seal and corporate books, shall sign, with the President, such instruments as require such signature and shall sign such documents and perform such other duties as are incident to his office or are properly required of him by the Board of Directors. The Secretary may delegate some of his duties with the approval of the Board of Directors.

   (c) The Treasurer shall have custody of all monies and securities of the Society and shall keep regular books of accounts and balance the same periodically. He shall sign or countersign such instruments as require his signature and shall perform all duties incident to his office or that are properly required of him by the Board of Directors. The Treasurer may also delegate some of his duties with the approval of the Board of Directors.

10/ SEAL The corporate seal of the Society shall consist of two concentric circles between which is the name: "Anthroposophical Society" and in the center: "Incorporated 1933 New York", and such seal as impressed on the margin shall be the corporate seal of the Society.

11. DUES* (a) The membership dues of this Society include the dues in the General Anthroposophical Society, Dornach, Switzerland, which shall be the equivalent of 15 Swiss francs annually, plus the dues for the American Society of not less than $2.00 annually for Group members and not less than $3.00

*Article 11 (a) The payment of 15 Swiss francs to the General
Anthroposophical Society as dues is mandatory on all members of
the General Anthroposophical Society. Under a special arrange-
ment with the Administration at Dornach, all the members of the
American Society receive the weekly English language News Sheet
by paying, in addition, a sum which makes the annual dues
amount to $6.00. This arrangement will continue unless another
seems desirable.

(b) All dues shall be due and payable on making application for
membership and they shall be thereafter payable on or about the
first day of each year.

(c) Dues shall cover the year in which they are paid, whatever may be
the date on which they are paid, except where members join during
the last quarter of the calendar year. In that case, the dues
shall be applied to the following year. The annual dues of the
Society may be altered from time to time by action of the Administrative Body and Initiative Council.

12. TRUSTEE FOUNDATION (a) There shall be a Trustee Foundation set
up within the Society known as the Rudolf
Steiner Foundation, Inc. This Foundation shall be composed of
seven members of the Society who shall be elected serially every
three years and serve seven. (In the first instance, the following members were elected for the given terms, beginning with the
last Monday in October, 1934: Mr. Henry B. Monges, who was to
serve for three years; Mr. Olin D. Wannamaker, for four years;
Mr. George Sumner Small, for seven years; Mr. Herbert Chaudiere,
for eight years; and Mr. Roger Hale, for nine years.) At the end
of the first three years, and every year thereafter, a new trustee
shall be elected to serve for seven years. Retiring trustees are
eligible for re-election.

(b) Any vacancy shall be filled by the members of the Foundation
submitting to the Society names of members who in their estima-
tion would be capable and willing to accept the office. If all
are rejected, the General Secretary shall be asked to name a
member, but only one acceptable to the members of the Foundation.

(c) No investment shall be made or altered unless instructions are
given at a duly constituted meeting of the trustees of the
Foundation.

(d) The Anthroposophical Society in America, Inc., may turn over or
transfer any or all gifts, legacies, or principal funds, or any
other of its property of whatever nature to the Rudolf Steiner
Foundation, Inc., as agent or trustee under an irrevocable or
revocable indenture of trust or otherwise, and the said Foundation shall invest, preserve and administer the same to the best
of its ability. In the case of gifts and legacies turned over
to the Foundation by the Anthroposophical Society in America, Inc
the income shall be paid over to the Anthroposophical Society in
America, Inc., from time to time as earned in whatever proportion
requested by it for carrying on the work of the Society. Over
this income the Society shall exercise full control and it shall
be its duty to direct its expenditure for the benefit of the work
and purposes of the Society through its Administrative Officers.
The Foundation shall, therefore, have no control or any say about
the manner or purpose of the expenditure of the income from said
gifts or legacies, and the administration of the income from such
other funds or property which the Anthroposophical Society turns
over to the Foundation shall be in accordance with any agreement
under which such funds are turned over to the Foundation.

(e) The said Foundation shall invest all principal funds in investments which in its opinion are suitable for the funds of the
Foundation, whether or not such investments are legal for Trust
Funds in the State of New York, except in the case of funds
otherwise restricted by the donor or testator or by the laws of
the State of New York.

-5-

(f) The removal of trustees of the Rudolf Steiner Foundation, Inc., may take place after charges have been served upon the same, who shall be allowed thirty days in which to answer. Removal shall be by two-thirds of the remaining trustees.

13. AMENDMENT OF THESE BY-LAWS These By-aws of the Anthroposophical Society in America, Inc., may only be amended by a two-thirds majority of the Administrative Body and the Initiative Council and visiting Group Heads meeting together after notice of the purpose of the meeting has been sent out thirty days in advance of the same. Such amendments must be passed by two consecutive such meetings held thirty days apart. They shall only become valid and be incorporated in these By-Laws after being confirmed in writing by a two-thirds majority of the Group Heads.

14. * EXPULSION OF MEMBERS Any member may, for cause, be expelled from the Anthroposophical Society in America, Inc., at any time by the affirmative vote of a majority of the Board of Directors. Such expulsion applies only to American membership and does not affect continued membership in the General Anthroposophical Society.

* Article 14. This has been inserted at the suggestion of our attorney who strongly advises it as a protection of ownership of valuables and property and to prevent exploitation of the Society and members.

AMENDMENT TO ARTICLE 6, paragraph (b):   (as of April, 1947)

But if there is no such agreement, the results of the last vote and a request for a new ballot shall be sent out for reply within two weeks. In the event that there is still no two-thirds majority agreement in these last returns, this process shall be continued until a two-thirds agreement is reached. Pending such agreement, the existing General Secretary-President or, in his absence, the Secretary or Treasurer - whichever shall be named by the President at the time of his or her nomination to office, or, in the absence of such nomination, the Secretary - shall act as General Secretary-President pro tem.

(This change is suggested merely to give more latitude in the choice of an executive officer at a possibly critical moment.)

END NOTE (2) – PAGE 35 – *"ANTHROPOSOPHY AT THE TIME OF NAZI GERMANY"* A COLLECTION OF ACTUAL NAZI DOCUMENTS FROM THE ARCHIV AM GOETHEANUM.
https://firebornecom.files.wordpress.com/2022/02/2.5-nazi-archive.pdf

These documents were provided in 2000 during a worldwide Michael Conference to the Anthroposophical Society in America by Uwe Werner, the Archivist at Archiv Am Goetheanum.

ARCHIV AM GOETHEANUM

Anthroposophy in the Time of Nazi Germany

Recent accusations of "racist" and "Nazi" undertones of anthroposophy and Waldorf Schools betray a curious case of history contradicting itself. To the Nazis themselves, Anthroposophists were persecuted as guilty of the opposite charges: "individualistic", "internationally oriented", and "pacifistic", they were accused of maintaining close ties to Jews. Their humanistic philosophy, contradictory to the ideas of race and "Volk" upheld by the Nazis, was determined to be "directly opposed to National Socialism". The following is a short excerpt from Uwe Werner's recent book "Anthroposophen in der Zeit des Nationalsozialismus" (Verlag R. Oldenberg, Muenchen, 1999), which sketches the historical circumstances of the anthroposophical movement in the time of Nazi Germany.

Anthroposophists belonged to the many groups of people who were persecuted under the Nazi regime. Hitler's own disdaining remarks regarding Rudolf Steiner and the Anthroposophists appeared as early as 1921.[1] By spring of 1933, articles criticizing the movement began appearing more frequently in National Socialist newspapers. By summer of that year, Steiner's books were banned from public libraries in Bavaria, and study groups and branches of the Anthroposophical Society, along with other cultural organizations, were ordered to submit to National Socialistic leadership.

During the years leading up to the 1935 prohibition of the German Anthroposophical Society and the closing of Waldorf Schools in the years thereafter, the society Council was faced with the question of whether to submit to pressure to dissolve the Society of their own accord, or whether to attempt to preserve the Society and to continue working as long and as effectively as possible. Choosing the second of these two paths made it necessary for them to make compromises in order to be tolerated by those in power. It is for this reason that, despite the fact that the main Council had unanimously renounced the National Socialist cause at an internal meeting at Easter 1933, there was never a public rejection of National Socialism on the part of the Anthroposophical Society.

Like the Anthroposophical Society, institutions based on anthroposophy (such as Waldorf Schools, schools for the handicapped, hospitals, schools of Eurythmy, etc.), for the most part adopted a strategy of peaceful and passive resistance. Waldorf Schools experienced serious financial strains and were forced to let go of Jewish teachers, but the remaining teachers could continue to create their own lesson plans. In homes for the handicapped, children could be cared for. It was still possible to publish and to have access to the work of Rudolf Steiner. In a manner of working not unlike that carried out by Anthroposophists today in regions with human rights violations, efforts aimed to uphold human dignity wherever possible.

Though the decision had been reached by July, 1934, it was not until November 1, 1935 that, through the efforts of Nazi leaders Heinrich Himmler and Reinhard Heydrich, the Anthroposophical Society was prohibited in Germany. The grounds for its prohibition read as follows:

> "According to its historical development, the Anthroposophical Society is internationally oriented and even today continues to maintain close contacts to foreign freemasons, Jews and pacifists. The methods of teaching developed by its founder, Steiner, and followed in the anthroposophical schools still existing today follow an individualistic and human-oriented education, which has nothing in common with principles of National Socialistic education. As a result of its opposition to the National Socialistic idea of Volk (*Voelkische Gedanke*), the continued activity of the Anthroposophical Society imposes the danger of injuring the National Socialistic State. The organization is therefore to be dissolved on account of its subversive character and the danger it poses to the public."[2]

The accusations had been carefully researched. Himmler ordered numerous investigative reports that serve to document the stand of the Nazis toward anthroposophy. Fifteen in-depth reports, as well as countless individual accounts, all come to the same conclusion: that anthroposophy is irreconcilable with the aims and ideologies of National Socialism.

"To briefly summarize my judgement," wrote Jakob Wilhelm Hauer, Professor of Religion at the University of Tuebingen and member of the Secret Service of the S.S.,

> "every undertaking and activity of anthroposophy necessarily arises out of the Anthroposophical world view. The anthroposophical worldview is in its most important points directly opposed to National Socialism. Therefore, schools which are built out of the anthroposophical worldview and led by anthroposophists mean danger to true German education."[3]

Perhaps the most persuasive adherent of National Socialism to formulate the incompatibility of anthroposophy and National Socialism was Alfred Bauemler, a distinguished philosopher and professor of education in Berlin. As part of his work within the Rosenburg Office "for the control of the intellectual life of the National Socialist Party", he was commissioned to conduct an in-depth investigation of the work of Rudolf Steiner. Unlike hasty and unstudied police reports, Bauemler's "Report on Waldorf Schools" and "Report on Rudolf Steiner and Philosophy" are noteworthy attempts to understand the thoughts underlying anthroposophy: Baeumler's hope was to find means to adopt aspects of Waldorf pedagogy into National Socialist education. He concluded, however, that the principles underlying anthroposophy contradict the aims of the National Socialist State. "The fateful distinction," he wrote, "occurs through the fact that Steiner replaces the theory of heredity with *a different, positive theory*. Steiner does not simply overlook the biological reality, but rather consciously converts it to its opposite. Anthroposophy is one of the most consequent antibiological systems." In that race and *Volk* are discounted in anthroposophy as the essential determining factor of individual capacity, Bauemler realizes that the objectives in Waldorf education, according to Steiner's principles, "can only be humanistic, and not based on race or ethnic group."[4]

In March, 1936, Waldorf Schools were prohibited from taking on new students; by summer of 1941, all Waldof Schools in Germany had been forced to close their doors.

On June 9, 1941, shortly before the attack on Russia, the Gestapo staged an action against the "inside opponents" of the Nazis. The Christian Community was prohibited from continued activity, and prominent Anthroposophists and members of the Christian Community were arrested, interrogated, and imprisoned or sent to concentration camps. The following fall, the Department of Security of the Reich published a 50 page brochure entitled "Anthroposophy and its Associated Institutions". The report's concluding statement read: "If one is to accept the totality of thinking embraced in a world-view and recognize its impact on the entire opinions and bearing of the people, then there can be no doubt that followers of Anthroposophy must necessarily become opponents of National Socialism."[5]

* * *

Documentary Material

1. Adolf Hitler about Rudolf Steiner and Three-folding

"In the course of the London affair, there gradually emerged such mysterious circumstances that it has become not only expedient but indeed necessary to look somewhat more closely at this Minister [Simons], the intimate friend of the Gnostic and Anthroposophist Rudolf Steiner, follower of Three-folding of the Social Organism and whatever all these Jewish methods of destroying the normal frame of mind of the people are called: to see whether that mindless face, as Lloyd George described it, is really just the result of a deficient intellect, or if it is the mask behind which something else is concealed... [*He continues with a protest against Simon's political activity, and particularly the movement to disarm the German people*] ... And who is the driving force behind all this devilishness? The Jew! Friend of Doctor Rudolf Steiner, the friends of Simons, the "mindless"..."

Adolf Hitler, Staatsmaenner oder Nationalverbrecher (Men of the State or National Criminals"), in: Voelkischer Beobachter, 35.Jg., 15. March 1921, S.2. (original German text)

2. Prohibition of the Anthroposophical Society in Germany, November 1, 1935

"Prussian Secret Police, Berlin, November 1, 1935. The deputy chief (*stell. Chef*) and Inspector II 1 B 2 69121?766 L/35.

Regarding: the Anthroposophical Society.

In accordance with paragraph 1 of the decree of 2.28.1933 for the Protection of People and State, issued by the President of the Reich, I hereby dissolve the Anthroposophical

Society within the territory of the German Reich, effective immediately. The organization's properties are to be confiscated. The re-establishment of the Society, as well as the creation of undercover successor organizations, is forbidden under threat of the penalties described in paragraph 4 of the above-named decree.

Grounds: According to its historical development, the Anthroposophical Society is internationally oriented and even today continues to maintain close contacts to foreign freemasons, Jews and pacifists. The methods of teaching developed by its founder, Steiner, and followed in the anthroposophical schools still existing today follow an individualistic and human-oriented education, which has nothing in common with principles of national socialistic education. As a result of its opposition to the National Socialistic idea of Volk (*Voelkische Gedanke*), the continued activity of the Anthroposophical Society imposes the danger of injuring the National Socialistic state.

The organization is therefore to be dissolved on account of its subversive character and the danger it poses to the public.

sig. *in absentia*, Heydrich."

BAK (German Federal Archives) R 43 II/822 (original German text)

3. Dr. J.W. Hauer on Waldorf Schools

"[…] To briefly summarize my judgement: Every undertaking and activity of anthroposophy necessarily arises out of the anthroposophical world view. The anthroposophical world view is in its most important points directly opposed to national socialism. Therefore, schools which are built out of the anthroposophical world view and led by anthroposophists mean danger to true German education, particularly through the relation of the anthroposophical communities to Dornach, the international center of anthroposophy, in which Jews also play an important role, or at any rate have played until the present. A survey of the teachers and leaders of the individual Waldorf Schools in Germany before the [Nazi] takeover indicates clearly that the Jewish impact was important in the German anthroposophical communities and schools."

Prof. Dr. J.W. Hauer, in an internal report for the Secret Service, Stuttgart on February 7, 1935. BAP R 4901-3285 (original German text)

4. From "Report on Waldorf Schools" and "Report on Rudolf Steiner and Philosophy" by Alfred Bauemler

The understanding of man (*Menschenkunde*) which underlies Waldorf education contain deep and correct insights, which R. Steiner derived mostly from his exceedingly fruitful study of Goethe's writings on natural science. The National Socialistic understanding of man can only be derived from race. To the extent to which race is a reality of nature, it could appear that already in the point of departure there lay an essential correlation between Rudolf Steiner's understanding of man, and that of National Socialism: Steiner departs from the formative forces of Nature and bases school-education on the development of natural forces. One might thereby call his education "biologically" founded. However, if one were to attempt to introduce the concept of race as we understand it into this biological foundation, it would explode Steiner's understanding of man. This is because National Socialism departs from the reality of blood, and from the *differences* that exist between groups of people of differing blood. We grasp these differences not only biologically/anthropologically, but primarily *historically*, in that we turn our attention to those things which people of varying blood-heritage have produced and developed: the cities, works of art, inventions, scientific systems, etc. Rudolf Steiner's understanding of man has no access to this *historical thinking* derived from knowledge of the reality of race. The position occupied in our world view by the man determined by the forces of race is occupied in the world view of Rudolf Steiner by the Spirit of Man, sovereign over all history. The thought of Rudolf Steiner is not biological-racist, but biological-cosmic."

Alfred Bauemler, *Report on Waldorf Schools*, 1937, in: Achim Leschinsky, "Waldorf Schools in National Socialism", *Neue Sammlung*, May/June 1983, p.280. (original German text)

"Steiner is not only an epigone of idealistic philosophy, but he builds upon the philosophy of the intellect (spirit) in a decided manner. The fateful turning point occurs through the fact that Steiner replaces the theory of heredity with *a different, positive theory*. He does not simply overlook the biological reality, but rather consciously converts it to its opposite. Anthroposophy is one of the most consequent antibiological systems in existence." (p.401)

"Objectives of pedagogical activity: According to the basic assumptions of anthroposophy, these objectives can only be humanistic, and not based on race or ethnic group." (p.403)

Alfred Bauemler, *Report on Rudolf Steiner and Philosophy*, 1938, in: Uwe Werner, *Anthroposophen in der Zeit der Nationalsozialismus 1933-1945*, Muenchen, 1999, p. 401, 403. (original German text)

5. "Anthroposophy and its Associated Institutions"

"Die Anthroposophie und ihre Zweckverbaende. Bericht unter Verwendung von Ergebnissen der Aktion gegen Geheimlehren und sogenannte Geheimwissenschaften vom 5. Juni 1941." RSHA ca. Oktober 1941. ("Anthroposophy and its Associated Institutions. Report applying evidence from the Operation against Secret Teachings and so called Occult Sciences of June 5, 1941." RSHA, ca. October 1941)

Preußische Geheime Staatspolizei
Der stellvertretende Chef u. Inspekteur

B.-Nr. II 1 B 2 69121/766 L/35

Berlin SW 11, den 1.November 1935.
Prinz-Albrecht-Straße 8

III P Zay. 222

<u>Betrifft</u>: Anthroposophische Gesellschaft.
<u>Im Nachgang</u> zu meinem Schreiben v.14.10.35 -
Tgb.Nr. wie oben -.

    Die im Reichsgebiet bestehende Anthroposophische Gesellschaft habe ich durch Erlaß vom heutigen Tage ihres staatsgefährdenden Charakters wegen unter gleichzeitiger Beschlagnahme ihres Vermögens auf Grund des § 1 der V.O. des Herrn Reichspräsidenten zum Schutze von Volk und Staat vom 28.2.33 aufgelöst und gleichzeitig die Gründung von Nachfolgeorganisationen unter Androhung der Folgen aus § 4 der V.O. verboten.

              I.V.
          gez.Heydrich.

Beglaubigt:

Kanzleiangestellte.

An den
Herrn Reichs- und Preußischen
Minister des Innern

Berlin NW 40
Königsplatz 6.

Abschrift   76

Geheime preussische Staatspolizei   Berlin, 1. November 1935
                                          (ausgehändigt 12. November)

Betrifft Anthroposophische Gesellschaft

Auf Grund des § 1 der V.O. des Herrn Reichspräsidenten zum Schutze von Volk und Staat vom 28.2.1933 löse ich mit sofortiger Wirkung die im Gebiete des deutschen Reiches bestehende Anthroposophische Gesellschaft auf. Das Vermögen der Organisation wird beschlagnahmt. Die Neu-Gründung der Gesellschaft sowie die Schaffung getarnter Nachfolgeorganisationen wird bei Androhung der Folgen aus § 4 dieser Verordnung verboten.

Gründe !

Nach der geschichtlichen Entwicklung der Anthroposophischen Gesellschaft ist diese international eingestellt und unterhält auch heute noch Beziehungen zu ausländischen Freimaurern, Juden und Pazifisten. Die auf der Pädagogik des Gründers _Steiner_ aufgebauten und in den heute noch bestehenden anthroposophischen Schulen angewandten Unterrichtsmethoden verfolgen eine individualistische, nach dem Einzelmenschen ausgerichtete Erziehung, die nichts mit den nationalsozialistischen Erziehungsgrundsätzen gemein hat. Infolge ihres Gegensatzes zu dem vom Nationalsozialismus vertretenen völkischen Gedanken besteht die Gefahr, dass durch die weitere Tätigkeit der Anthroposophischen Gesellschaft die Belange des nationalsozialistischen Staates geschädigt werden.

Die Organisation ist daher wegen ihres staatsfeindlichen und staatsgefährdenden Charakters aufzulösen.

                                          I.V. Heydrich
Stempel.   Beglaubigt : gez. Bosse
                                          Kanzleiangestellte

Reichsgesetzblatt
Teil I

| 1933 | Ausgegeben zu Berlin, den 28. Februar 1933 | Nr. 17 |

Inhalt: Verordnung des Reichspräsidenten zum Schutz von Volk und Staat. Vom 28. Februar 1933...... S. 83

Verordnung des Reichspräsidenten zum Schutz von Volk und Staat. Vom 28. Februar 1933.

Auf Grund des Artikels 48 Abs. 2 der Reichsverfassung wird zur Abwehr kommunistischer staatsgefährdender Gewaltakte folgendes verordnet:

§ 1

Die Artikel 114, 115, 117, 118, 123, 124 und 153 der Verfassung des Deutschen Reichs werden bis auf weiteres außer Kraft gesetzt. Es sind daher Beschränkungen der persönlichen Freiheit, des Rechts der freien Meinungsäußerung, einschließlich der Pressefreiheit, des Vereins- und Versammlungsrechts, Eingriffe in das Brief-, Post-, Telegraphen- und Fernsprechgeheimnis, Anordnungen von Haussuchungen und von Beschlagnahmen sowie Beschränkungen des Eigentums auch außerhalb der sonst hierfür bestimmten gesetzlichen Grenzen zulässig.

§ 2

Werden in einem Lande die zur Wiederherstellung der öffentlichen Sicherheit und Ordnung nötigen Maßnahmen nicht getroffen, so kann die Reichsregierung insoweit die Befugnisse der obersten Landesbehörde vorübergehend wahrnehmen.

§ 3

Die Behörden der Länder und Gemeinden (Gemeindeverbände) haben den auf Grund des § 2 erlassenen Anordnungen der Reichsregierung im Rahmen ihrer Zuständigkeit Folge zu leisten.

§ 4

Wer den von den obersten Landesbehörden oder den ihnen nachgeordneten Behörden zur Durchführung dieser Verordnung erlassenen Anordnungen oder den von der Reichsregierung gemäß § 2 erlassenen Anordnungen zuwiderhandelt oder wer zu solcher Zuwiderhandlung auffordert oder anreizt, wird, soweit nicht die Tat nach anderen Vorschriften mit einer schwereren Strafe bedroht ist, mit Gefängnis nicht unter einem Monat oder mit Geldstrafe von 150 bis zu 15 000 Reichsmark bestraft.

Wer durch Zuwiderhandlung nach Abs. 1 eine gemeine Gefahr für Menschenleben herbeiführt, wird mit Zuchthaus, bei mildernden Umständen mit Gefängnis nicht unter sechs Monaten und, wenn die Zuwiderhandlung den Tod eines Menschen verursacht, mit dem Tode, bei mildernden Umständen mit Zuchthaus nicht unter zwei Jahren bestraft. Daneben kann auf Vermögenseinziehung erkannt werden.

Wer zu einer gemeingefährlichen Zuwiderhandlung (Abs. 2) auffordert oder anreizt, wird mit Zuchthaus, bei mildernden Umständen mit Gefängnis nicht unter drei Monaten bestraft.

§ 5

Mit dem Tode sind die Verbrechen zu bestrafen, die das Strafgesetzbuch in den §§ 81 (Hochverrat), 229 (Giftbeibringung), 307 (Brandstiftung), 311 (Explosion), 312 (Überschwemmung), 315 Abs. 2 (Beschädigung von Eisenbahnanlagen), 324 (gemeingefährliche Vergiftung) mit lebenslangem Zuchthaus bedroht.

Mit dem Tode oder, soweit nicht bisher eine schwerere Strafe angedroht ist, mit lebenslangem Zuchthaus oder mit Zuchthaus bis zu 15 Jahren wird bestraft:

1. Wer es unternimmt, den Reichspräsidenten oder ein Mitglied oder einen Kommissar der Reichsregierung oder einer Landesregierung zu töten oder wer zu einer solchen Tötung auffordert, sich erbietet, ein solches Erbieten annimmt oder eine solche Tötung mit einem anderen verabredet;

2. wer in den Fällen des § 115 Abs. 2 des Strafgesetzbuchs (schwerer Aufruhr) oder des § 125 Abs. 2 des Strafgesetzbuchs (schwerer Landfriedensbruch) die Tat mit Waffen oder in bewußtem und gewolltem Zusammenwirken mit einem Bewaffneten begeht;

3. wer eine Freiheitsberaubung (§ 239) des Strafgesetzbuchs in der Absicht begeht, sich des der Freiheit Beraubten als Geisel im politischen Kampfe zu bedienen.

§ 6

Diese Verordnung tritt mit dem Tage der Verkündung in Kraft.

Berlin, den 28. Februar 1933.

Der Reichspräsident
von Hindenburg

Der Reichskanzler
Adolf Hitler

Der Reichsminister des Innern
Frick

Der Reichsminister der Justiz
Dr. Gürtner

Herausgegeben vom Reichsministerium des Innern. — Gedruckt in der Reichsdruckerei, Berlin.

Anlage 4: Klassen-, Lehrer- und Schülerzahlen der Waldorfschulen in Deutschland 1919 bis 1945 (1941).[1]

Schuljahr	Rudolf Steiner Schule Altona			Rudolf Steiner Schule Berlin			Rudolf Steiner Schule Breslau			Rudolf Steiner Schule Dresden			Freie Waldorfschule Kassel			Freie Goethe Schule Wandsbek			Freie Waldorfschule Hannover			Freie Waldorfschule Stuttgart		
	Klas	Lehr	Schü	Klas	Lehr	Schü	Klas	Lehr	Schü	Klas	Lehr	Schü	Klas	Lehr	Schü	Klas	Lehr	Schü	Klas	Lehr	Schü	Klas	Lehr	Schü
1919/20																						8	12	256
20/21																						11	23	420
21/22																						15	30	536
22/23													1	2	7							19	38	640
23/24													2	3	22							22	47	687
24/25													4	5	88							23	52	784
25/26													5	7	103							26	56	894
26/27													6	9	182	1	2	52				28	60	1023
27/28													8	11	241	2	3	90				28	60	1019
28/29				2	3	56							9	13	311	3	5	136				28	63	1120
29/30				–	–	–				–	–	65	10	17	372	5	8	186				28	64	1124
30/31				7	12	323	3	–	–	5	9	206	–	9	151	11	18	356	6	11	228	28	60	1061
31/32	5	5	107	8	–	–	5	–	–	–	–	–	6	11	243	12	19	382	8	14	288	28	60	1060
32/33	–[2]	–	–	8	–	369	–	–	–	–	–	289	–	14	268	12	20	388	9	14	310	28	60	1.003
33/34	–	–	–	9	16	367	7	–	227	8	–	300	–	16	305	13	19	421	10	15	329	27	58	963

[1] Quelle: Zusammengestellt aus Archiv Bund der Waldorfschulen und Schulaufsicht Hannover (StAH).

Anlage 4: Klassen-, Lehrer- und Schülerzahlen der Waldorfschulen in Deutschland 1919 bis 1945 (1941).[1] (Fortsetzung)

Schuljahr	Rudolf Steiner Schule Altona			Rudolf Steiner Schule Berlin			Rudolf Steiner Schule Breslau			Rudolf Steiner Schule Dresden			Freie Waldorfschule Kassel			Freie Goethe Schule Wandsbek			Freie Waldorfschule Hannover			Freie Waldorfschule Stuttgart		
	Klas	Lehr	Schü	Klas	Lehr	Schü	Klas	Lehr	Schü	Klas	Lehr	Schü	Klas	Lehr	Schü	Klas	Lehr	Schü	Klas	Lehr	Schü	Klas	Lehr	Schü
34/35	8	12	287	10	17	394	8	11	240	9	17	340	9	15	293	–[2]	–	–	11	15	305	23	54	870
35/36	10	–	360	–	–	–	–	–	–	–	–	–	–	20	320	–	–	–	11	–	291	23	–	804
36/37	–[3]	–	–	–	–	335	–	–	–	–	–	220	–	–	–	12	–	420	10	14	238	19	47	667
37/38	–	–	–	–	–	–	–	–	–	–	–	202	–	–	–	–	–	–	9	–	186	17	43	555
38/39				5[3]	5	90	–	–	–	–	–	308	–	–	100	7	–	–	6[3]	–	81	11[3]	19	322
39/40										–	–	447	–[3]	–	–	11	–	200	4[3]	–	30			
40/41										–	–	450												
41/42										–	–	–												
42/43																								
43/44																								
44/45																								
	Selbstschließung (06.04.36)			Selbstschließung (26.08.37)			Selbstschließung (24.03.1939)			Zwangsschließung (05.07.41)			Selbstschließung (27.06.38)			Selbstschließung (21.03.40)			Selbstschließung (09.07.37)			Zwangsschließung (01.04.38)		

[1] Quelle: Zusammengestellt aus Archiv Bund der Waldorfschulen und Schulaufsicht Hannover (StAH).
[2] –: Zahlenangaben fehlen.
[3] Umschulungskurse nach Schließung der Schule.

END NOTE (3) – PAGE 38 – 1938 AN "ORGANIC ARMY" RALLIED AROUND A SPIRITUAL SCIENTIFIC TRUTH – "FARM AS ORGANISM" AND LAUNCHED "ORGANIC AGRICULTURE" WORLDWIDE

https://firebornecom.files.wordpress.com/2022/02/03-organic-army.pdf

1938 THE ORGANIC ARMY

In 1938, Pfeiffer published his book, "*Bio-Dynamic Farming and Gardening*"(1). It was Lord Northbourne who coined the term "organic "in his book, *"Look To The Land"* published a year later in 1939.

A key contribution of Northbourne was to take Rudolf Steiner's idea of 'the farm as organism' and derive from it a named practice, a differentiated agriculture, 'organic farming' (Paull, 2006; Steiner, 1924).(2)

Northbourne's underlying concept of 'the farm as organism' can be traced back to Ehrenfried Pfeiffer's book Bio-Dynamic Farming and Gardening (1938), and Pfeiffer had it from Rudolf Steiner's 1924 Agriculture Course. Steiner (1861-1925) declared, in the series of eight lectures held at Koberwitz, that: "Truly, the farm is an organism" (1924, lecture VIII, p.7). (3)

Northbourne was keen to organize an "organic Army" willing to do cultural battle with the forces of chemical science, economic profit and political muscle.

In January 1939, Northbourne visited Pfeiffer in Switzerland to organize the first biodynamics conference in England, and at which Pfeiffer was the lead lecturer (Northbourne, 1939b). The outcome was the Betteshanger Summer School and Conference on Bio-Dynamic Farming conducted over nine days, 1-9 July 1939, at Northbourne's estate. One of Pfeiffer's lectures at the conference was "The Farm as a Biological Organism" (Northbourne, 1939a; Paull, 2011b).(4)

Northbourne conducted a first and then a second Betteshanger Summer School and Conference on Bio-dynamic Farming on his estate in England. These conferences "summoned" an Organic Army of influential individuals with international forces drawn by a morality which bubbled along secret cultural and interpersonal pathways.

- Ehrenfried Pfeiffer, "the Bio-dynamic Agricultural Method," 1938.
- Lord Northbourne, "Look To the Land," 1939.
- J. I. Rodale. His periodical, Organic Farming and Gardening appeared in May 1942.
- Sir Albert Howard, "An Agricultural Testament," 1943.
- Lady Eve Balfour, "The Living Soil," 1943. Her book led directly to the founding in 1946 of the Soil Association which became the UK's leading organic advocacy group. (Brander 2003)

Each had the openness to the idea of "biologic or organic thinking" as Pfeiffer sometimes called it.

" *... three fundamental characteristics become evident in every phenomenon of life ...*

The third fundamental characteristic can be approximately outlined in the following sentence: *The whole is not merely the sum of all its parts, but a harmonic unity of a higher order, which as organic being, as an organism with laws of a higher order, lifts the world of the physio-chemical inorganic to the world of the organic-living.* Expressed consciously for the first time by Goethe, this truth today affects more and more all our biological thinking. From it, we learn not only that a man, an animal, a plant is an organism, but that the living together of the plant world and earth, of plant with plant in certain groupings, of plant and with animal and man forms itself likewise into an organic unity. Indeed the entire development of the "living space," let us say of a folk, of a continent is fashioned according to the same fundamental laws of the "will to evolve," of the proper interactivity of all factors."(5)

The leading English farming magazine said this about Lord Northbourne's book, *Look To The Land* when it was first published in 1939: "This book sounds an alarm. Lord Northbourne knows that for life and for wellbeing man is dependent upon the soil. In this book he warns us that we are making improper use of our heritage ... He believes that salvation will come not through government, not through individual labors of love."(6)

1. At the time he published his Bio-Dynamic Farming and Gardening, Pfeiffer was the Director of the Bio-chemical Research Laboratory at the Goetheanum, the headquarters of the Anthroposophy movement, in Dornach, Switzerland. Pfeiffer played a key role in testing and evolving Steiner's ideas into biodynamic agriculture, a system which eschewed synthetic fertilizers and pesticides (Paull, 2011c).
2. LORD NORTHBOURNE THE MAN WHO INVENTED ORGANIC FARMING, A BIOGRAPHY, John Paull, Journal of Organic systems, School of Land and Food, Tasmania, Australia, June 2014, pg. 32
3. ibid
4. ibid ORGANIC ARMY PAGE 2
5. BIO-DYNAMIC FARMING AND GARDENING, Ehrenfried Pfeiffer, Anthroposophic Press, 1938. Introduction pg. vi.
6. Leading British agricultural periodical THE FIELD, 1940, p. 104 (PAULL pg. 33)

END NOTE (4) – PAGE 39 – **1942 INVESTIGATION BY THE OFFICE OF SECRET SERVICE (O.S.S.), HONOLULU**
https://firebornecom.files.wordpress.com/2022/02/1943-diversity.pdf

CONFIDENTIAL INVESTIGATION BY THE O.S.S. (OFFICE OF SECRET SERVICE)
One can see that the elements of Euro-centrism were naturally strong within some Society members. However, investigations over the years have shown that the Society was patriotic and American.

As the Second World War loomed, all organizations with foreign connections were subject to particular scrutiny. Because Americans were encouraged to "spy" on one another for the good of "national security" you can imagine that citizens would be suspicious of an Eurocentric organization with some German speaking members.

A January 2001 FOIA request to the Justice Department / Federal Bureau of Investigation (F.B.I.) did result in a 134 page file about the Society. The file contained dozens of investigations about alleged anti-American activity, anti-Semitism and so forth dating back to the 1940's which were all investigated.

Here is one example:

> "Attached are two copies each of the two concluding reports on the Anthroposophical Society which you requested. Our investigator is convinced that this is one of the many

psychical organizations in the city and that there is nothing subversive so far as can be learned."

"Personally, I was a bit suspicious because the organization was known by Mrs. VM of the Aloha Bookshop whose place is the hub of all subversive and anti-Semitic activity in this city. However, acting on the latest report, I checked with Dr. O, whom I know, and he advises that he has known M for a considerable time and he does not know him to be either un-American or anti-Semitic and does not believe he is such."

(O.S.S. "Confidential" file dated January 4, 1943)

END NOTE (5) – PAGE 39 – **1943 – THE WHITE ROSE**

THE WHITE ROSE:
Resistance to Fascism and Anti-Semitism

Compiled by Jean W. Yeager

The White Rose was a Nazi resistance organization run by medical students in Munich during World War II which made headlines around the world when it was discovered in 1943 and six of its leaders guillotined.

The White Rose resistance group were middle-class students who defied Hitler by printing a series of illegal pamphlets denouncing Hitler and the atrocities of the Gestapo-run society, travelling throughout Germany to distribute them.

Their efforts had results. For example, a demonstration in 1942 in Munich was broken up by the SS. Several students were arrested, brutally mistreated, and taken before the Military Court. Agitation continued through the pamphlets of the White Rose and came to a head in February 1943.

Terrible Justice

In February 1943, after weeks of intense Gestapo searching, three White Rose members were arrested. Hitler assigned his "hanging judge" Roland Freisler, to personally get "justice". After trials which lasted only an hour or so, the three young people were found guilty and beheaded before the day's end. Hans and Sophie Scholl and Christopher Probst, who were the first White Rose members to be executed, died on February 22, 1943, just two days before the anniversary of the founding of the Nazi party.

Despite considerable interrogation at Gestapo headquarters, the three gave no names of additional conspirators. The Gestapo increased their efforts to "stamp out" the White Rose.

Hitler so feared the White Rose resistance effort, that immediately following the first executions, he sent a proclamation to Munich which exhorted loyal party members to remain steadfast despite the attacks, and to strengthen German resolve by ruthless annihilating saboteurs. "The Party has to break terror with tenfold terror," Hitler's message shrieked. "It has to extinguish the traitors -- whoever they are, whatever their disguise."

On February 27, Propaganda Minister Goebbels demanded that all university students be subjected to the free use of corporal punishment. As if to underscore his meaning, three additional White Rose members were executed: Alexander Schmorell, Kurt Huber and Wilhelm Graf.

The Gestapo arrested everyone who could have known those executed. And additional White Rose members who were identified as having played an active part in the resistance effort were identified, arrested, tried and sentenced to prison. Under Nazi law, all family members of anyone who had been found guilty of "crimes against the state", were also arrested. Many family members served prison sentences as well.

Traute LaFrenze

Traute LaFrenze was one of the first students to be arrested in the Gestapo sweeps to discover others in the White Rose. She was a long-time friend and colleague of all who had been executed and had been an active White Rose member. She was tried and sentenced to prison.

LaFrenze and the other members of the White Rose, were young people who had grown up in Nazi Germany but who had not succumbed to Hitler's attempt to "brainwash" the youth of the country.

Following her prison sentence, and after the war ended and she was released, LaFrenze went on to complete her medical training, eventually becoming a physician. She specialized in Anthroposophical medicine and studied and practiced in Switzerland. In the 1950's she emigrated to the United States.

Her Work In America

Traute (LaFrenze) Page, M.D., was one of the few physicians practicing Anthroposophically-extended medicine in the U.S. in the 1950's. She traveled extensively, sharing her knowledge with the growing Waldorf school communities springing up throughout the U.S.

Dr. Page co-founded the Esperanza School for handicapped children in Chicago, IL.

Dr. Page also served for many years on the General Council (Board of Directors) of the Anthroposophical Society in America during the 1970s.

Dr. Page is an active member of the medical work in the U.S.

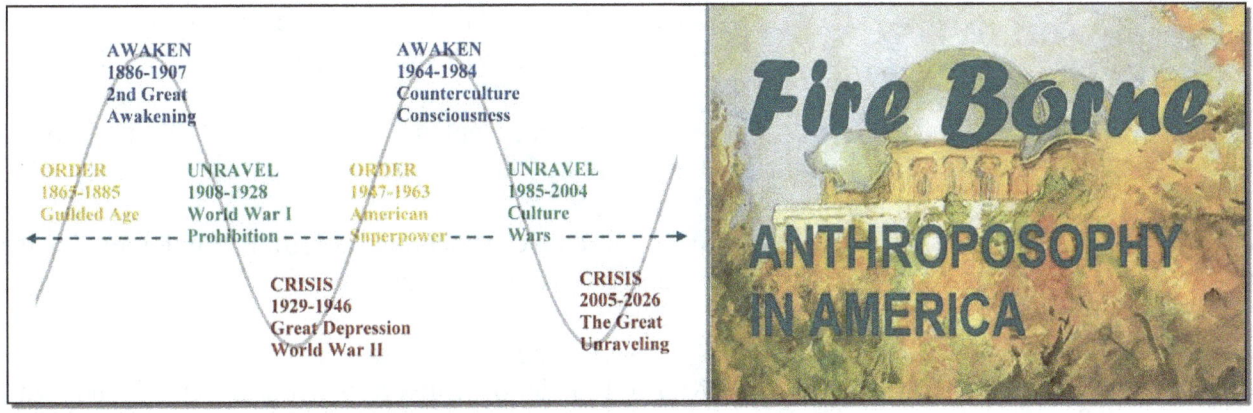

CULTURAL WAVE CHART © 2016 Jean W. Yeager[4]

1946-1964 "American Superpower"
PHASE: ORDER (Stability)

U.S. GENERATION commonly called *"The Baby Boomers"* grow up in a Moral Ecology of suburbia, green lawns, shopping malls. Segregation by race and socially by gender social class or sexual orientation is the norm.[5] Corporations and "industry" won WWII and television has won the family life.

Abbreviations:	RS Rudolf Steiner	ED Education	MED Medical	ASiA Anthroposophical Society in America
AG Agriculture	SM Spirit Matters	TF Threefold	SCI Science	GAS General Anthroposophical Society

All timeline entries are for U.S. events unless otherwise noted.

1946
– U.S. microwave oven developed by Percy Spencer

– **U.K. Sir Albert Howard's *The War In The Soil* is published by Rodale Press, Emmaus, PA.**

1947
– U.S. President Truman signs executive order investigating the loyalty of all Federal employees. Three million investigations, 308 are fired, 1 arrested for "spying" but this case is dismissed because of illegal FBI actions.

AG – Rodale publishes Ehrenfried Pfeiffer's book *The Earth's Face And Human Destiny*

– *Howdy Doody* children's television show premiers.

"THE WAR IN THE SOIL"
"The downfall of the artificial manure industry and of its satellites will mark the end of the war in the soil ... the last episode of the war in the soil will be the conversion of ... agricultural experiment stations ... and agricultural colleges ... from inorganic to organic farming."

---

[4] Dates / phases from THE FOURTH TURNING, William Strauss and Neil Howe, Broadway Books, 1997
[5] BOWLING ALONE, pg. 177

> ### WORLDVIEW
> ### AMERICA SUPERPOWER
>
> **1947** – *Foreign Assistance Act* called the "Marshall Plan," extends $1.3 billion in aid to rebuild Europe and Japan. This puts the U.S. industry in the "driver's seat" for the global economy for decades.

– COLD WAR – The CIA is created by Congress through the *National Security Act* to fight the Soviet Union.

– U.S. Airforce Captain Chuck Yeager breaks the sound barrier in the Bell X-1 jet.

AG – Rodale contracts with Pfeiffer to write articles for *Organic Gardening* magazine.

AG – Pfeiffer's "Pennsylvania Project" with Alarik Myrin, founder of Kimberton Waldorf School, ends with interpersonal conflict.

1948
– U.S. Supreme Court abolishes Bible reading in all public schools declaring it to be a violation of the First Amendment.

– USSR blockades all non-Communist areas of Berlin.

– U.S. There are an estimated 500,000 television sets in the U.S. Most watched tv show: *Texaco Star Theatre* starring Milton Berle: *"The Thief Of Bad Gags."*

– U.S.-Rural electrification complete.

END NOTE (1) – 1949 – FROM HEROES OF PRODUCTION TO HEROES OF CONSUMPTION

1949
– French fashion designers introduce the bikini.

– USSR tests first nuclear bomb. This ratcheted up fear of the U.S. Communist Party.

– U.S. signs onto the North American Treaty Organization (NATO).

1950
– U.S. Senator Joseph McCarthy (R, WI) latches onto the issue of a crusade against Communism with the support of J. Edgar Hoover's FBI.

– The House Un-American Affairs Committee (HUAC) chaired by McCarthy began hearings to root out "Reds."

– The Los Angeles *Times* tells its readers that if approached by a peace advocate: *"Don't punch him in the nose. Reds are used to that. Get his name and address and phone the FBI."*

ED – WALDORF EDUCATION – there are 5 schools in North America.

AG – Pfeiffer forms General Compost Corporation with Philadelphia attorney, Andrew Farnese, Esq. Farnese accompanies Pfeiffer to visit east coast anthroposophists to raise funds for this business.

– **Oakland** – *"The City With Golden Garbage"* – COLLIER'S MAGAZINE 1950 reports Ehrenfried Pfeiffer's General Compost project in Oakland CA for composting municipal, household kitchen waste. >>>>

AG – Farnese negotiates contract for Pfeiffer to develop and direct a municipal composting project to transform household garbage into pelletized agriculture fertilizer with the Oakland "Scavengers."

AG – Pfeiffer given patents for various "bacteriological" formulas (called 'bacts') including Barrel Compost.

AG – Pfeiffer develops compost starters and other products for commercial "compost teas" for Bio-dynamic and household use. These are used on wide-spread basis in central valley CA and sprayed from airplanes as "bacts" (bacteriological sprays).

– KOREAN CONFLICT – Ground forces land in Korea, pass the 38th Parallel and invade North Korea going all the way to the Chinese boarder. China put 850,000 troops into a *"Police Action."*

– *McCarran Internal Security* Act passed by Congress and establishes the Subversive Control Board which, as directed by the Attorney General, requires registration of individuals and groups judged to be "Communist" affiliated. The act also established "emergency concentration camps."

END NOTE (2) – W.E.B. DuBois *"A GREAT SILENCE HAS FALLEN ON THE REAL SOUL OF THIS NATION"*

– Black men were 12 times more likely to be homicide victims than white men. (*Chokehold*, pg. 21)

1951
– 12-million television sets in American household.

– *22nd Amendment to the Constitution* – no person can serve as President for more than two terms.

Military World View
"We are living in the midst of a permanent wartime economy. The most important capital good produced in the West today is weaponry. The most important sector in international trade is not oil for automobiles or airplanes. It is armaments."
— Robert McNamara
Voltaire's Bastards: The Dictatorship of Reason in the West, John Ralston Saul, pg. 152

– General Douglas MacArthur, Commander in Chief of U.S. forces in Korea, dismissed by President Truman. MacArthur had publicly challenged Truman and advocated bombing China and invading mainland China.

– A delegation of prominent black Americans present a petition to the U.N., which charges the U.S. government with a policy of genocide against its black citizens.

<<<< **Eisenhower names Robert McNamara, former CEO of Ford Motor Company as**

Secretary of State and asks him to apply "industrial efficiencies" to the military.

1952
– Dwight Eisenhower elected President. Vice President Richard Nixon admits to an $18,000 "slush fund" rich people had set up for his campaign.

1953
– CIA leads coup in Iran to overthrow the popularly elected government and nationalize the oil industry. Kermit Roosevelt named chairman of Gulf Oil.

ASiA – *AMENDMENT TO ARTICLE 12 OF THE ANTHROPOSOPHICAL SOCIETY BY-LAWS – related to the membership of the Board of Trustees of Rudolf Steiner Foundation, Inc. was distributed in 1951 and finally approved in 1953.* (To be published separately in the Administrative Collection).

MED – Traute (Lafrenze) Page MD, who as a young student in Germany was incarcerated by the Nazis, has become a medical doctor and relocates to Chicago to work in anthroposophical medicine and creates the Esperanza School. (*Into The Heart's Land*, pg. 361) See also **END NOTE (5)** on page 39.

– **McNamara leads Eisenhower to surrender oil and gas reserves to oil corporations.**

– Fidel Castro leads an attack in an attempt to overthrow the Batista dictatorship in Havana Cuba.

– Armistice in Korean military action.

1954
– Thoreau's *Walden* banned by U.S. Information Service libraries worldwide as being "socialistic."

> **LARGEST TRANSFER OF WEALTH IN U.S. HISTORY**
> Secretary of State, Robert McNamara arranged for President Eisenhower to surrender $80-billion of offshore oil and gas reserves to oil corporations – the largest transfer of wealth in U.S. history.

– Army/McCarthy hearings televised. Thirty-six days of bitter argumentation. McCarthy discredited and "condemned" by a vote of 67-22.

– French defeated by the North Vietnamese at Diem Bien Phu and withdrew. Vice President Nixon urges direct intervention by the U.S.

ASiA – *MAY 8, 1954 – BY-LAWS OF ANTHROPOSOPHICAL SOCIETY REVISED TO CREATE "A FORUM OF ACTIVE MEMBERS" AND HAVE MEMBERS ELECT THE GENERAL COUNCIL.* (To be published separately in the Administrative Collection).

– *Brown v. Board of Education* Supreme Court rules unanimously against segregation.

– The *Church of Scientology* created by L. Ron Hubbard.

– Guatemala government falls in a coup supported by CIA.

1955
– Emmett Till, a 14 year old black youth, is brutally killed in Mississippi.

END NOTE (3) – EMMIT TILL BRUTALLY MURDERED 'WHAT IT WAS LIKE' BY ROSA PARKS

– Rosa Parks, a black woman in Montgomery, AL, refuses to give up her bus seat to a white man and is arrested. This sparks a non-violent bus boycott led by Martin Luther King, Jr.
– CBS airs first TV news segment alleging links between smoking and lung cancer.

AG – DDT SPRAYING. The state of New York, in an effort to stop a plague of fire ants, conducted wide-spread and indiscriminate aerial spraying of DDT mixed with fuel oil on Long Island, NY. Mary T. Richards and Marjorie Spock whose biodynamic garden was sprayed, sued New York State to stop spraying. >>>>

> **BIODYNAMIC GARDENERS SUE N.Y. STATE FOR AERIAL DDT SPRAY**
> The Theodora Richards lawsuit eventually goes to the U.S. Supreme Court. Pfeiffer gathers scientific research important for the case. This is shared with Rachael Carson for her book *"Silent Spring."*

END NOTE (4) – TWO COURAGEOUS BIODYNAMIC GARDENERS SUE NEW YORK STATE

ASiA – Pacific Regional Anthroposophical Conference in Hawaii. (*Into The Heart's Land, pg. 323*)

1956
AG – Richards and Spock made sure that the misuse of pesticides by New York State filled local newspapers. This attracted the attention of Rachael Carson.

END NOTE (5) – 1958 PFEIFFER – THE UN-NAMED EXPERT WITNESS PAGE 33

AG – Pfeiffer assembles hundreds of international scientific references about the dangers of pesticides and DDT for the support of the Richards and Spock court case. This provided Carson with one of the largest troves of data for her book, *Silent Spring*. Pfeiffer publishes the abstracts of the research in Issue Number 43 of the Journal for Bio-dynamics, Winter 1958.

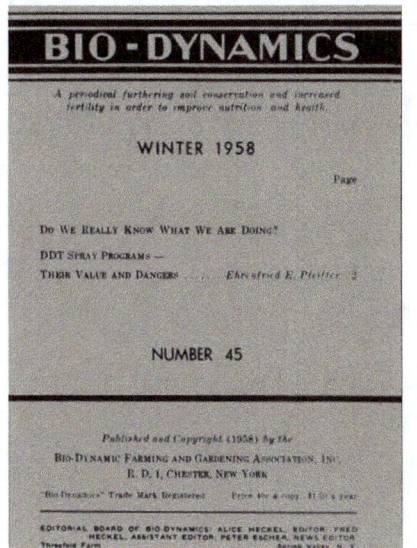

END NOTE (6) – ABOUT ISSUE #45 OF BIO-DYNAMICS – COURT CASE 1956-1957

– 60% of all American households own televisions.

– Optical fiber essential for digital communications developed.

– Video tape developed by Ampex.

1957
– 1,000 Army paratroopers sent by President Eisenhower to Central High School for school integration.

– Soviet Union begins "space race" by launching Sputnik I.

1958
– *Silent Spring* published.
"Silent Spring" published and environmental consciousness arises worldwide. Industry attacks Rachael Carson and tries to denigrate the science of environmentalism. >>>>

END NOTE (7) – *SCIENCE AND SPIRT* **THE OBLIGATION TO ENDURE,** Rachael Carson, From *SILENT SPRING*

ASiA – Rudolf Steiner Group, 528 West Grant Place, Chicago incorporated. (*Into The Heart's Land, pg. 308*)

– Silicon chip patented by Jack Kilby and Robert Noyce.

– US & USSR launch 6 satellites.

1959
– US & USSR launch 14 satellites.

– Fidel Castro marches triumphantly into Havana.

– Alaska becomes 49th State.

– Hawaii becomes 50th State.

ED – Sacramento Waldorf School founding with lectures by Hermann von Baravalle. (*Into The Heart's Land, pg. 259*)

SILENT SPRING
Environmental World View
"It (Silent Spring) polarized government, science, and industry, and made people stop in their tracks and see the world in a new way. With it's publication, 'ecology' became part of everyday vocabulary"
Linda Lear, environmental historian.
(1) *Environmental History Review* 17 (Summer 1993): 23-48, Linda J. Lear, University of Maryland, Baltimore County.
https://go.elib.com/NkJpK

1960
– A survey says three in four Americans said *"you could trust the government in Washington to do what is right all or most of the time." (Bowling Alone*, p. 47)

END NOTE (8) – **WHAT IT WAS LIKE IN 1960** – BEFORE ROE v. WADE – TO BE A PREGNANT, TEENAGE GIRL – Ursula K. Leguin
https://firebornecom.files.wordpress.com/2022/02/1950-leguin-what-was-it-like-2.pdf

GAS – In 1960 the Dutch and British Anthroposophical Societies which had been excluded from the G.A.S. in 1925, decided to return to the Goetheanum and the Anthroposophical Society.

– US & USSR launch 19 satellites.

– 15.6 million farms, down 10-million from 1950.

– 7% of all children live with one parent. >1% experience divorce.

– John Kennedy and Richard Nixon televised debates seen by 8-million viewers.

– Robert McNamara leads the decision by the United States and France, followed by Britain and then the Soviet Union, to convert arms production into a major export industry.

1961
– U.S. breaks diplomatic relations in Cuba, bans travel to Cuba, CIA fails the Bay of Pigs attack.

– John F. Kennedy inaugurated President

– Twenty-nine electrical firms including G.E. and Westinghouse and 44 executives found guilty and convicted of price rigging U.S. government bids. The case is defended as "free enterprise vs. state dictatorship."

> *"Age of Science"*
> *TIME Magazine*
> "The era of polarization ... occurred at a time when problems in soil fertility and crop pest control were being treated as so-called 'miracles' of chemistry ... . Atomic power, for example, was being sold to the public as safe and almost unlimited power source would be too cheap to meter."
> www.westonprice.org

<<<< *"Age of Science," TIME* **Magazine**

– Thirteen *"Freedom Riders"* leave Washington DC for New Orleans to test desegregation of public facilities. Two buses attacked, one firebombed. President Kennedy sends 350 National Guard to protect the buses.

– *BERLIN WALL:* Berlin crisis of East/West German treaty standoff leads to building "Berlin Wall."

– First U.S. military companies arrive in South Vietnam to preserve Vietnam's independence starting the "Vietnam conflict."

– Stauffer Chemical develops glycophosphate as a "descaling" agent to clean mineral deposits out of water pipes.
– Civil rights march in Montgomery, AL results in 737 arrests.

AG – Ehrenfried Pfeiffer dies.

1962
ASiA – Maulsby Kimball, the Executive Director of Anthroposophical Society in America (ASiA) (*Into The Heart's Land, pg. 291*)

ASiA – Anthroposophical Society direct mail – 2,000 name mail list. (*Into The Heart's Land, pg. 291*)

– US & USSR launch 70 satellites.

– By Federal court order, University of Mississippi accepts James Meredith, first black student.

– U.S. blockades Cuba after photos of missiles capable of sending nuclear bombs.

– Newspapers go on strike.

1963

– George Wallace sworn in as Alabama governor and pledges *"Segregation now Segregation tomorrow. Segregation forever!"*

– **16th Street Baptist church bombing, Montgomery, AL kills four girls.** >>>>

– Civil rights demonstrations throughout the South lead to bombings of leaders, clubbing and shooting incidents.

– Detroit anti-civil rights demonstration draws 125,000.

– Washington DC pro-civil rights demonstration draws 200,000. Martin Luther King, Jr. proclaims "Now is the time."

– "Learning Disabilities," a "new" disease introduced.

– Ngo Dinh Diem, Vietnamese President, assassinated in CIA organized coup with knowledge and approval of U.S. President.

> *"… The death of these little children may lead our whole Southland (Yeah) from the low road of man's inhumanity to man to the high road of peace and brotherhood. (Yeah, Yes) These tragic deaths may lead our nation to substitute an aristocracy of character for an aristocracy of color. The spilled blood of these innocent girls may cause the whole citizenry of Birmingham (Yeah) to transform the negative extremes of a dark past into the positive extremes of a bright future. Indeed this tragic event may cause the white South to come to terms with its conscience. (Yeah)"*
>
> **Eulogy For The Victims Of the 16th Street Bombing – Martin L. King, Jr.**

President John Kennedy assassinated in Dallas, TX.
Lyndon Johnson becomes President.

– Public schools in the south peacefully integrate except Alabama where Gov. George Wallace sends State Troopers to close schools.

1964

– *Civil Rights Act* signed by President Johnson.

– Race riots: Philadelphia, New York and New Jersey.

– *In 1964 Dr. Konig, (founder of Camphill Villages for handicapped individuals), warned: We are placed into apocalyptic events; we have to behold death and destruction, the outer tumult, the inner stillness. Every one, every single person, is a piece of apocalypse. Every one of us is, in this sense, of apocalyptic nature. Nevertheless we carry within this apocalypse the immaculate pure image of God whereby we can recognize each other. (Karl Konig, Advent 1964 at Fohrenbuhl).*

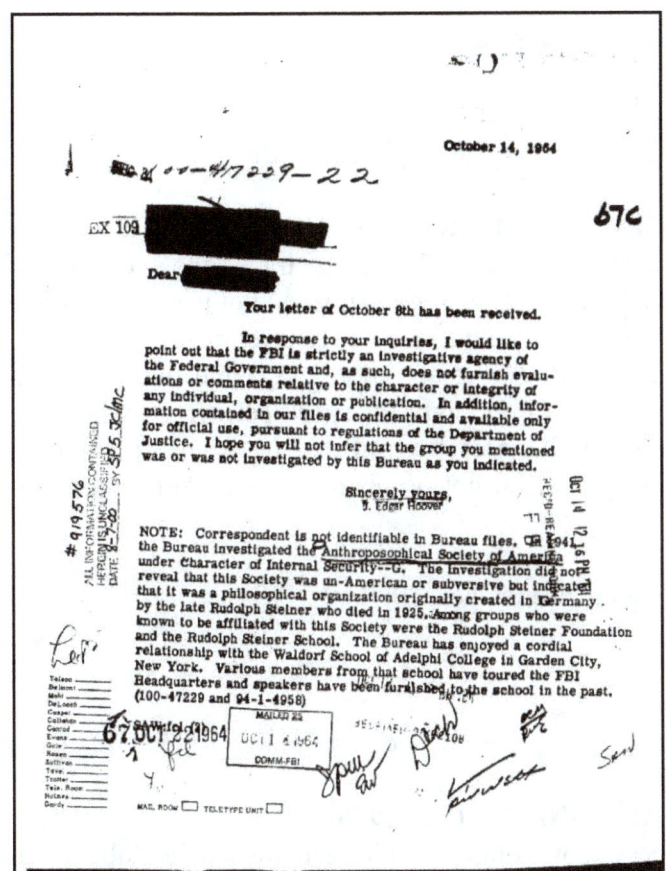

<<<<

END NOTE (9) – 1964 FBI REPORT ABOUT THE ANTHROPOSOPHICAL SOCIETY AND WALDORF EDUCATION (obtained under the Freedom of Information Act [FOIA])

ASiA – END NOTE (10) – GEOGRAPHIC REGIONALIZATION OF ANTHROPOSOPHICAL SOCIETY IN AMERICA LEADS TO AMENDMENT OF BY-LAWS which means that the future of the Society is "… in the hands of the COUNCIL whose members are (regional) group leaders and subject group leaders and individual members.." The Council will act as a coordinating group.

NOTES:

Into The Heart's Land, Henry Barnes, Steiner Books, 2013

"The City With Golden Garbage" – COLLIER'S MAGAZINE 1950

Chokehold: Policing Black Men, Paul Butler, 2017

Bowling Alone, Robert D. Putnam, Simon & Schuster, 2000

Organic Gardening and Farming Magazine, J.I. Rodale

Silent Spring, Rachael Carson, 1958

Voltaire's Bastards, John Ralston Saul, Simon & Schuster Paperbacks, 1992

Rudolf Steiner Library, https://rudolfsteinerlibrary.org/

LINKS AND END NOTES:

END NOTE (1) – PAGE 62 – 1949 – FROM HEROES OF PRODUCTION TO HEROES OF CONSUMPTION
https://firebornecom.files.wordpress.com/2022/02/1949-heroes-of-production.pdf

1949 – FROM "HEROES OF PRODUCTION" "TO HEROES OF CONSUMPTION"

"In 1949, Leo Lowenthal wrote a much discussed essay in which he traced the evolution of profile stories in popular magazines such as Saturday Evening Post. His point was that at some point in the early point in the century the "heroes of production" were celebrated, people who made bridges, built dams, and built companies. But more and more magazines were shifting their attention to "heroes of consumption," such as movie stars and sports celebrities, who were the superstars of the leisure world. Even when politicians were profiled, he observed, attention was on the hobbies and private personality of subject, not on his or her accomplishments or behavior.

BOBOS IN PARADISE, David Brooks, Simon & Schuster, 2000, pg. 113

END NOTE (2) – PAGE 63 – 1950 – "A GREAT SILENCE HAS FALLEN ON THE REAL SOUL OF THIS NATION" W.E.B. DuBois
https://firebornecom.files.wordpress.com/2022/02/1951-a-great-silence-has-fallen-on-the-soul.pdf

THE PEOPLE'S ALMANAC – 1951 1950

The McCarran Internal Security Act was passed by Congress which established the Subversive Control Board (SCB) which was required individuals or groups judged by the Attorney General to be "Communist" affiliated to register. The Act also established emergency concentration camps."

"W.E.B DuBois was handcuffed, fingerprinted and searched for concealed weapons was brought to trial for not registering as a "subversive."

He was acquitted. DuBois said: "A great silence has fallen on the real soul of this nation."1
THE PEOPLE'S ALMANAC, pg. 241

END NOTE (3) – PAGE 64 – 1955 – EMMETTT TILL BRUTALLY MURDERED – "WHAT IT WAS LIKE" by Rosa Parks
https://firebornecom.files.wordpress.com/2022/02/1955-emmett-till.pdf

1955 – EMMETT TILL

December 5, 1955, was the day of Rosa Park's court appearance. "Months before, in Mississippi, fourteen-year-old Emmett Till had unintentionally whistled at a white woman shopkeeper (he had a speech defect from polio) and was lynched three nights later by a party led by the woman's husband. He was mutilated, castrated, and shot, his skull crushed beyond recognition. The lynch mob was arrested, tried, and set free. This incident, though highly publicized, was not anomalous; there had been on average one lynching per week in the ninety-year period since Reconstruction.(1)

In every community in the south, poor whites took it upon themselves to be enforcers of the apartheid system while the middle class averted its eyes. Anytime a march, demonstration or gathering occurred, blacks would be stared down and called out by people who knew them."(2)

1 Burns, TO THE MOUNTAINTOP, pg. 9-11
2 BLESSED UNREST, Paul Hawkin, Viking, 2007. pg. 81

END NOTE (4) – PAGE 65 – 1956 TWO COURAGEOUS BIODYNAMIC GARDENERS SUE NEW YORK STATE
https://firebornecom.files.wordpress.com/2022/02/1-4pg-b-d-and-silent-spring.pdf

FROM A BIODYNAMIC ASSOCIATION FLYER DISTRIBUTED IN WHOLE FOOD STORES

Next year (2006) will mark the 50th anniversary of an act of state-supported environmental pollution which prompted outrage and resistance by two Biodynamic gardeners and eventually led to a worldwide change in consciousness.

In 1956, the state of New York, in an effort to stop a plague of fire ants, conducted wide-spread and indiscriminate aerial spraying of DDT mixed with fuel oil (so that it would adhere better) on Long Island, New York. Mary T. Richards and Marjorie Spock (sister of the noted Pediatrician, Benjamin Spock) whose garden on Long Island had been tended for many years in a non-chemical, Biodynamic fashion, sued the government to stop the spraying and for damages.

The case went to trial in Long Island, and Richards and Spock made sure that the shocking misuse of pesticides by the government filled the local newspapers. Richards and Spock brought together a wide-range of scientific experts in documenting the enormous damage that pesticides had done to fish, birds, wildlife, dairy cattle, gardens, livestock, and perhaps to children.

The enormous press coverage caught the attention of Rachael Carson who, at that time, was just beginning her research into the effects of pesticides. Carson attended the trial and soon became friends with Richards and Spock who, when they found out about her scientific and literary background, provided Carson with transcripts and research data which they had assembled for the trial. As Linda Lear an environmental historian puts it: "It (the trial) provided Rachel Carson with 'mountains of material,' important collaborators such as Mary Richards and Marjorie Spock, and a wealth of expert contacts in medical and agricultural fields previously unknown to her." (Lear)

"*Silent Spring* (published in 1958) indicted the chemical industry, the government, and agribusiness for indiscriminately using pesticides ... There are very few books that can be said to have changed the course of history, but this was one of them. It polarized government, science, and industry, and made people stop in their tracks and see the world in a new way. With its publication, 'ecology' became part of everyday vocabulary." (Lear) It took the U.S. government until 1972 to ban the use of DDT in the United States.

Environmental awareness was fired by Carson's book and continued in worldwide political / cultural movements. By the 1970's, the concern with the on-going environmental pollution caused by agrichemicals resulted in increased attention of alternative, non-chemical methods of farming which have today come to be known as "organic" farming.

We are grateful for the example of Mary T. Richards and Marjorie Spock, whose principled stand in 1956 is an example of how citizens can change the world.

Biodynamic farming and gardening has insisted on conscious and pro-active avoidance of chemical fertilizers, pesticides and herbicides in agricultural practices since it was originated by Dr. Rudolf Steiner in 1924. But, the Biodynamic® method is more than just avoiding chemicals. It is a well-established method for working with the dynamic, health-giving forces of nature.

– Jean W. Yeager

© 2006, The Biodynamic Farming & Gardening Association, Inc. All Rights Reserved
NOTES: (1) Environmental History Review 17 (Summer 1993): 23-48, Linda J. Lear, University of Maryland, Baltimore County.
https://www.history.vt.edu/Barrow/Hist3706/readings/lear.html

END NOTE (5) – PAGE 65 – **1958 PFEIFFER – THE UN-NAMED EXPERT WITNESS**
https://firebornecom.files.wordpress.com/2022/02/1958-pfeiffer-the-unnamed-witness.pdf

1958 PFEIFFER – THE UNNAMED EXPERT WITNESS

"In 1958 Rachel Carson wrote Spock and Richards in February at a time when they were preparing evidence for the trial. At least 57 letters have survived from Carson to Spock and Richards. The letters have subsequently been deposited at the Beneke Rare Book and Manuscript Library, Yale Collection of American Literature, of Yale University."

In a letter Carson writes "many thanks for the ... Very excellent Pfeiffer paper ... With its many references. It is a gold mine of information" (Carson, 1958). In the same letter, Carson states "You have been so enormously helpful to me, and apparently are so familiar with the vast amount of material." (Carson, 1958).

'The "Goldmine" to which Carson refers was the Winter issue of Bio-Dynamics, #45.

"Many of the references and authors cited by Pfeiffer later reappeared in Carson's reference list. Of one of his references (viz., Read, and generally, 1956), Pfeiffer (1958) commented, "this is one of the most comprehensive reports, with almost 1000 references" (page. 19 39). It reappeared in Carson's references. In her exchanges with Spock, Carson makes multiple references to Pfeiffer to his correspondence. With Spock and Richards as intermediaries Pfeiffer was queried by Carson about sources, references, and his own tests and experiments, although he received no acknowledgment in Silent Spring."

NOTES:

(1) *Environmental History Review* 17 (Summer 1993): 23-48, Linda J. Lear, University of Maryland, Baltimore County.

https://www.history.vt.edu/Barrow/Hist3706/readings/lear.html

Pfeiffer also appeared as an expert witness in the Long Island Spray Trial (Spock and Richards, 1962). When he was challenged by a defense attorney as to what fee he was receiving, he responded that no fee was involved; and when further challenge as to why he was there, he risked responding, "because I am interested in the future of the human race" (page. 25).

One can see the influence of Rudolf Steiner's "biological thinking" on which Pfeiffer's work is based and it flows through to Carson's work when you read Silent Spring.

END NOTE (6) – PAGE 65 – **1958 ABOUT ISSUE #45 OF BIO-DYNAMICS – COURT CASE 1956-1957**

BIO-DYNAMICS WINTER 1958 – PAGE 33

https://firebornecom.files.wordpress.com/2022/02/4.3-page-33.pdf

PAGE 33 - BIO-DYNAMICS, Number 45, Winter 1958, pg. 33-34

One philosophy, the direct outflow of dialectic materialism, sees the creation of an artificial realm. As a result of human intelligence, applied technology, production methods, and, the progress of civilization. This creation born from human intellect is superimposed on nature. The other philosophy still looks upon nature as the greatest teacher, for in it, in growth, in its wisdom, we see the finger of a higher intelligence. The wisdom of the Creator.

We human beings can strive - at our best - to comprehend only, rather than to imitate or improve upon higher wisdom which, after all, is the foundation to which we owe our existence. If the wisdom and biological balance of nature are violated, for instance, by agricultural production methods geared to the so-called most economic mass production, loss of growth of said biological balance are upset and nature goes her way to teach a lesson.

The increase of pests is faster than the increase of crop yields, for the methods used in agricultural production to increase crops have disturbed the natural balance. We have harvested only what we have sown, and the wider sense we have introduced one-sided fertilization methods - monoculture - in order to produce more. This attitude has created the increase of pests. To think now that by "killing" the pest we will remove the causes, is our error. The disturbed balanced is only more disturbed and the vicious cycle continues. No problem in human or natural life, in history as well as in the life of the individual, whether physiological or psychological, or in problem between nations has ever been solved by killing.

END NOTE (7) – PAGE 66 – **1958 *SCIENCE AND SPIRT* "THE OBLIGATION TO ENDURE," Rachael Carson, From *SILENT SPRING***
https://firebornecom.files.wordpress.com/2022/02/1962-silent-spring-obigation.pdf

THE OBLIGATION TO ENDURE
SILENT SPRING, Houghton Mifflin, 1962
Rachel Carson

The history of life on earth has been a history of interaction between living things and their surroundings. To a large extent, the physical form and the habits of the earth's vegetation and its animal life have been molded by the environment. Considering the whole span of earthly time, the opposite effect, in which life actually modifies its surroundings, has been relatively slight. Only within the moment of time represented by the present century has one species – man – acquired significant power to alter the nature of his world.

During the past quarter – century this power has not only increased to one of disturbing magnitude but it has changed in character. The most alarming of all man's assaults upon the environment is the contamination of air, earth, rivers, and sea with dangerous and even lethal materials. This pollution is for the most part irrecoverable; the chain of evil it initiates not only in the world that must support life but in living tissues is for the most part irreversible. In this now universal contamination of the environment, chemicals are the sinister and a little – recognize partners of radiation in changing the very nature of the world – the very nature of its life … pg. 25. …

Along with the possibility of the extinction of mankind by nuclear war, the central problem of our age has therefore become the contamination of man's total environment with such substances of incredible potential for harm – substances that accumulate in the tissues of plants and animals and even penetrate the germ cells to shatter or alter the very material of heredity upon which the shape of the future depends.

Some would-be architects of our future look forward a time when it will be possible to alter the human germ plasm by design. But we may easily be doing so now by inadvertence, for many chemicals like radiation, bring about genetic mutations. It is ironic to think that man might determine his own future by something so seemingly trivial as the choice of an insect spray.

All this has been risked – for what? Future historians may well be amazed by our distorted sense of proportion. How could intelligent beings seek to control a few unwanted species by a method that contaminated the entire environment and brought the threat of disease and death even to their own kind? Yet this is precisely what we have done. We have done it, moreover for reasons that collapse the moment we examine them. We are told that the enormous and expanding use of pesticides is necessary to maintain farm production yet is our real problem not one of over-production? ... pg. 25-26

There is still very limited awareness of the nature of the threat. This is an era of specialists, each of whom sees his own problems and is unaware of or intolerant of the larger frame into which it fits. It is also an era dominated by industry, in which the right to make a dollar at whatever cost is seldom challenged. When the public protests, confronted with some obvious evidence of damaging results of pesticide applications, it is fed little tranquilizing pills of half truth. We urgently need an end to these false assurances, to the sugar coating of unpalatable facts. It is the public that is being asked to assume the risks that the insect controllers calculate. The public must decide whether it wishes to continue on the present road, and it can do so only when in full possession of the facts. In the words of Jean Rostard's time, "the obligation to endure gives us the right to know." pg. 29-30

SILENT SPRING, Rachael Carson, Penguin Books Paperback edition, 1965

END NOTE (8) – PAGE 66 – 1960 WHAT IT WAS LIKE IN 1960 – BEFORE ROE v. WADE – TO BE A PREGNANT, TEENAGE GIRL – Ursula K. Leguin
https://firebornecom.files.wordpress.com/2022/02/1950-leguin-what-was-it-like-2.pdf

Ursula K. Le Guin
2004 Oregon NARAL Meeting
NARAL Pro Choice Foundation

My friend at NARAL asked me to tell you what it was like before Roe v. Wade. They asked me to tell you what it was like to be 20 and pregnant in 1950 and when you tell your boyfriend you're pregnant he tells you about a friend of his in the Army whose girl told him she was pregnant, so he got all of his buddies to come and say, "we all fucked her, and so who knows who the father is?" And he laughs at the good joke.

They asked me to tell you what it was like to be a pregnant girl – we weren't "women" then – a pregnant college girl who, if her college found out she was pregnant, would expel her, there and then, without plea or recourse.

What it was like, if you are planning to go to graduate school and get a degree and earn a living so you could support yourself and do the work you love – what it was like to be a senior at Radcliffe and pregnant and if you bore this child, this child which the law demanded you bear and would then call "unlawful," "illegitimate," this child whose father denied it, this child which would take from you your capacity to support yourself and do the work you knew it was your gift and your responsibility to do: What was it like?

I can hardly imagine what it's like to live as a woman under Fundamentalist Islamic law, I can hardly remember now, 54 years later, what it was like to live under Fundamentalist Christian law. Thanks to Roe v. Wade, none of us in America has lived in that place for half a lifetime.

WORDS ARE MY MATTER, Ursula K. Le Guin, Small Beer Press, 2016. pg. 7

END NOTE (9) – PAGE 69 – 1964 FBI REPORT ABOUT THE ANTHROPOSOPHICAL SOCIETY AND WALDORF EDUCATION (obtained under the Freedom of Information Act [FOIA])

https://firebornecom.files.wordpress.com/2022/02/1964-diversity-fbi.pdf

1964 DIVERSITY – F.B.I. REPORT

One concluding exchange was a 1964 letter from a citizen requesting the F.B.I.'s opinion of the Anthroposophical Society and Waldorf Schools. Typed beneath a boiler-plate acknowledgment of the letter was this succinct summary of the information about the Society which is contained in the previous 130-some pages of the F.B.I. file:

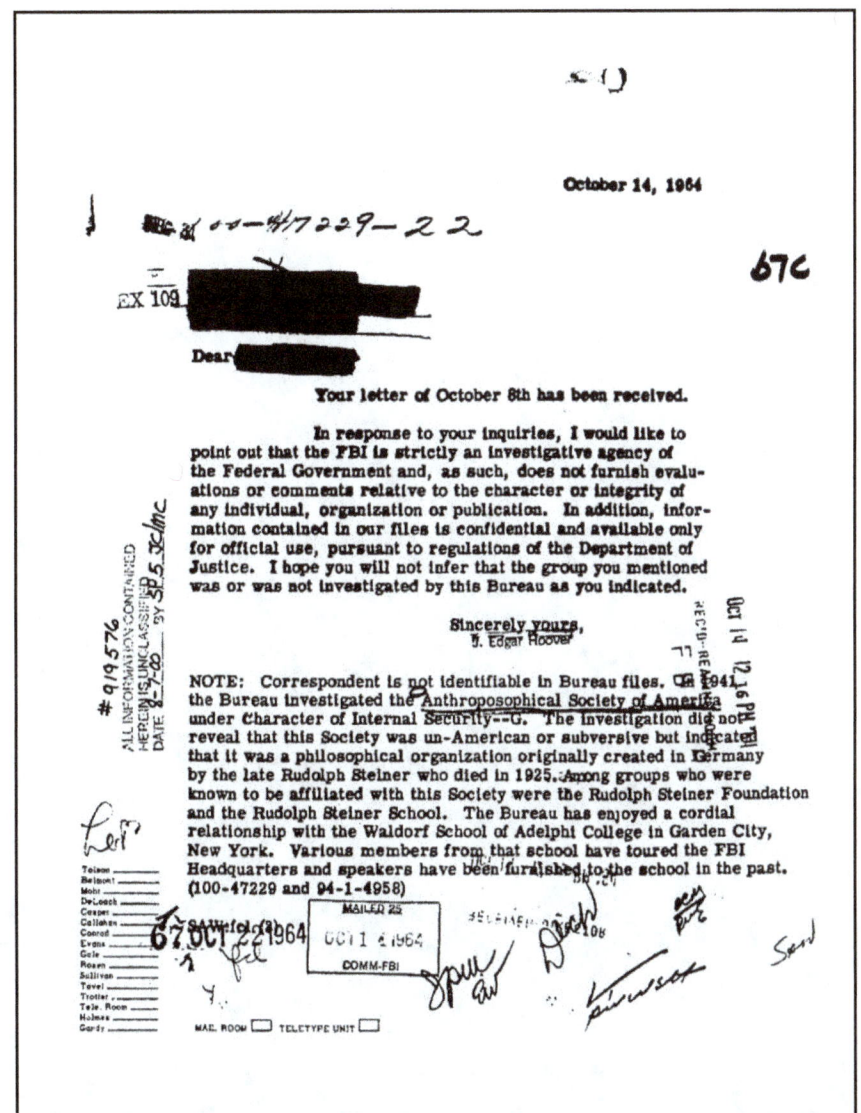

FOIPA No. 919576 / 190-HQ-1323192 File: 100-47229

In 1941 the Bureau investigated the Anthroposophical Society in America under Character of Internal Security – G. The investigation did not reveal that the Society was un-American or subversive but indicated that it was a philosophical organization originally created in Germany by the late Rudolph Steiner who died in 1925. Among groups who were known to be affiliated with this Society were the Rudolph Steiner Foundation and the Rudolph Steiner School. The Bureau has enjoyed a cordial relationship with the Waldorf School of Adelphi College in Garden City, New York. Various members of the school have toured the F.B.I. Headquarters and speakers have been furnished to the school in the past.

(100-47722 and 941-1-4958) SAW:fel (5)

END NOTE (10) – PAGE 69 – 1964 MEMORANDUM TO APPROVE GEOGRAPHIC REGIONALIZATION OF ANTHROPOSOPHICAL SOCIETY IN AMERICA
https://firebornecom.files.wordpress.com/2022/09/1964-asa-bylaws.pdf

---

May 28, 1964

MEMORANDUM

AMENDMENT OF BY-LAWS OF THE ANTHROPOSOPHICAL SOCIETY IN AMERICA 1964

During the last two years some changes have taken place with regard to the organization of the Anthroposophical Society in America and the time has now come to make the Society's By-Laws comply with the new situation.

The impulse behind these amendments is to render the by-laws as simple as possible, to provide maximum flexibility for new initiatives and at the same time to insure continuity of administration and of the activities. A conscious effort has been made to formulate the amendments in accordance with the spirit of the Christmas Foundation Meeting of the General Society in 1923.

Responsibility for the affairs of the Society will be in the hands of the Council whose members are group leaders, subject group leaders and individual members. The Council will appoint its Executive Committee.

The work throughout the country will be carried by the initiative of groups and individuals. With the help of its Executive Committee, the Council will act as a coordinator of this work and attend only to those things which the individual centers cannot do on their own. It will be a sounding board for what lives in the minds and hearts of members throughout the country and take

-2-

appropriate action. It will listen to the needs of our times and try to respond to them.

On the basis of this general thinking and the practical experience gained during the last two years, the Council at a Special Meeting held on May 16 decided on amendments to the by-laws which are explained further below. In this memorandum, frequent reference will be made to the "old" by-laws - adopted in 1954 - some of which can be retained in their present form. Others will have to be changed or deleted.

Article I (NAME) and Article 2 (RELATIONSHIP TO THE GENERAL ANTHROPOSOPHICAL SOCIETY) will remain substantially as they are now. As suggested by the Vorstand, Article 2 will also make reference to the By-Laws of the General Anthroposophical Society. By recommendation by the Vorstand some changes are suggested for Article 3 (MEMBERSHIP). Application for membership should be endorsed by one member instead of two. Membership cards will be signed by an officer of the American Society and countersigned by the Head of the Vorstand in Dornach. The "old" by-laws have this order reversed.

As the Council consists of the leaders of Geographical Groups and Subject Groups, a new article for Groups has been added:

Article 4. GROUPS

(a) Geographic Groups will each consist of seven or more members of the Anthroposophical Society in America who meet regularly for active group work. Such groups re-

(Article 4 continued)

quire recognition by the Council.

(b) Subject Groups will consist of seven or more members of the Anthroposophical Society in America engaged in a particular field of the work who come together in order to coordinate and intensify their efforts. Such Groups require recognition by the Council.

(c) New Groups consisting of at least seven members will apply for recognition by the Council in a letter from the Group Leader carrying the signature of all Group members.

(d) Any Group of less than seven members may apply to the Council for associate non-voting membership of its leader or delegate.

(e) A member may hold membership in more than one Geographic Group provided the membership dues of the General Anthroposophical Society are paid in each Group to which the member belongs. This principle shall not apply in instances of transfer of residence if a member wishes to maintain his fellowship in a Group with which the member can no longer participate actively. Continuance of such a membership shall concern only the member and the Group from which distance has separated him.

-4-

Article 5 covers the organization, and will now read as follows:

Article 5. ORGANIZATION

The conduct of the affairs of the Society shall be in the hands of:

(a) The Council
(b) The Executive Committee of the Council consisting of at least three officers, who are also the Board of Directors of the Corporation.
(c) A General Meeting of the members of the Society.

The next article covers the Council and is worded as follows:

Article 6. THE COUNCIL

(a) The Council will comprise Group Leaders or one Delegate each of Geographic and Subject Groups, and of Individual Members chosen by the Council.
(b) The Council will choose its Chairman from its own membership.
(c) A quorum of the Council shall be 12 of its members assembled in a meeting.

Article 7 deals with the duties of the Council as follows:

-5-

Article 7. DUTIES OF THE COUNCIL

(a) The activities of the Council shall be directed toward the furthering of the aims of the General Anthroposophical Society as expressed in Statute One of the Principles of the General Anthroposophical Society. It shall conduct the administration of the Anthroposophical Society in America in the light of its character as a national branch of the General Anthroposophical Society. It shall consider itself a part of the General Anthroposophical Society in Dornach, Switzerland - and cooperate with its leadership.

(b) The Council will select its Executive Committee.

(c) The Council will establish its own rules of procedure.

(d) The duties of the Chairman of the Council shall be to preside at all meetings of the Council when present and to designate another member of the Council as Chairman pro tem when unable to be present. He will remain in close contact with the Executive Committee.

(e) The Council will remain in close relationship with the membership.

The following Articles 8 and 9 cover the composition and duties of the Executive Committee.

-6-

Article 8. THE EXECUTIVE COMMITTEE.

(a) The Executive Committee shall consist of
   The Executive Director
   The Treasurer
   The Secretary
   And additional members as may be selected by the general consent of the Council.

Article 9. DUTIES OF THE EXECUTIVE COMMITTEE

(a) The Executive Committee shall administer the affairs of the Anthroposophical Society in America in accordance with the general policies adopted by the Council.

(b) The Executive Committee will meet regularly to transact such business as may come before it.

Articles 10 and 11 covering the Board of Directors are substantially the same as in Article 7 and 8 of the old by-laws.

Article 12 deals with the General Meeting which remains substantially unchanged, except for one change. In an effort to strengthen the role of the General Meeting and the voice of the members at large, Article 12f has been reworded to the effect that any resolution made, seconded and carried by a two-third majority of those present must be given "serious consideration" by the Council. Under the "old" by-laws such resolutions could only be acted upon if they were submitted two weeks in advance by three official working groups.

-7-

The provisions in the previous by-laws covering the Executive Secretary (Article 9), the Duties of the Executive Secretary (Article 10) will be deleted.

It is hoped that membership organizations, such as the Forum, will continue to be active. They will result from the free initiative of members and, therefore, need not be legislated by the Society's By-Laws. Article 11 covering the Forum of Active Members will, therefore, be deleted.

A new article is offered to cover elections. It is believed that the election of individual members to the Council must be limited. Each year a maximum of five members are to be elected to serve on the Council for a period of three years. Officers of the Executive Committee will be chosen for terms not exceeding three years.

Article 13. ELECTIONS

(a) The Council

Group Leaders or Delegates of Geographic and Subject Groups will be appointed to the Council by their Groups.

The Council may select a maximum of five Individual Members per year to serve for a period of three years beginning at Easter. They may be reelected to successive terms.

The Chairman of the Council is chosen by its members from their own number to serve a maximum of three

-8-

(Article 13 continued)

        years beginning at Easter. He is eligible for successive terms.

  (b) The Executive Committee

        Members of the Executive Committee will be selected by the Council to serve for a maximum of three years beginning at Easter. They may be reelected for successive terms.

        The election of officers to the Executive Committee becomes final upon ratification by the members assembled in the General Meeting or in an Extraordinary General Meeting.

        Members of the Executive Committee and the Chairman of the Council will remain in office until their successors have been duly elected.

No changes are suggested for the articles covering the Seal of the Society, Dues and Trustee Foundation, which will become Articles 14, 15 and 16 under the new By-Laws. Article 18 of the "old" by-laws deals with the expulsion of members. Subject to the advice of legal counsel, this article will become Article 17 in substantially the same form. Any member to be expelled should have a fair hearing and have the right to state his case prior to any action by the Council.

Article 17. EXPULSION OF MEMBERS

Any member deemed by the unanimous judgment of the Council to endanger the well-being of the Anthroposophical Society in America shall be permitted to make any statement this member may desire to make to the Council. Decision in favor of any action, including expulsion from the Society, by two-thirds of the Council shall be binding upon the member and the Anthroposophical Society in America. Whatever action shall be taken shall be reported to the <u>Vorstand</u> (Executive) of the General Anthroposophical Society in Dornach, with request for information as to any action that may be taken by that body.

Finally, the article covering Amendments of By-Laws will have to be adapted to the new situation.

Article 18. AMENDMENT OF BY-LAWS

These By-Laws of the Anthroposophical Society in America, Inc. may be amended at the suggestion of a two-third majority of the Council in a duly constituted meeting after intention to consider amendment has been announced at least 30 days in advance. Such amendment shall go into effect if ratified by a majority of all members of the Society who vote within three months.

D. V. Asten
For the Council

Anthroposophical Society in America

211 MADISON AVENUE
NEW YORK, N. Y. 10016
MURRAY HILL 5-4618
CABLE: ANPOSOF

July 20, 1964

Dear Friends:

The Council of the Anthroposophical Society in America has now completed its work on a set of revised By-Laws.

A detailed description of the new organization, which has been thoroughly tested for more than two years, was mailed to you with our letter of May 28th.

In accordance with the 1954 By-Laws, Amendments "shall come into effect if ratified by all members of the Society who vote within three months."

The suggestions received have been considered, and our lawyer assures us that no conflict with the law exists. He also made a number of minor recommendations, some of which we accepted.

A set of the new By-Laws is enclosed. Kindly let us have your vote on the attached form below.

Very sincerely yours,

D. V. Asten Maulsby Kimball
For the Council For the Executive

To the Council
The Anthroposophical Society in America
211 Madison Avenue
New York 16, N. Y.

I Approve_____ I Disapprove_____
The new By-Laws of the Anthroposophical Society in America as proposed in your letter of July 20th, 1964.

COMMENTS:

 (Signed)_____
Date_____1964.

The General Anthroposophical Society: The Goetheanum, Dornach, Switzerland

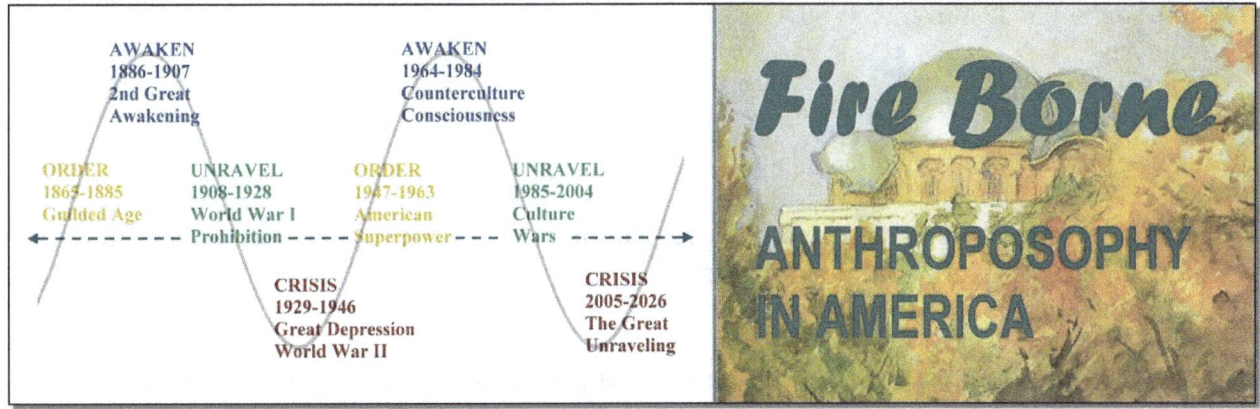

CULTURAL WAVE CHART © 2016 Jean W. Yeager[6]

1965-1984 "Counterculture Consciousness"
PHASE: AWAKEN

U.S. GENERATION commonly called *"The 13th Generation"* – they rebel against the Moral Ecology of segregation, the Vietnam war, sexual restrictions, divorce and abortion. They embrace risk and freedom over loyal corporatism create a counterculture. Personal computing and personal technology originate in this era. It is a period of growth for many small spiritual groups.

Abbreviations:	RS Rudolf Steiner	ED Education	MED Medical	ASiA Anthroposophical Society in America
AG Agriculture	SM Spirit Matters	TF Threefold	SCI Science	GAS General Anthroposophical Society

All timeline entries are for U.S. events unless otherwise noted.

1965

ED – 9 Waldorf Schools in North America.

ED – The Detroit Waldorf School was founded by Rudolf and Amelia Wilhelm, who wanted to provide Detroiters more choices in educating their children. (*Wikipedia.*)

<<<< **First gathering of Waldorf Schools forms Association of *Waldorf Schools of North America (AWSNA)*.**

– First generation raised on television.

– Use of home computers begins. IBM executives originally say there is no market for such devices but later are proved wrong.

– *Gulf of Tonkin Incident* – Johnson orders troops into Vietnam. U.S. bombs North Vietnam until 1969.

– *Voting Rights Act* signed by President Johnson.

---

[6] Dates / phases from THE FOURTH TURNING, William Strauss and Neil Howe, Broadway Books, 1997

– "Back To the Land" movement (60s-70s) migration to smaller, rural towns.

– *Organic Gardening Magazine* subscriptions **UP 500%** from **260,000 to 1.3 million**

– Anti-war protesters surround the Pentagon.

– *Conservative Caucus* initiates direct-mail revolution for Christian evangelical conservatives and generates a database of 20 -30 million names.

1966
– Average membership in 32 national chapter based associations peaked in the 1960s and declined precipitously. [7]

– American Independent Party established and nominates former Alabama Governor George Wallace for President. Wallace's pro-segregation policies had been rejected by the mainstream Democratic Party.

1967
– *Miranda v. Arizona* Supreme Court decision rules arrested people have rights.

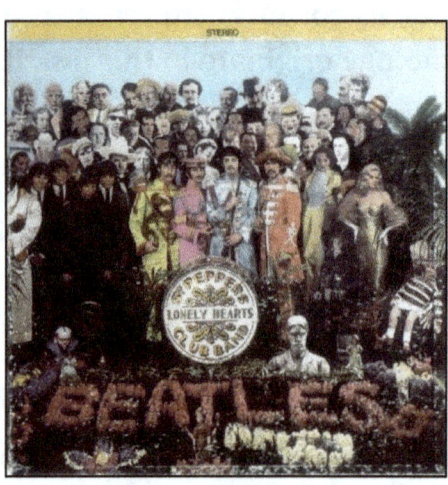

<<<< *Sergeant Pepper's Lonely Hearts Club Band* **album is released by the Beatles. Changes the course of Rock & Roll.**

– LONG HOT SUMMER – 159 RIOTS which started with the Twelfth Street Riot, Detroit.

– 500,000 soldiers fighting in Vietnam. 42% were draftees who suffered 58% of the casualties.

– Hypertext developed by Andries van Dam and Ted Nelson.

– 93% of all American households own a television set.

ED – In 1967, Werner and Barbara Glas start the Waldorf Institute at the Detroit Waldorf School. The Waldorf Institute was the first Waldorf teacher-training institution in the United States, and only the second English-speaking one. In 1979, the Waldorf Institute moved to Southfield, Michigan, and in 1986 moved to Chestnut Ridge, New York. (*Into The Hearts Land, pg. 926*)

1968
– *TET OFFENSIVE* – The CIA fails to detect in advance the Viet Cong attack on South Vietnam. The turning point of the war. Deaths of U.S. soldiers shown on evening TV.

Martin Luther King, Jr. assassinated.

– Machine guns are placed on the steps of the nation's capital.

---

[77] BOWLING ALONE, Robert D. Putnam, Simon & Schuster, 2000 pg. 54 Includes: League Of Women Voters, Grange, elks, Moose, Knights of Columbus, Rotary, Optimists, PTA, B'nai B'rith, to name a few.

Draft declared universal, all men over age 18 required to register with Selective Service >>>>

– Black Power movement recognized.

– *Whole Earth Catalog I* published.

Robert F. Kennedy Jr. assassinated.

– *Democratic Party National Convention in Chicago.* Chicago Police club thousands of demonstrators on national television. Hubert Humphrey nominated.

– CHICAGO EIGHT indicted for conspiracy and inciting a riot during the 1968 Democratic National Convention in Chicago: Jerry Rubin, Abbie Hoffman, Tom Hayden, Rennie Davis, Bobby Seale, Lee Weiner, John Froines and David Dellinger, circa 1968. The Chicago Seven, after Seale was severed from the case.

> **STUDENTS CREATE CULTURE WAR**
>
> *In various forms and fashions, students seek to reclaim their cultural influence, politically, spiritually, culturally, and economically.*

1969

– *Days Of Rage* – conducted by the *Weather Underground,* a radical, violent student group which was a segment of the Students For A Democratic Society (SDS).

– *Woodstock*, three-day music festival in Rural New York. Pivotal moment in popular music.

– Crime rate up 135%, 1960-70.

– Richard Nixon inaugurated.

– Moon landing – Neil Armstrong sets foot on the moon.

1970

ED – 11 AWSNA member schools in North America.

– *Mother Earth News* begins publishing

– Protestant Christian evangelism arises. Seek to reclaim cultural influence of the 1920s-30s.

– "Campus Crusade For Christ" movement sweeps college campuses across the country. Oral Roberts, Billy Graham, Jimmy Swaggart and other radio ministries very widespread.

– 50% DIVORCE RATE – One out of two American marriages divorced

– *Women's Liberation Movement* goes public.

– Koch Industries agrees to largest civil fine, $30 million, to settle claims related to 300 oil spills from its pipelines in six states.

FIRE BORNE 1965-1984

END NOTE (1) – **TECHNOLOGY CHANGE FROM AM TO FM RADIO**
And The Lord Gave Us TALK RADIO

A Great Awakening – ecstatic spiritualism, fundamentalists, evangelicals capture public attention.

– *"New Right"* meets Christian Conservatism and awakes to political power offered by electronic media such as databases and talk radio. Spawns movement which re-invents AM radio into "Talk Radio."

– Unconventional new religious groups emerged during the late 1960s and into the early 1970s accompanied by widespread media coverage of these "cults," their supporters, and their critics. The surge of new religious movements continued to flourish in the 70s' and 80s.
https://www.encyclopedia.com/religion/legal-and-political-magazines/anti-cult-movement

END NOTE (2) – **ANTI-CULT MOVEMENT – MORAL PANIC**
According to Susan P. Robbins writing in the IPT Journal (Issues In Child Abuse Accusations), media gave special attention to a variety of non-traditional religious groups that proliferated during the 1960s and 70s. Reporting activities of these groups provided content for "Talk Radio" increasing audiences and advertising revenue."

Protestant Christian Evangelism On The Rise Launches Talk Radio "Culture War"

CAMPUS CRUSADE FOR CHRIST a nationwide, Christian evangelical campus organization, one of many socially active evangelical groups connected by the "New Right" electronic church.

Key political issues which draw listeners to talk radio ministries:
- Prayer In Schools banned
- 50% divorce rate
- Abortion (which dramatically heated up after *Roe v. Wade* 1973)
- Drugs, Sex and Rock & Roll Music
- Disrespect for authority
- Women's Lib

– **Kent State Massacre** of student protesters by National Guard troops.

– The agriculture industry touts increased productivity via agriculture chemicals and rejects organic farming as a viable alternative.

– Glyphosate (glycophosphate) promoted as a weedkiller after Monsanto scientist John Franz discovered this new use. Monsanto patents it in 1971.

– Opioids Percocet and Vicodin melded with acetaminophen and widely prescribed.

– *Clean Air Act* passed by Congress which charges the Environmental Protection Agency (EPA) with regulating toxic emissions.

ASiA – Anthroposophical Youth Conference in Spring Valley, NY – *"Self-Development and Social Responsibility"* – 600 participants. (*Into The Heart's Land*, pg. 452)

EARTH DAY*, April 22, 1970 – *AUTO ENGINE BURIAL, Colorado State University (CSU). Shown at the microphone, delivering the eulogy, State Representative Richard Lamm who would later become governor. PHOTO UPI – Art Levy. *(AUTHOR NOTE: As a college student, I helped organize this event. The engine was from my roommate's Mustang and had to be returned.)*

1971
– DISINFORMATION – *Pentagon Papers* leaked to the Washington Post. The report reveals that President Johnson systematically lied "not only to the public but to Congress."

AG – First U.S. Biodynamic Conference, UCLA. (*Into The Heart's Land*, pg. 291.)

– First DAVOS International Business Technology conference promotes "Globalism."

– President Richard Nixon unilaterally withdraws the U.S. from the Bretton Woods international monetary agreement which causes worldwide economic chain reactions.

– Email created by Ray Tomlinson.

– Surgeon general funds studies about the effect of television on children.

– Liquid Crystal Display (LCD) developed by James Fergason.

– Floppy disk, invented by David Nobel / IBM.

1972
– WATERGATE OFFICE BUILDING BREAK-IN – operatives arrested. This starts the long trail toward Nixon's resignation.

IFOAM, *International Federation of Organic Agriculture Movements* founded, includes 120 countries >>>>

– Fewer than 350,000 people in U.S. prisons and jails. (*The New Jim Crow*, pg. 8)

ED – School for Eurythmy founded in Spring Valley, NY.

– Title IX of the Education amendment for gender equality is enacted.

FIRE BORNE 1965-1984

– *Whole Earth Catalog II* published.

ASiA – Anthroposophical Society in America sold its headquarters building at 211 Madison Ave. in New York City and moved to the Fine Arts Building in Chicago. At that time the Rudolf Steiner Library moved from 211 Madison Ave. to the "Carriage House" in Harlemville, NY. *(2017 Anthroposophical Society in America Annual Report Online, pgs. 22-23)*

1973
– Ethernet created by Bob Metcalf and David Boggs.

– *Roe v. Wade* Supreme Court landmark decision making laws which criminalize abortion unconstitutional.

ED – Parents from Hawthorne Valley Farm (NY), neighbors, Farm Store workers, and Camphill Village residents started the Hawthorne Valley Waldorf School Initiative.

– Paris Accords end Vietnam war, but the war continues.

– Universal military service ends in U.S.

– Watergate Hearing conducted in House of Representatives.

<<<< ***Endangered Species Act (ESA)*** **passed by Congress. Gives the EPA authority to block Federal projects which do not protect "Endangered Species."**[8]

– Personal Computer, Xerox.

– General Agreement on Trade and Tariffs (GATT) breaks down. Replaced by World Trade organization (WTO).

– Yom Kippur War (Arab/Israeli War) leads to oil embargo and price rises.

– National Advisory commission on Criminal Justice recommends no new prisons be built and existing juvenile prisons be closed. (*The New Jim Crow*, pg. 8)

– *THE MACK*, the first hip-hop film about racist cops by Michael Campus is released.

1974
– Richard Nixon resigns presidency rather than face impeachment.

– Monsanto introduces glyphosate as a commercial herbicide in 1974, and it quickly becomes the leading pesticide in the global agrochemical market.

---

[8] "SAVE A LIVING THING" first *Cause Marketing* promotion and was conducted by 7-Eleven for Slurpee "Endangered Species Cups and embedded the concept of "extinction" in culture. Poster from the author's collection.

1975
– Vietnam War ends with fall of Saigon. The U.S. withdraws, defeated. 58,000 American dead. Several hundred thousand vets return to a U.S. public which is bitter and disrespectful. Post-Traumatic Stress Disorder (PTSD) affects vets their marriages, families and children.
END NOTE (3) – LONG TERM EFFECT OF THE VIETNAM DEFEAT Lt. Col. Dave Grossman, *"On Killing"*
– **The U.S. military is re-designed as a business by Robert McNamara. Arms production becomes leading U.S. export business >>>>**

WALDORF UP 150% IN 10 YEARS – From 9 schools in 1965 to 24 AWSNA member schools in North America.

> **VIETNAM WAR CALLED "McNAMARA's WAR"**
>
> *Robert McNamara reacted to the fall of Vietnam like any excellent businessman and saw that war needed a "re-design" of war itself. Arms production became the leading export U.S. industry and wars, now called "irregular wars," are America's #1 business.*

– Apple Computer founded April 1.

ED – Chicago Waldorf School founded.

AG – Biodynamic Conference Sacramento State (*Into The Heart's Land*, pg. 177.)

ED – Sacramento State University, full credit courses in Waldorf education. (*Into The Heart's Land*, pg. 291.)

SCI – Woods End Research Laboratory started by William Brinton PhD. *(Into the Heart's Land, pg. 537)*

1976
– **BICENTENNIAL OF THE U.S.**

– *MOTHERING Magazine* begins publishing.

ED – Rudolf Steiner College forms in Fair Oaks, CA. Programs for Waldorf teacher training, the arts, and Biodynamic agriculture get underway.

1977
– James Earl (Jimmy) Carter inaugurated President.

<<<< PERSONAL COMPUTERS INTRODUCED – Radio Shack TRS-80, Commodore PET, Apple II successful.
(Photo: TANDY / RADIO SHACK TRS-80 Model 1 – oldcomputers.net)

ASiA – Anthroposophical Women's Conference – *A Woman's Incarnation In The 20th Century.* (*Into The Heart's Land*, pg. 177.)

1978
– Christian Broadcasting Network (CBN) formed with 10-million subscribers.

– Pat Robertson dubbed *"The Vicar Of The Electronic Church."*
"If Christian people work together, they can succeed during this decade and win back control of the institutions that have been taken from them ..." Pat Robertson
– "DEAD, DEAD, ALL DEAD – DETAILS AT 10" A Dallas Newscaster's Promo for the report about the 1978 mass suicide / murder of the followers of Jim Jones in Jonestown, Guyana. This tragedy is credited by some researchers with solidifying the "anti-cult" (small religious movements) concept in the worldwide cultural mindset.

– President Carter defeated on consumer protection legislation.

– Filibuster defeats Union Organizing bill.

1979
– Soviets invade Afghanistan.

END NOTE (4) – CAMPHILL SERVICE AWARD

– Three Mile Island nuclear disaster. More than 140,000 residents evacuated.

– "Nuclear Winter" Soviet disinformation campaign targets U.S. allies and says Carter would use nuclear weapons on them if necessary.

– Energy crisis as Iran reduces oil exports. (*See 1953 Iranian coup.*)

– Soviet disinformation campaign says Carter administration supports South African apartheid.

ASiA – U.S. – Anthroposophical West Coast Youth Conference (*Into The Heart's Land*, pg. 177.)

WEST COAST ANTHROPOSOPHICAL YOUTH CONFERENCE
ORC ANTHROPOSOPHICAL YOUTH NEWSLETTER 1979 MAY VOLUME 1 NUMBER 2
RUDOLF STEINER LIBRARY ONLINE COLLECTION
https://nyheritage.contentdm.oclc.org/digital/collection/nyrud/id/2278/rec/9
<SNIP> "Look at the last 2 or 3 years: all over the world are very clear tendencies of an awakening to a new task and situation. We have experienced our separations so much – Are sufficient inner forces already there from this suffering and tragedy? Or, is it that a new generation is coming from the spiritual world willing this cooperation? Is the whole spiritual Goetheanum, where our friends are joined so strongly, working together with us and wanting this so strongly that we are all already beginning to go in this direction?"

1980
– U.S. population 263,423,000

– 1 million farms – down 80% from 1970. 2,987,522 farmers.

AG – Frey Vineyards – 3 generations of Biodynamic wine.

– *Talk Radio* breathes new life into AM radio in the 80s.

```
USDA begins surveying
the organic farming
sector with purpose of
increasing communication
between organic farmers
and the USDA.
```

– Christian Coalition meets Young Republicans, forming *New Right*.

USDA AND ORGANICS?
The USDA has been responsible for promoting all aspects of U.S. agriculture since 1862 including all governmental agricultural statistics. BIODYNAMIC AND ORGANIC AGRICULTURE grew independently worldwide since the 1930s-40s without any USDA acknowledgement until it reached a point where the total numbers of U.S. farms fell so low that organic was the only growing segment of agriculture and so began making measurable in-roads into the market statistics.

– John Lennon shot to death on street in New York City.

– 4 out of 10 Americans divorced.

WALDORF UP from 24 schools in 1975 to 39 AWSNA member schools in North America.

– *Conservative Caucus* mass mailings generated a database of 20-30 million names.

– New Right strategy targets electing Christian conservatives to local school boards.

October 31, 1980
The Rudolf Steiner Archive
is founded by James Stewart, an anthroposophist in Michigan who was a data base analyst for the auto industry, to offer Steiner's published works in a searchable data base. Stewart was inspired by Rudolf Steiner's quote:

"In the meetings of the Anthroposophical Society a great truth can be experienced. When human beings meet together seeking the spirit with unity of purpose then they will also find their way to each other – they will find the path from soul to soul."

OPIOIDS INTRODUCED
Pharmaceutical manufacturers lobby medical journals to say that all types of pain should be treated aggressively. Oxycodone released with multi-million dollar sales and public relations push and starts epidemic of opioid pain killers. Illustration: Wong-Baker pain scale

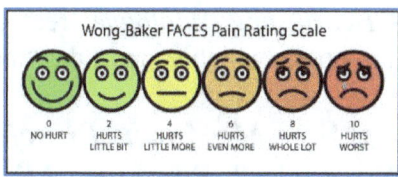

1981
– Ronald Reagan inaugurated.

– Recession due to Iran Oil crisis and tight money policy.

– YES GMOs! NO ORGANICS!

ASiA – Financial deficit is one factor in approval of the sale of 211 Madison Avenue (New York City). Council Minutes and Memos describe the transaction between the national Society and the New York City branch. ADMINISTRATIVE COLLECTION.

```
YES GMOs! NO ORGANICS!
New attention and recognition
of organics in 1980 lead to a
backlash from the incoming
Reagan administration which
tried to abolish the previous
positive position on organics.
```

ASiA – Regionalization of the Anthroposophical Society is complete and members vote to change the by-laws at the Annual General Meeting.

END NOTE (5) – MEMORANDUM TO MEMBERS – HISTORY OF REGIONALIZATION
https://firebornecom.files.wordpress.com/2022/09/1981_1-regionalization-a-brief-summary-of-history-of-growth.pdf

Two typescript, photocopied pages of a very poor quality – however it is of interest historically for who were the seven General Council members at the time – each was a founder of colleges, communities, enterprises, healing practices that substantially created the future of the Anthroposophical Society in America for decades.

Dietrich Asten, Henry Barnes, Werner Glas, Traute Page, Carlo Pietzner, Rene Querido, and Virginia Sease. They wrote: *"It is clear to us that By-Laws cannot create a Society. Only spiritually active members can do that. But By-Laws can provide the framework in which spiritual life can unfold."*

Included in the ADMINISTRATIVE COLLECTION of documents.

END NOTE (6) – 1981 BY-LAWS approved at the Annual General Meeting, December 20, 1981
https://firebornecom.files.wordpress.com/2022/09/1981_3-asa-bylaws.pdf
Strengthen the organizational form of "Regionalization."
Seven pages and are included in the ADMINISTRATIVE COLLECTION of documents.

1982
– Monsanto creates genetically modified plants (GMOs) which are not killed by (are resistant to) *Roundup*, glyphosate herbicide. Seeds named: *"Roundup Ready."*

1983
– EPA lists glyphosate as a carcinogen and Monsanto counters with legal action to block efforts to suspend use.

– *Hearthsong Catalogue* created by Barbara Kane in black & white to offer carefully selected toys and books which support the "magic of childhood," adventure in play for young children.

– U.S. – *McMartin Preschool "Satanic Cult" lawsuit*[9] causes international media "hysteria." Spawns anti-cult, anti-New Age, and anti-small spiritual groups movement which grows rapidly and internationally. This case built the audiences for religious right talk shows.

AG – Nicanor Perlas / Philippines founds International Alliance for Sustainable Agriculture. Coins phrase "sustainable agriculture."

SCI – Woods End Research lab Will Brinton is contracted by Prince Charles to "lead him on a tour of compost piles of England." *(Personal conversation – JWY.)*

---

[9] Stories flooded mainstream media and launched the large audiences of religious right talk shows. A lawsuit went on for eight years, cost millions of tax payer dollars and in the end there was no crime, no abuse, but people did time. The *Los Angeles TIMES* investigated itself and found that they chose salacious headlines in order to sell newspapers rather than seek the truth.

ED – Barnabas Youth Opportunities Center bounded by Bart Eddy, former Waldorf Class Teacher at the Detroit Waldorf School to bring social renewal to a lower income part of Detroit. *(SEE LILIPOH Fall 2021, pg. 30.)*

TF – Rudolf Steiner Foundation (RSF) trustee Sigfried Finser begins working with John Alexandra to look for ways to work with money that are more consistent with spiritual and social insights of Rudolf Steiner. Gradually others join this founding group. (*A History Of RSF Social Finance, Spring 2014, RSF Quarterly*, pg. 4)

ED – Pine Hill (NH) Waldorf School burns.
The school requests funding from the Rudolf Steiner Foundation (RSF) which only has $6,000 cash in assets. The founding group reaches out to the community to fundraise, and RSF makes its first loan commitment in the amount of $500,000. The Foundation is in John Alexandra's garage in Spring Valley, New York. (*A History Of RSF Social Finance, Spring 2014, RSF Quarterly*, pg. 4)

1984

Rudolf Steiner Foundation, founded 1938, re-forms for innovative, socially responsible financing. Raises $500,000 to rebuild Pine Hill Waldorf School. A "Three Fold" example of "crowdfunding" in the Anthroposophical community.

UTNE READER created by Eric Utne to offer *"conversations that transcend traditional labels, biases, and stereotypes; conversations that demonstrate there's still plenty of room for all of us to grow, to be educated ... to be cured of ignorance."*

– Digital / analog telephone switches make digital communications over analog "twisted pair" phone systems, by Northern Telecom.

– FBI anti-drug funding up over 10 times from $8 to $95 million.(*The New Jim Crow*, P. 497.)

– Dept. of Defense anti-drug funding from $33 million to 1,042 million in 1991.

– Drug Enforcement Administration (DEA) anti-drug spending up from $86 million to $1,026 million.

– DEA drug treatment spending down from $224 million to $54 million. (New Jim Crow, pg. 49-50)

AG
<<<< **Michael Fields Ag Institute (MFAI) formed for organic / biodynamic research.**

– President Reagan rolls back auto emission standards.

– Mcintosh computer introduced by Apple.

– Reagan White House hired staff to publicize the emergence of crack cocaine as part of a strategic effort to build a public and legislative "war on drugs."

– IRAN-CONTRA SCANDAL. This messy, complicated affair involved the CIA illegally selling guns to Iran and using those funds to arm a Nicaraguan army for regime change. The Nicaraguans then provided cocaine which was sold, with CIA assistance to inner-city black Americans who were then targeted by increased anti-drug agencies. (New Jim Crow, pg. 49-50
https://en.wikipedia.org/wiki/iran%E2%980%93Contra_affair

ED – Emerson Waldorf School, Chapel Hill, NC formed (*Into The Heart's Land*, pg. 318.)

– Bophal, India Union Carbide plant major chemical leak which killed 15,000 and seriously injured 200,000. In addition 500,000 had long-term health disabilities. The CEO of Union Carbide flew in to Bophal to sympathize and was shocked to be arrested and held responsible for the actions of the corporation.

– James Stewart's **Rudolf Steiner Archive** begins offering Rudolf Steiner lectures on the Internet (ARPAnet). First one sent out was "Good Fortune. Its Reality and Its Semblance" GA# 61, December 7, 1911.
https://wn.rudolfsteinerelib.org/Lectures/Dates/19111207p01.html

NOTES:

Into The Heart's Land, Henry Barnes, Steiner Books, 2013

Chokehold: Policing Black Men, Paul Butler, 2017

Bowling Alone, Robert D. Putnam, Simon & Schuster, 2000

Rudolf Steiner Library, https://rudolfsteinerlibrary.org/

LINKS / END NOTES:

END NOTE (1) – PAGE 90 – 1970 TECHNOLOGY CHANGE FROM AM TO FM RADIO
https://firebornecom.files.wordpress.com/2022/02/0.5.2-1970s-am-fm.pdf

1970s TECHNOLOGY CHANGE FROM AM RADIO TO FM RADIO

AM radio was introduced in the 1920s. It was the ONLY broadcast technology until FM was introduced in the mid 1950s.

Unfortunately for FM broadcasters, television was emerging at the same time. FM got lost in the shuffle. Most of the early FM stations went off the air in the fifties.

Those that survived had sister AM's and simulcasted their programming with the AM.

FM stereo was came out about 1960. It was expected to revitalize the FM band, but failed to do so.

GM offered its first FM car radios in 1963. Cadillac first offered FM Stereo radios in 1966. In the late sixties, some FM stations began to have moderate success with progressive rock and jazz which did not fit in well with the heavily formatted AM business.

AM dee-jays were seeing the handwriting on the wall by the mid to late 60s – early 70s. That was an era of wild and crazy promotions on AM radio. FM stations began in the seventies originated their own programming such as album Oriented rock (AOR) and became successful.

In the 1980s the Fairness Doctrine was allowed to expire under President Reagan. Also, AM radio was languishing under the higher quality sound of FM. What was needed was a way to gather listeners.

By the late eighties, AM was in free fall. AM stereo was introduced to fight this, but did not catch on.

What did catch on was a programming shift to Talk Radio.

END NOTE (2) – PAGE 90 – ANTI-CULT MOVEMENT – MORAL PANIC

According to Susan P. Robbins writing in the IPT Journal (Issues In Child Abuse Accusations), media gave special attention to a variety of non-traditional religious groups that proliferated during the 1960s and 70s.

"The popular use of the term 'cult'; generally carries with it extremely pejorative connotations, and such groups are viewed as essentially deviant and controversial due to their unconventional beliefs and lifestyles ..." (Beckford, 1985, Robbins, 1992; Shupe & Bromley, 1991)[10]

With the 1978 mass suicide / murder of the followers of Jim Jones in Jonestown, Guyana, the anti-cult sentiment was solidified in the worldwide cultural mindset.

By the 1980s, formal, anti-cult groups had arisen and drawn media attention to their cause. They forged an alliance with sympathetic social workers, psychologists, psychiatrists, social scientists, lawyers and police and began generating sophisticated newsletters, journals and utilizing a host of talk-radio shows for promoting their businesses.

---

[10] THE SOCIAL AND CULTURAL CONTEXT OF SATANIC RITUAL ABUSE ALLEGATIONS, Susan P. Robbins, www.ipt-forensics.com/journal/volume10/j10_8.htm, pg. 3

FROM WIKIPEDIA https://en.wikipedia.org/wiki/McMartin_preschool_trial
The **McMartin preschool trial** was a day care sexual abuse case in the 1980s, prosecuted by the Los Angeles District Attorney Ira Reiner.[1] Members of the McMartin family, who operated a preschool in Manhattan Beach, California, were charged with hundreds of acts of sexual abuse of children in their care. Accusations were made in 1983, arrests and the pretrial investigation took place from 1984 to 1987, and trials ran from 1987 to 1990. The case lasted seven years but resulted in no convictions, and all charges were dropped in 1990. By the case's end, it had become the longest and most expensive series of criminal trials in American history.[2][3] The case was part of day-care sex-abuse hysteria, a moral panic over alleged Satanic ritual abuse in the 1980s and early 1990s.

END NOTE (3) – PAGE 93 – **1975 LONG TERM EFFECT OF THE VIETNAM DEFEAT – Lt. Col. Dave Grossman,** *"On Killing"*
https://firebornecom.files.wordpress.com/2022/02/1975-vietnam-defeat.pdf

1975 THE LONG-TERM EFFECT OF THE DEFEAT IN VIETNAM

In his book, ON KILLING, Lt. Col. Dave. Grossman, pg. 288, Grossman describes two soldiers at the end of the Vietnam war.

"Our two Vietnam veterans departed ... with a mixture of joy at having survived and shame at having left their buddies behind. Instead of returning to parades, they found antiwar marches. Instead of luxury hotels, they were sent to locked and guarded military bases ... the media prepared the American people by calling returning veterans 'depraved fiends' and "psychopathic killers," and beautiful young movie stars led the accusing chant of a nation that echoed through the veteran's soul: 'Baby killers ... murderers ... butchers ...' They were rejected by girlfriends, spit on, and accused by strangers and finally dared not even admit to friends they were veterans."

"... for the Vietnam infantry man in the example in the last chapter, the condemnation upon his return amplified the horror of his combat experiences to result in a staggering degree of war. By the very nature of its unique historical causation, the existence of any significant number of individuals in such a condition is unprecedented in the history of Western civilization. Although this model only crudely reflects what has happened it begins to represent the relative forces. Statistics on the horrible number of suicides among Vietnam vets, on the tragic number of homeless who are Vietnam vets, on divorce rates, drug use rates and so on, give evidence that something has occurred that is significantly, start willingly different from what occurred after World War II and on any other war our nation has ever encountered.

Thus, the long-term legacy of the Vietnam War upon American society is not just hundreds of thousands of troubled veterans, it is also hundreds of thousands of troubled marriages impacting women, children and future generations. For we know the children of broken families are more likely to be physically and sexually abused, and that children of divorce are more likely to become divorced as adults, and that victims of child abuse are more likely to become child abusing adults. And this is only one facet of the price this nation will pay for those personal kills in the jungles of Vietnam.

1   ON KILLING, Lt. Col. Dave Grossman, pg. 290-291

END NOTE (4) – PAGE 94 – 1979 CAMPHILL SERVICE AWARD

1979 SERVICE AWARD CAMPHILL
From NEWSLETTER of the
Anthroposophical Society in America, Summer 1979

TURNING THE NIGHTMARE OF THE HOLOCAUST INTO THE DREAM OF HUMAN COMMUNITY
U.S. CAMPHILL COMMUNITIES
RECEIVE 1979 SERVICE AWARD
OF THE
AMERICAN ASSOCIATION ON MENTAL DEFICIENCY

The Award ceremony took place in Miami, Florida on May 31, 1979 at the 103rd Annual Meeting of the American Association on Mental Deficiency. Past AAMD Award recipients include President John F. Kennedy, Mrs. Muriel Humphry, and Whitney Young, Jr.
The wording of the citation reads:

SERVICE AWARD
Camphill Village, USA

Camphill Villages. Yours are communities which remind us what many more of our cities and towns could be like in the best of all possible worlds. The very act of sharing this award illustrates the reason for it, and the reason why it does more to announce the wisdom within this Association than your desire for the recognition. You have made it clear to all that your special mission is to demonstrate that people of diverse interests and needs can engage in a life sharing experience, and that service to our fellows is derivative from such an experience and not vice versa. Your creations are proof that an intentional community can be normal if the main purpose of that community is NOT only to serve others but to live and share together, to serve each other. Forty years ago, as the Holocaust was kindled in the heart of Europe and tested with mixed effect the conscience of the world, a group of young people near Aberdeen, Scotland answered the nightmare with a dream. The Camphill movement was born. Under the guidance of Dr. Karl Koenig, these refugees from Nazism established a community dedicated to the value and importance of each human being regardless of race or creed, of social status or degree of, intellectual endowment. Twenty years ago, one of those present at the original community, Carlo Pietzner, brought the now-flourishing movement to the United States. Today, of between 50 and 60 Camphill centers all over the world, there are three Camphill communities in the UNITED STATES which share this Association's Service Award for 1979: Children's Village in Beaver Run, Pennsylvania, Camphill Village in Copake, New York, and Camphill Village in Kimberton, Pennsylvania. The Achievements of Camphill are based firmly on the work and vision of Rudolf Steiner. His influence is quietly evident in every aspect of each community, from education to architecture, from agriculture to worship. The wisdom of Rudolf Steiner's influence is felt by every visitor to these splendid communities in which life is shared equally by everyone. About half of the residents would be considered handicapped elsewhere, yet no one is handicapped in Camphill because service to fellow human beings is part of everyone's life. At Camphill, each person has meaningful work and holds a value placed in the lives of others.

For bringing to life a vision of hour human beings can live more purposefully, yours has been a contribution that goes beyond a field and touches everyone. By proving again that ALL human beings are valuable and that the future for EACH OF US holds nothing but good, you deserve more than what a mere award is permitted to convey.

END NOTE (5) – PAGE 96 – MEMORANDUM TO MEMBERS – HISTORY OF REGIONALIZATION
https://firebornecom.files.wordpress.com/2022/09/1981_1-regionalization-a-brief-summary-of-history-of-growth.pdf

Two typescript, photocopied pages of a very poor quality – however it is of interest historically for who were the seven General Council members at the time – each was a founder of colleges, communities, enterprises, healing practices that substantially created the future of the Anthroposophical Society in America for decades.

Dietrich Asten, Henry Barnes, Werner Glas, Traute Page, Carlo Pietzner, Rene Querido, and Virginia Sease. They wrote: *"It is clear to us that By-Laws cannot create a Society. Only spiritually active members can do that. But By-Laws can provide the framework in which spiritual life can unfold."*

Included in the ADMINISTRATIVE COLLECTION of documents.

END NOTE (6) – PAGE 96 – 1981 BY-LAWS approved at the Annual General Meeting, December 20, 1981
https://firebornecom.files.wordpress.com/2022/09/1981_3-asa-bylaws.pdf
Strengthen the organizational form of "Regionalization."
Seven pages and are included in the ADMINISTRATIVE COLLECTION of documents.

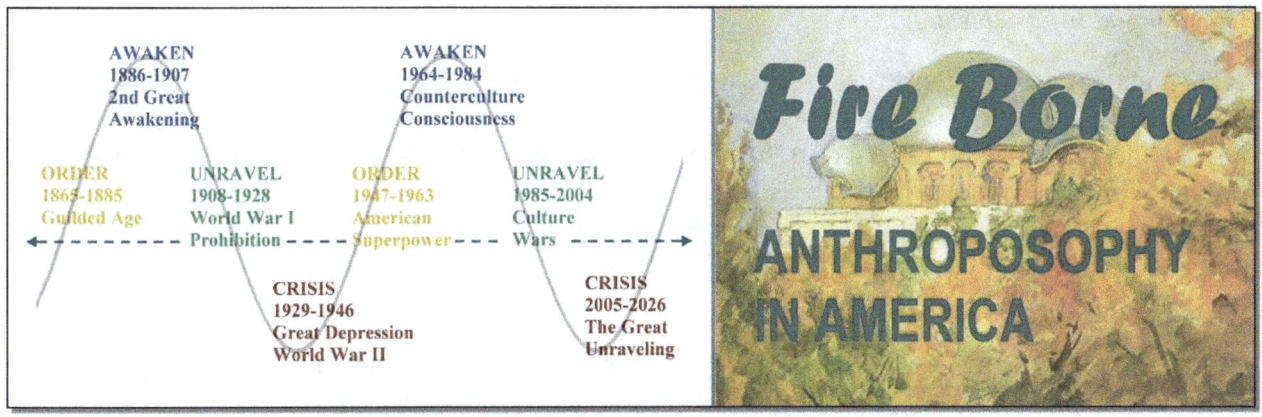

CULTURAL WAVE CHART © 2016 Jean W. Yeager[11]

1985-2004 "Culture Wars"
PHASE: UNRAVEL

In this phase the Moral Landscape, the counterculture deepens and "old ways of doing things" come unraveled. The term "Cultural War" was coined in 1992 by then Presidential candidate Patrick Buchanan and describes the dramatic cultural and social unraveling which may continue through the 2020s. NGOs shift the terrain and a "Third Sector" arises.

Abbreviations:	RS Rudolf Steiner	ED Education	MED Medical	ASiA Anthroposophical Society in America
AG Agriculture	SM Spirit Matters	TF Threefold	SCI Science	GAS General Anthroposophical Society

All timeline entries are for U.S. events unless otherwise noted.

1985
AG – *THE FIRST COMMUNITY SUPPORTED AGRICULTURE FARM*

Jan Vander Thun brought the model from Zurich. "In Switzerland there are presently five groups, primarily urban, with 100-200 households in each. The members or shareholders as they are called, have agreed to find land together, to capitalize the operation, and to pay all of the operating costs. In two cases they have expanded from gardens to full farms with dairy, grains and fruits."

"Imagine an agricultural experience that can inspire young people to pursue an agricultural path, both because of the private rewards and because of the social and economic respect. Imagine providing for those with less in the community by allocating shares for that purpose. Imagine a place for the handicapped to be appreciated and integrated within a broad community. All these imaginings and more exists now in various locales around the world and they lead to one primary point. *Quality food.* For there is more to food than its purity, taste and beauty. If you can imagine, then you connect. The examples are there. (pg. 64) *1987 Summer – Journal for Biodynamics*, Number 163, Page 58-64)

Jan Vander Thun, Robyn Van En and Hugh Ratcliffe started Indian Line Farm in 1984-85. (2) Photo by Patti Barrett PHOTO © Copyright, 1987, *Journal for Biodynamics*)

---

[11] Dates / phases from THE FOURTH TURNING, William Strauss and Neil Howe, Broadway Books, 1997

– Lead in gasoline banned.

– Conventional farmers converge on Washington DC to demand economic relief.

BD – Demeter Association formed in the U.S. – "seventeen years before the USDA established the National Organic Program (NOP)."
https://www.demeter-usa.org/about-demeter/demeter-history.asp

– 58% of all households married.

END NOTE (1) – 1985 CIA COCAINE SMUGGLING The New Jim Crow, Michelle Alexander, pg. 5-6
https://fireborneecom.files.wordpress.com/2022/02/1985-cia-cocaine-smuggling.pdf

– 5 divorces per 1,000 people.

– 22% of all births out of wedlock.

– 18 abortions per 1,000 females age 15-44.

– U.S. – first mandatory seatbelt law.

– Internet Domain Name System (DNS) created.

TF – THE THIRD SECTOR ARISES
An estimated 1,600 Non-Governmental Organizations (NGOs) spent $2.8 billion on environmental, social justice, and other programs they supported.
  "The *International Herald Tribune* said, "they (the NGOs) are called the 'Third Sector,' alongside the state and private sector. They offer a new channel to introduce both social responsibility and a democratic approach where either government or commerce has always dominated ellipses (they are an energetic force in the conduct of international relations and the spread of civil society across borders." -"*The Emergence Of A Global Threefold Society And The Future Task of the Michaelic Movement*, Jesiah Ben-Aharon, an essay in THE FUTURE IS NOW: Anthroposophy At The New Millennium, Temple Lodge, 1999, pg. 49

– 20 countries (but not the U.S.) sign a treaty banning torture.

– 66% of *Fortune* 500 companies (roughly 300+) were involved in illegal activities according to *U.S. News and World Report.* (*The Ecology of Commerce*, pg. 116)

ED - 72 AWSNA member schools in North America.

– U.S. performs nuclear testing in Nevada. USSR performs nuclear testing in Kazakh/Semiplitinsk.

– ATF raid: *"The Covenant, The Sword, The Arm Of The Lord"* compound in northern Arkansas.

– *"New Coke"* debuts with new secret flavor formula.

-- RJ Reynolds merges with Nabisco to become the largest food company in the U.S. >>>>

– Michael Jordan named NBA rookie of the year.

– 17th Space Shuttle Mission *Challenger 7* lands safely at Edwards AFB.

– Coca-Cola announces it will bring back *"Old Coke."*

– EPA classifies glyphosate as a carcinogen (Class C). Monsanto provides "scientific" research (later proved to false in a court of law) to persuade the EPA that it was not possible for glyphosate to be a carcinogen.

> ### *The Other Economic Summit*
> ### *(TOES)*
> Sustainable agriculture proponents report virtually no research or conversation about sustainable agriculture. No recognition of the need to even begin talking about sustainable agriculture. – Joan Dye Gussow. *(Chicken Little, Tomato Sauce and Agriculture, 1991)*
>
> Rod Shouldice, Biodynamic Exec Director says, *"Someone out there is feeding you." (Probably RJR and Nabisco)*

– Louisiana Catholic priest pleads guilty to 11 counts of sexual molestation of boys. This is the first case of child sexual abuse reported nationally.

1986
– Challenger 10 space shuttle explodes 73 minutes after liftoff.

– Reagan administration directs the FCC to allow the Fairness Doctrine to lapse allowing broadcasters to ramp up pointed political discourse with no requirement for a rebuttal. SEE 1987.

– Reagan administration launches disinformation campaign internationally about how U.S. may attack Muammar Gaddafi with bombs or oust him in a coup.

– Reagan signs gun control legislation banning sale of new machine guns. The existing guns in the U.S. estimated to be 200,000 and their value skyrocketed.

– OIL EMBARGO – Price falls from $78.20 to $26.89. Then the Organization of Petroleum Exporting Countries (OPEC) reduce production to drive up prices. This causes gas shortages, lines at pumps, and is seen as a threat to the "American way of life!"

– Ice-T makes *"6 In The Morning"* first gangsta rap song.

– Reagan administration's "Iran-Contra Affair" leaks out and is originally denied.

– Microsoft Initial Public Offering (IPO).

– New York City passes first pro-lesbian and gay rights legislation.

– IBM produces 1-megabyte chip.

– U.S. nuclear tests in Nevada for the second year.

– Bluebonnet Whole Foods grocery in Dallas, TX merges with Texas Wholefood Distributors (Austin) to launch Whole Foods Inc., retail grocery chain.

ED – The Waldorf Institute of Detroit, MI moves to Chestnut Ridge, NY and changes its name to Sunbridge Institute. *Into The Heart's Land,* Henry Barnes, Steiner Books, 2013

1987
– The FCC abolished the FAIRNESS DOCTRINE. The doctrine was implemented in 1949 and required broadcasters to air opposing views. (There was no requirement for "equal time."). This allowed broadcasters to air opinions without rebuttal. "AM radio was languishing in the shadows of higher quality sound of FM ... into this perfect storm of opportunity rode Rush Limbaugh with his fiery and anti-intellectual brand of liberal-bashing and conservative talking points." This article gives a lengthy list of the most notable "talk radio" broadcasters many of whom are household names today.
https://rationalwiki.org/w/index.php?title=Conservative_talk_radio&oldid=1778541"

– First *Intifada* (Arabic literally meaning "shake off") conflict with Israeli occupiers in Palestinian territories.

– Chernobyl (Soviet Union) nuclear reactor disaster. Radiation clouds go worldwide.

– U.S. Disinformation Media Campaign for "war on drugs" campaign extraordinarily successful and launched an *actual* inner-city war. When the War on Drugs hits high gear, employment of black men drops 28%. (*The New Jim Crow,* pg. 51)

– *"Go-Go Eighties"* on Wall Street as a time for fast fame and easy money with corporate buy-outs using "junk bonds."

> Anthroposophical Society in America Newsletter
> Tables of Contents
> Spring 1987 – 2008 No. 2
> **LINK ALSO IN APPENDIX**
> RUDOLF STEINER LIBRARY ONLINE COLLECTION
>
> https://nyheritage.contentdm.oclc.org/digital/collection/nyrud/id/1785/rec/4
>
> Includes regional newsletters: Eastern, Midwestern and Western

– *"Junk Bond King"* Michael Miliken drew highest corporate paycheck in history of half-billion a year while he was in his thirties.

– 1987-94 estimated 50,000 new Non-Governmental Organizations (NGO's) are chartered and gain cultural/political power as activists.

– Teen suicides quadrupled between 1982 and 1987.

– *Acquired Immune Deficiency Syndrome* (AIDS) spreads among adolescents.

– STOCK MARKET CRASH fueled by over-leveraged major corporations using junk-bonds, and sub-prime mortgages. It was triggered by electronic programmed trading.

– CIA admits to Iran/Contra affair and interfering with law enforcement attempting to stop crack cocaine sales.

– Pat Robertson places second in Iowa caucuses for Republican President.

– Fall of the Berlin Wall, breakup of the Soviet Union.

AG – SOUTHEAST BIODYNAMIC CONFERENCE with Hugh Lovell, Harvey Lisle, Hugh Courtney and Jeff Poppen.

1988
– HTTP (HyperText Transfer Protocol) created which gives rise to the world-wide web.

– Organic Valley becomes nation's largest member-owned dairy co-operative.

ED – Hawthorne Valley Waldorf school heavily damaged by fire.

– George H.W. Bush inaugurated President.

– *The Simpsons* premiers.

– Pat Robertson forms the Christian Coalition as a political movement after his defeat by Bush.

– A "whistleblower" tells the press how Brown & Williamson (and other) tobacco companies manipulate nicotine content to cause addiction and increase sales. B&W, who owned American Express, used credit card records to identify the whistleblower.

– Business Week / Lou Harris poll – 9 out of 10 Americans surveyed believe that business will lie and deceive, harm, endanger or cheat to make more money. (*The Ecology of Commerce*, pg. 118)

– Politicians of both parties (at the Republican convention) met with sustained applause when they demanded the right to invade almost anybody's privacy; to search without a warrant almost anybody's automobile or boat; to bend the rules of evidence, or hire police spies, and attach (without a warrant) electronic surveillance. (*The Age of Folly*, pg. 16)

– ABC / Washington Post poll indicated 55% supported mandatory drug testing for all Americans, 52% were willing to have their homes searched, and 83% favored reporting suspected drug users to the police, even if they happen to be a member of your family. (*The Age of Folly*, pg. 60)

1989
– GMO SEEDS – Monsanto testing genetically modified (GMOs) commodity crops which are not killed by (are resistant to) glyphosate herbicide – "Roundup Ready" corn and soybeans which will generate high volume product and increase profitability.

– ORGANIC SEEDS – Seeds Of Change, Santa Fe, NM starts a national organic seed company, funded by M&M / Mars and which gives 1% of all profits to organic enterprises.

– Berlin Wall comes down.

RSF SOCIAL FINANCE (1989)

Total Assets: $5,067,000   Investor Funds: $3,564,000
Loan Portfolio: $2,893,000   Client Accounts: 264

ED – Denver Waldorf High school forms. (*Into The Heart's Land*, pg. 315)

ED – Shining Mountain Waldorf school, Boulder, CO forms. (*Into The Heart's Land*, pg. 316)

1990
– World-Wide Web (WWW) designed by Tim Berners-Lee.

– Soviet Union unravels. Vladimir Putin, head of the KGB, named President and stops "power grab" by oligarchs.

– Kweisi Mfume, president of the NAACP, sends a letter to the Secretary General of the United Nations calling for a public health rather than criminal approach to drug addiction.

> *"Three out of four Americans did not "trust the government to do what is right most of the time."* Bowling Alone, pg. 47

AG – "By the mid-sixties, many homey little farms that dotted the countryside were either going through expansion in order to survive or were closing their barn doors. ... Angelic Organics (Caledonia, IL) was reborn (as a CSA) out of my great losses in the 1980s, reborn with an eye to the well-being of the earth we live on and the food we eat" (1)

Farmer John Peterson quoted in the *Journal for Biodynamics*, Summer 1987.

By 1990 there were 60 Community Supported Agriculture (CSA) gardens.

– 50% divorce rate. 27% of children live with one parent.

– Financial recession due to oil prices.

– **Clean Air Act up for revision. Corporations battle the Act because of liability costs. An infamous Texas refinery created a 1 in 10 chance for neighbors to contract cancer.**

MED – THE HOUSE OF PEACE, Ipswitch, MA, founded by Carrie and John Schuchardt, provides physical and spiritual shelter to victims of war in a small healing community in companionship with adults with special needs, and provides education for peace and moral awakening.

– Greenpeace tripled its membership to 2,350,000 then lost 85% by 1998. (*Bowling Alone*, pg. 161)

AG – Organic Food Production Act (OFPA) publishes organic standards for public comment. Biodynamic Association (BDA) and the Demeter Association respond.

1991
– Rodney King being clubbed by L.A. cops caught on home video and shown on local TV. This sets off LA Riots.

TF – RS Foundation changes name to RSF Social Finance and becomes premier socially responsible investing organization.

> **1991 –** *Cult Awareness Network (CAN)* has twenty three chapters dedicated to collecting information on New Religious Movements and monitoring two hundred groups that it refers to as "mind control cults." This includes the Anthroposophical Society in America. CAN denigrates small spiritual groups on the worldwide web through their "flame" site.

– "Open World" digital switch makes digital / analog technology link. By Northern Telecom.

ED – Milwaukee Urban Waldorf School (a public school) project gets underway. (*Into The Heart's Land,* pg. 415.)

– From November through December, Czechoslovakia, Poland, Romania and E. Germany "fall" through televised revolutions.

– Clarence Thomas, first African American confirmed to the Supreme Court confirmed after hearings which contended sexual misconduct.

– "Summer of Mercy" – pro-life activists, conservative Christians and evangelicals launch nationwide effort to shut down abortion clinics through mass demonstrations and harassment of clients.

SCI – Water Research Institute established by Jennifer Greene. (*Into The Heart's Land,* pg. 538)

– Iraq invaded Kuwait to defend itself against financial threats from Kuwait. This triggers the first Gulf War and throws petroleum prices and availability into worldwide turmoil.

ED – The Sunbridge Institute, a Waldorf teacher training center, which moved to Chestnut Ridge, NY in 1986, changes its name to Sunbridge College and begins to offer M.A. degrees. *(Wikipedia)*

1992
– 935,459 organic acres.

TF – THE POWER SHIFT

"In an article with this title in *Foreign Affairs,* Jessica Matthews, a leading Central Senior Fellow at the Council on Foreign Relations, wrote: "The end of the Cold War has brought (a) novel redistribution of power among states, market, and civil society." Non-Governmental Organizations (NGOs) as, the driving power of civil society, "deliver(s) more official development assistance than the entire UN system. In many countries they are delivering the services in urban and rural community development, education, and healthcare – that faltering governments can no longer manage ... Increasingly, the NGOS are able to push around even the largest governments."

> **1992**
> **The e.Lib and the Rudolf Steiner Archive**
> James Stewart brings his database collection of Rudolf Steiner's works to the World Wide Web through his Bulletin Board service, The e.Lib. Researchers from around the world now have searchable access to Rudolf Steiner's works. Volunteers throughout the world submit texts and help to edit the on-line works.

Matthews points to the place and time in which she believes civil society, via its NGOs, irrevocably entered the power structure of global society. This happened at Earth Summit in Rio de Janeiro in 1992. (*"The Emergence Of A Global Threefold Society And The Future Task of the Michaelic Movement*, Jesiah Ben-Aharon, an essay in THE FUTURE IS NOW: Anthroposophy At The New Millennium, Temple Lodge, 1999, pg. 47)

EARTH SUMMIT
The United Nations Conference on Environment and Development, also known as the Rio de Janeiro Earth Summit, the Rio Summit, the Rio Conference, and the Earth Summit, was a major United Nations conference held in Rio de Janeiro from June 3 to June 14, 1992. Wikipedia

END NOTE (2) – REPORT FROM THE URBAN WALDORF PROGRAM, Ann Pratt – AWSNA NEWSLETTER, SPRING/SUMMER 1992, "A school psychologist with 12 year's experience reported walking into the Waldorf kindergarten by saying, "*'I have been amazed at the calmness."*
https://fireborne com.files.wordpress.com/2022/02/1992-awsna-milwaukee.pdf

– Rap music explosion – "Cop Killer" rap song by Ice-T becomes culturally defining statement about inner city life.

– RUBY RIDGE SIEGE – FBI agents and U.S. Marshalls engage in an 11 day standoff with white separatist Randy Weaver, his family and Kevin Harris in Idaho. Weaver's wife is killed by an FBI sharpshooter.

– Vice President Dan Quayle attacks Murphy Brown television show for "glamourizing unwed motherhood."

– *Christian Coalition* newsletter predicts religious battle. Presidential candidate Pat Buchanan echoes the same.

END NOTE (3) – PAT ROBERTSON ARTICLE PREDICTS BLOODY RELIGIOUS BATTLE BUT SAYS THAT CHRISTIANS WILL BE VICTORIOUS
https://fireborne com.files.wordpress.com/2022/02/3.5.4-1992-pat-robertson-culture-war.pdf

– CULTURE WAR – Pat Buchanan runs for president and calls for "*Culture War*" during Republican Convention.

– Pat Robertson gives Republican convention speech stating *"The campaign before us is save the soul of America – for the destiny of America."*

1993
 – William Jefferson (Bill) Clinton wins Presidential election.

– Pro-Abortion activist David Gunn is shot to death in Pensacola, FL.

– *THE WACO SIEGE*, a 51 day standoff between Branch Davidian Church members and FBI and ATF agents at the church's compound near Waco, TX. Nearly 80 people are killed.

BD -A 1993 study comparing Demeter Certified Biodynamic® farms and conventional farms in New Zealand, published in *Science Magazine* determined that Biodynamic® farms had superior soil health. (*"Soil Quality and Financial Performance of Biodynamic and Conventional Farms in New Zealand,"* by John P. Reganold, Alan S. Palmer, James C. Lockhart and Nate Macgregor, *Science*, April 16, 1993, Volume 260, pp. 344-349)

– 1 in 5 high school students carry a handgun to school.

– *Southeastern Pennsylvania Planned Parenthood vs. Casey* Supreme Court decision reaffirms right to abortion with certain limitations.

– Media sensationalism, especially via conservative Christian talk radio, driven by profit motive, pushes the message that non-traditional spiritual groups are immoral or illegal.

– The Treaty on European Union, commonly known as the Maasctricht Treaty.

1994
– *European Critics* – European Congress of Skeptical Organizations (ECSO) formed with hundreds of local affiliated groups in European countries. They begin targeting small religious groups and lobbying governments against them.

– Nicole Browne Simpson and Ronald Goldman murdered. The arrest and trial of O.J. Simpson becomes a daily television show.

– *Michigan Militia*, a well-armed and organized group with 2,000 members, is called before a Congressional Sub-Committee on Terrorism.

RSF SOCIAL FINANCE (1994)
Total Assets: $9,022,000   Client Accounts: 445
Loan Portfolio: $4,458,000

– Two California Waldorf-Inspired Public schools are formed.

– Amazon founded as an online bookstore.

– Two abortion clinic workers gunned down in Brookline, MA.

– Newt Gingrich unites Republican Party with *"Contract With America."* Conservative Political Action Conference drew 4,000 attendees.

ASiA – LACK OF DIVERSITY SURFACES AS A "PUBLIC QUESTION" AT THE SOCIETY'S AGM The question of "lack of diversity" within the Society first arose publicly in 1994 at the Society's Annual General Meeting in Chicago. At that time, members expressed a strong wish to take up issues of diversity and racism and their implications within the wider society as well as within the Anthroposophical Society. The general feeling of the membership in 1994 was: *"... if humanity is to move forward in a Michaelic way and develop the consciousness soul forces, the forces of racism need to be transformed."*
https://firebornecom.files.wordpress.com/2022/02/1994-diversity-lack-of-diversity-question.pdf

1995
END NOTE (4) – **NOT MUCH MORE COULD BE CHANGED – Anthroposophical Society in America New Approach To Leadership: Arthur Zajonc, Joan Almon and Mark Finser.**

ASiA – STRATEGIC PLAN – Anthroposophical Society in America Builders Group called together by Arthur Zajonc created a committee to draft a Strategic Plan. The group is Coleman Lyles (Camphill), Beth Dunn Fox (Eurythmy Association) and Jean Yeager (Biodynamic Assoc. / Envision Associates).

GAS – *European Critics:* Governments of France and Belgium are successfully lobbied by the European Council of Skeptical Organizations (ECSO). They put Anthroposophical Societies (and related organizations) along with the Church of Scientology, Jehovah's Witnesses and dozens of other small spiritual groups, on *"dangerous cult"* lists. SEE WIKIPEDIA LIST OF CULTS

> *ANTHROPOSOPHICAL BUILDERS GROUP*
> The ASiA Leadership Group hosts a gathering of 33 leaders of related initiatives: Waldorf [AWSNA], Biodynamics, Physicians [PAAM], and others; to imagine the future and foster an entrepreneurial spirit to turn vision into action in the new Millennium.

– 1995 BY-LAWS REVISION eliminates a specific requirement (in effect since 1933) for the Society to deposit bequests (or other funds) in the Rudolf Steiner Foundation due to the fact that Mark Finser, an RSF Board Member, has been appointed to the leadership of the Anthroposophical Society. See Administrative Collection.

– The CAO is an on-going committee of the General Council. The history document is 30+ pages long and is included in the Administrative Collection or follow the link below.
https://firebornecom.files.wordpress.com/2022/02/02-1995-cao-history.pdf

"The 1994-95 school year marks the 75TH Anniversary of Waldorf Education in the world and the sixty-sixth birthday of the Rudolf Steiner School in New York – the first Waldorf School in North America." *David Alsop, Chairman the Association Of Waldorf Schools of North America (AWSNA), RENEWAL Journal for Waldorf Education, Spring/Summer 1993, pg. 2*

ED – **There are 109 Private Waldorf schools in North America.**

ED – Two public schools chartered to add Waldorf methods after receiving staff training at Rudolf Steiner College since 1991.

– *U.S. Critics* – People for Legal and Non-Sectarian Schools (PLANS) founded. PLANS web site listed links to groups which were connected with the European actions against anthroposophy and Waldorf: ECSO, San Francisco Skeptics Society, Cult Action Network (CAN), atheist and Secular Humanist groups.

– Financial "housing bubble" starts in 1995 and bursts in 2006.

– Monsanto buys Calgene plus an array of genetically modified foods.

– GMO / "Frankenfoods" widely panned.

– 63 million untrained computer users.

AG – Robert Parker *Wine Advocate* newsletter lauds Biodynamic wine and Rudolf Steiner. Parker reviews the Biodynamic wines of Michael Chapoutier, *WINES OF THE RHONE VALLEY* pg. 139.

– Mexican peso's plunge triggers worldwide financial crisis.

– LILIPOH (an acronym for Life Liberty And The Pursuit of Happiness) magazine is launched by Christine Murphy formerly of Weleda.
Read about the founding online in the Anthroposophical Society in America Newsletter 1996 Autumn, Page 39
https://rudolfsteinerlibrary.org/

– Pat Robertson's Christian Coalition and 700 Club grows viewership dramatically.

1995 – Demeter Certified Biodynamic wine from France becomes touted internationally.

– Timothy McVeigh bombs the Oklahoma City Federal building as "payback" for 1993 "Waco Siege" Branch Davidian massacre of 85+ church members by FBI and ATF.

1996
ASiA – A GIFT OF A BUILDING -The Rudolf Steiner House at 1923 Geddes Ave. is given by the Great Lakes Branch of Ann Arbor to become the headquarters building for the ASiA.

ASiA – headquarters moved from The Fine Arts Building in Chicago to Ann Arbor, MI. New staff is hired.

– A GIFT OF $92,000 – *"The New Initiative's Fund"* – comes from a fund at the GAS to support the ASiA expanded plan of activities.

ASiA – Anthroposophical Society in America – The Builders Group Strategic Plan committee returns draft plan which recommends hiring an Administrative Director to help the ASiA Leadership Group and General Council achieve and expanded agenda.

ASiA – A nationwide call for applications for the ASiA Administrative Director position is published. After an interview process of all applicants, Jean Yeager is hired. Yeager's first task – move the headquarters from Chicago to Ann Arbor.

– *Defense of Marriage Act* passed by Congress defining marriage as the "legal union between one man and one woman."

– *Members of the Church of Scientology* file 51 separate legal actions against Cult Awareness Network (CAN) and wins a judgment of $2 million. CAN goes bankrupt and gives all assets, including their web site and files, to Scientology.

END NOTE (5) – 1996 – FORMING THE THIRD REALM ASiA – A Council of Anthroposophical Organizations (CAO) was formed from those who had attended the "Builders Group" plus additional representatives from major organizations – Waldorf Schools, Biodynamics, Camphill, Anthroposophical Medicine, Eurythmy Association, and others. A series of meetings which lead to the forming of the Council of Anthroposophical Organizations (CAO) to strengthen the relationship of the National Anthroposophical Society and Initiatives arising out of Anthroposophy.
https://firebornecom.files.wordpress.com/2022/10/1996-forming-the-third-realm.pdf

– *European Critics*, Grandt Brothers, publish *"Blackbook Anthroposophy,"* blocked by European court for defamation. >>>>

1997
GAS – News From The *Goetheanum*, Spring 1997,
END NOTE (6) – "RUDOLF STEINER'S EFFORTS TO ENCOURAGE CULTURAL DIVERSITY" By Detlef Hardorp
https://go.elib.com/yPjAz

ASiA – END NOTE (7) – Charges of Racism / Anti-Semitism leveled at Anthroposophical Society. – Anti-Defamation League Criteria adopted to ask critics: *"Is There A Pattern of Behavior?"*
https://go.elib.com/ie67t
– In 1997 Arthur Zajonc PhD and General Secretary of the Society served as coordinator for the Mind and Life dialogue The New Physics & Cosmology in Dharmsala, India with the Dalai Llama.

EUROPEAN CRITICS:
ANTHROPOSOPHY
"AN INCOMPATABLE WORLD VIEW"

The Grandt brothers appealed to German Federal Parliament, European Parliament, UNESCO and UNICEF to use democratic controls to withdraw supports from anthroposophical initiatives: *"Anthroposophy is incompatible with our democratic constitution, German law, the 1989 UN Convention on the Rights of Children and General Declaration of Human Rights."*

1,000 CSAs reported by Rodale Institute.

– 1,364,000 acres organic (USDA)

– National Organic Protocol (NOP) issued by USDA to "universal repudiation." (Keating)

TF – RSF Social Finance moves to The Presidio in San Francisco and expands and innovates in the growing world of social finance. *(Into The Heart's Land*, pg. 414)

-*U.S. Critics* – PLANS targets Mien speaking Hmong community in Sacramento at Oak Ridge elementary for "action" to block Waldorf and public school funding.

END NOTE (8) – **U.S. Critics – People For Legal And Non-Sectarian Schools (PLANS) demonstrate at Oak Ridge public school in Sacramento**

– Kyoto Accord – 150 nations reach agreement against heat-trapping greenhouse gasses.

END NOTE 9)
<<<< *"The attack on Oak Ridge,"* **Sacramento BEE editorial**.

– Acteal Massacre of Roman Catholics by paramilitary forces in Mexico.

– Microsoft buys Hotmail and re-launches it as MSN Hotmail.

– Heaven's Gate cult suicides result in 39 deaths.

– UN Climate Conference, Kyoto, Japan – 150 countries reach agreement on climate remedies.

– School shooting, Bethel, AR.

– School shooting, Pearl, MS.

– School shooting, Paducah, KY.

– Oak Ridge School Principal Mrs. Jue invites parents to parent forums after demonstration.

– *U.S. Critics* – PLANS sends local television crew to Rudolf Steiner College, the "college which teaches witchcraft."

– *U.S. Critics:* PLANS starts aggressive letter writing campaign to all California school boards about "Waldorf, a New Age cult."

PLANS FUNDRAISING DOCUMENT STATES THEIR INTENTIONS (FROM THEIR IRS TAX EXEMPTION APPLICATION – ARTICLE INCLUDED IN "AKNIGHTS" COLLECTION.

– *"School Charged With Witchcraft." UCSD Guardian.*

– *U.S. Critics* – PLANS launches a "flame" web site that is linked to other skeptics' web sites. Charges Anthroposophy, Rudolf Steiner as being "cult," "satanic," "racist" and "anti-Semitic." And that Waldorf education "indoctrinates" children worldwide.

– NEW CENTURY BANK, a local bank inspired by Steiner's ideas on banking, founded by Kenneth Mumma in Phoenixville, PA.

– **Anthroposophical Prison Outreach (APO) founded by Fred Janney, a psychologist in Michigan, becomes a program of the Anthroposophical Society in America with support by General Council Member, Eileen Bristol.**
***Journal For Anthroposophy*, 2000 Easter, No. 70 Easter**
https://cdm16694.contentdm.oclc.org/digital/collection/nyrud/id/7849/rec/1
Rudolf Steiner Library Online Collection

– *1997 – THE JERUSALEM TIMES " Can children learn tolerance while being called 'Nazis'?"* >>>>

– HTML 4.0 published by Internet Consortium.

ED – DETROIT COMMUNITY HIGH SCHOOL AND KINDERGARTEN co-founded by Candyce Sweda and Bart Eddy to bring Steiner's educational principles into the educational domain in the Brightmoor/Cody Rouge neighborhoods of the northwest side of Detroit.

– Urban Waldorf Program in Milwaukee issues report of reading increases the Curriculum Specialist wrote the School Board Chair saying: *"We are convinced that the approach taken at the Waldorf school, as well as at our arts centered school, is good for children in the urban setting. We know that behaviors are changing, as well as attitudes toward learning. Now our confidence is soaring as the children in this program are also excelling academically."*
https://fireborncom.files.wordpress.com/2022/11/1997-milwaukee-public-reading-scores.pdf

1998
– *WALDORF / ANTHROPOSOPHY TRIAL* – Pacific Justice Institute (PJI), a religious right-wing legal defense fund which supplies funding for attorneys, accepts PLANS application for funding for First Amendment lawsuit. Application says students are required to do "Wicca based practices." Attorney Scott Kendall Esq. selected by PJI to litigate Sacramento Unified / Twin Ridges trial.

– *U.S. Critics* – PLANS files First Amendment court case challenging public schools which use Waldorf methods and claim the schools *"indoctrinate children using "Anthroposophy, a cult-like religion."*

– PJI promotes a nationally syndicated religious talk radio show hosted by PJI founder, Brad Dacus, Esq., *"The Dacus Report."* This show reports on the PLANS First Amendment legal action against the *"cult of Anthroposophy."*

HOW THE CRITICS (PLANS) MONETIZE THEIR ATTACKS see "AKNIGHTS" COLLECTION.

– Christian Talk Radio – WCBM (Baltimore) hosts a show about PLANS claiming Waldorf Schools are teaching witchcraft and that Anthroposophy is a "cult-like religion. The on-air confrontation is between PLANS founder, Dan Dugan, Betty Staley (Rudolf Steiner College) and David Alsop (AWSNA).

– The first Harry Potter book, *"Harry Potter and The Sorcerer's Stone"* is released bringing the terms witchcraft and the occult into the public.

`Google` formally incorporated by Larry Page and Sergey Brin, two Stanford students.

– Open Directory Project (ODP) and DMOZ begin to categorize WWW websites so search engines can operate. This makes Yahoo, Netscape and others possible.

– U.S. Internet – DMOZ (Directory Mozilla.org) becomes the fundamental architecture for the internet search engines is targeted by skeptic groups to encourage their "experts" to volunteer to rank URLs of critical groups ahead.

– School shooting, Jonesboro, AR.

– School shooting, Edenboro, PA.

– School shooting, Fayetteville, TN.

– School shooting, Springfield, OR.

– School shooting, Richmond, VA.

– Clinton White House scandal erupts around Monika Lewinsky.

– Dow plunges 518 points as financial crisis worsens.

– Brokerage houses ordered to pay $1.3 billion for price fixing.

– Oprah Winfrey found not guilty in "beef defamation" SLAPP *(Strategic Lawsuits Against Public Participation).* lawsuit.

– **FRANCE: "DANGEROUS CULT MATERIAL"** Police raid and close down Anthro Medical Clinics, Waldorf schools and Biodynamic farms seizing computers and records. *(See 1997 Grandt Brothers)*
In describing the raid to the press, a French Minister defamed the Waldorf School Association and the Anthroposophical Society, was sued and lost his job.

– WHO DEFENDS RUDOLF STEINER AND ANTHROPOSOPHY? In Media, the U.S. Federal Court Case and Social Media?: David Alsop, AWSNA chair, writes the Anthroposophical Society in America and asks Society to defend Steiner in social media, media and legal actions including an expected First Amendment Federal Court legal action.

– Anthroposophical Society General Council takes actions to counter claims that Anthroposophy is a "cult" and Rudolf Steiner is a racist. See "AKNIGHTS" COLLECTION.
https://firebornecom.files.wordpress.com/2022/02/1998-press-release-diversity.pdf

– *United States vs. Microsoft* + 20 states file antitrust case.

– Roman Catholic sex abuse case in Dallas pays $23.4 million to 9 former altar boys.

– Eric Robert Rudolph charged with 6 bombings including Olympic Park, Atlanta.

– Earth Liberation Front sets fire to Vail Mountain ski lodge causing $12 million damage.

– Lewinsky Scandal – impeachment proceedings against President Clinton.

SCI – The Nature Institute, studying the foundations of science and technology is started. (*Into The Heart's Land,* pg. 533)

1999

– **ASiA Letter to Members -***"How Should One Respond To Criticism?"* – **Arthur Zajonc, General Secretary. INCLUDED IN "AKINGHTS" COLLECTION.**
https://firebornecom.files.wordpress.com/2022/02/jan99-how-to-deal-with-criticism-of-anthroposophy-zajonc.pdf

– European Union (EU) issues currency: "The Euro."

– **ASiA DIVERSITY** – PAN AMERICAN CONFERENCE, SAN DIEGO, CA The first Pan American Conference, *"The Spiritual Mission of the Americas"* was held in August 1999 in San Diego, California and sponsored by the Anthroposophical Society in America. Activities included a special performance by the Brasil Eurythmy troupe. Preparatory meetings had been held in Buenos Aires, Argentina with representatives from anthroposophical societies in Argentina, Brasil, Chile, Ecuador, Peru and Mexico. Columbia and Uruguay were unable to attend but expressed their interest in participating. Canada and Hawaii were being kept informed.

– **ASiA DIVERSITY** – INTERCULTURAL YOUTH CONFERENCE took place in July 1999 at Mt. Madonna retreat center near Santa Cruz, CA as an impulse of the Anthroposophical Youth Initiative. The Conference was a "grass roots" effort at attracting young persons involved in a wide variety of cultural activities. Jesse Osmer of Berkeley, CA chaired the organizing committee. The conference was attended by some several hundred young people.

– DMOZ has indexed over 1 million URLs.

– Largest drug bust in American history, U.S. Coast Guard intercepts a ship carrying 4,300 kg of cocaine.

– Impeachment trial of Pres. Bill Clinton.

– SUB-PRIME MORTGAGES: Countrywide Financial begins "beefing up sub-prime mortgage loans with very risky "NINJA" loans (no income, no job).

– Kansas board of education votes to delete any reference to evolution from state science curriculum.

124 AWSNA Member Schools in North America.

– School shooting, Conyers, GA.

– School shooting, Deming, NM.

– School shooting, Fort Gibson, OK.

– *Anti-World Trade Organization (WTO) Protest* in Seattle, WA. Protests against WTO meeting by anti-globalism forces catch police unprepared.

– Dec 31, Boris Yeltsin resigns as president of Russia leaving Prime Minister Vladimir Putin as acting President.

RSF SOCIAL FINANCE (1999)

Total Assets: $30,608,000   Investor Funds: $12,569,000
Loan Portfolio: $14,253,000   Client Accounts: 535

2000

ASiA – *A VISION FOR THE MILLENIUM* – a publication released by the Anthroposophical Society.

ASiA – *An Anthroposophical Internet Anti-Defamation task group formed.* Worldwide effort to counter wide-spread false and defamatory claims of occultism, "anthroposophy is a religion," racism, anti-Semitism in Steiner's work and Waldorf practices. Led by volunteers funded by Anthroposophical Society in America. Names itself the *"AKnights."*

– **ASiA DIVERSITY** – ASIA-PACIFIC FRIENDS CONFERENCES Penelope Robert had been making trips to the annual Asian-Pacific Friends conferences since 2000. The Pacific region plays a unique role in the life of the United States and these conferences have an unique role in connecting the U.S. Society with those of Hawaii, Japan, New Zealand, Singapore, India and elsewhere in the Pacific region. In many cases the struggles to keep anthroposophical initiatives going often in conditions of extreme poverty, social opposition and conflict are described. Strength, inspiration and encouragement are often what can be offered in these circumstances but are gratefully received.

CULTURAL CREATIVES

"Since the 1960s, 26 percent of the adults in the United States -- 50 million people -- have made a comprehensive shift in their worldview, values, and way of life -- their culture, in short. These creative, optimistic millions are at the leading edge of several kinds of cultural change, deeply affecting not only their own lives but our larger society as well. We call them the Cultural Creatives because, innovation by innovation, they are shaping a new kind of American culture for the twenty-first century."

AMAZON.COM BOOK REVIEW

"THERE IS A NEW COUNTRY ...

... just as big and just as rich in culture, but no one sees it. It takes shape silently and almost invisibly, as if flown in under radar in the dark of night. But it's not from somewhere else. This new country is decidedly American. And unlike the first image, it is emerging not only in the cornfields of Iowa but on the streets of the Bronx, all across the country from Seattle to St. Augustine. It is showing up wherever you'd least expect it: in your brother's living room and your sister's backyard, in women's circles and demonstrations to protect the redwoods, in offices and churches and online communities, coffee shops and bookstores, hiking trails and corporate boardrooms."

"Cultural Creatives" Paul H. Ray and Sherry Anderson, 2000 – Book Review – Amazon.com

12 Waldorf-Inspired Public schools.

– *ANTI-DEFAMATION AKnights* research DMOZ search protocols to discover why PLANS web site comes up first on searches. It is found that certain categories are administered by anti-Waldorf individuals. AKnights works with DMOZ to change their system.

– Anthroposophical Society Administrative Director report" *"No Critic Left Behind."* (will be in the AKnights Collection)
https://firebornecom.files.wordpress.com/2022/11/2000-no-critic-left-behind.pdf

– The AKnights counter a *San Francisco Chronicle* article: *"Religion or Philosophy"* which quotes the PLANS defamations about Anthroposophy and Rudolf Steiner. This article is included in "AKNIGHTS" COLLECTION. https://go.elib.com/yyKCo

ASiA – COMMUNITY RELATIONS PROJECT – A direct result of the "Critical Path" project, was sponsored by the Council of Anthroposophical Organizations (CAO).

– The AKnights counter a *SF Gate* article saying *"Biodynamics could be another 'wacked out New Age' gardening method,"* but with engagement, the article was changed. The articles will be in AKnights Collection.

– *"ANTHROPOSOPHY AND THE QUESTION OF RACE" – DUTCH SOCIETY REPORT ON RACISM* – is a 14-page summary of a 720 page report issued by a special Commission by the Anthroposophical Society in the Netherlands. It was intended, exclusively for the media. An interim report was issued in 1998. The Commission found 245 quotations from the 89,000 pages of the collected works of Rudolf Steiner published 1861-1925. The conclusion of the Commission is that sixteen statements would be discriminatory under Dutch law. The Commission found that any suggestion that racism is an inherent part of Anthroposophy is categorically wrong.
https://go.elib.com/iCV0Q

MED – MISTLETOE CANCER THERAPY APPROVED FOR USE

EXCERPT FROM *MISTLETOE THERAPY*, Beth W. Orenstein, *RADIOLOGY TODAY, DECEMBER 23, 2002*

"… the scientific and clinical review committees of the Kimmel Cancer Center at Thomas Jefferson University Hospital, Philadelphia, Pa., looked at available research on the use of mistletoe as a supportive treatment for cancer patients.

"They concluded that it was an acceptable supportive therapy for patients seeking such options.

"Ever since, the prescription-only medicine made from the extracts of the European mistletoe plant has been offered as part of care to cancer patients through Jefferson's Center for Integrative Medicine. 'I believe it is helpful, and I suggest it to my patients,' says Steven Rosenzweig, MD, founding director of the center, which integrates complementary therapies into patient care to reduce symptoms and enhance quality of life. He is also principal investigator of a National Institutes of Health-funded clinical trial of mistletoe in lung cancer.

"… In the United States, Iscar is the only mistletoe product approved for distribution by the FDA in accordance with its requirements for homeopathic medicines. Hiscia Institute, a Swiss-based pharmaceutical company, manufactures Iscar, which is distributed worldwide by Weleda, Inc."

– *Bush v. Gore* – Controversial Presidential election resolved by the Supreme Court who named George W. Bush President.

– School shooting, Littleton, CO.

– School shooting, Mt. Morris Twp, MI.

– School shooting, New Orleans, LA.

– New Patent Law Treaty signed.

– Y2K COMPUTER "BUG" affects coding around the world.

2001
– The U.S. is voted off the U.N. Commission On Human Rights, a position it has held for 50 years.

– School shooting, Oxnard, CA.

– School shooting, Santee, CA.

– School shooting, Williamsport, PA.

– School shooting, Caro, MI.

– Digital satellite radio begins.

– Apple releases iTunes.

– **Dot.com financial investment bubble bursts.**

– Wikipedia launched by Jimmy Wales and Larry Sanger.

– First draft of human genome published in *Science* magazine.

– OPEC oil ministers announce they will cut production by 1 million barrels a day to maintain prices.

– Vice President Dick Cheney calls for increased domestic fossil fuel production and increased usage of nuclear energy.

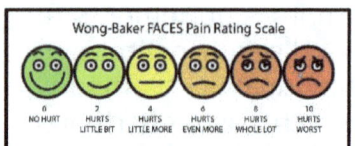

<<<< **Pharmaceutical lobbyists get Congress to declare the 2000s to be *"The Decade Of Pain Control and Research"* helping drug makers promote opioid pain killers.**
(WONG BAKER PAIN SCALE SHOWN)

– Bush Administration announces it will let oil companies drill on 1.5 million acres in the Gulf of Mexico.

– **SEPTEMBER 11 ATTACK – Two hijacked passenger planes fly into New York's World Trade Towers causing collapse of both and death of over 2,752 people. A third plane crashes into the Pentagon causing 125 deaths. A fourth plane crashes in Pennsylvania causing 64 deaths.**

– Article V of NATO agreement for "collective defense" is invoked.

– President Bush establishes Office of Homeland Security.
– Pentagon establishes the Information Awareness Office (IAO) to secure America against future terrorist attack. Plans include computers programmed to conduct "truth maintenance." (pg. 333)

– Apple releases iPod.

– Windows XP becomes available.

– Congress passes USA PATRIOT ACT.

ASiA – END NOTE (10) – ANNUAL REPORT – "AN INITIATIVE SOCIETY" General Secretary Arthur Zajonc quoted one of Rudolf Steiner's most powerful addresses to members. "Throughout our Society the mood should prevail that welcomes genuine initiatives, be they outer actions or equally as decisive inner initiatives."
NEWS FOR MEMBERS, AUTUMN 2001, pg. 14
https://firebornecom.files.wordpress.com/2022/10/2000_2001-initiative-society.pdf

– President Bush signs executive order allowing military tribunals against foreigners suspected of terrorism.

– Convention on Cybercrime signed in Budapest, Hungary.

– Enron files for Chapter 11 Bankruptcy in the Southern District of New York.

– People's Republic of China joins *World Trade Organization* (WTO).

– Richard Reid attempts to bomb a passenger airliner with explosives in his shoe.

– People's Republic of China granted permanent normal trade relations with the U.S.

2002
– *Organic standards adopted by USDA.*

– 3,045,000 acres of organic farmland.

– **1,700 COMMUNITY SUPPORTED GARDENS.**

– Rodale Institute estimates 1,700 CSAs. USDA estimates 12,398 alternative economic gardens.

– 61 largest newspapers in California run nearly 2,000 stories of Catholic sexual abuse, mostly about past allegations. During the same period these newspapers ran four stories about a larger – and ongoing – sexual abuse scandal in public schools uncovered by the Federal government.

– *AKnights Counter* PLANS defamatory letter to the Benicia School District board. (will be in the AKnights Collection)
https://firebornecom.files.wordpress.com/2022/10/020404beniciausd.pdf

ASiA – Joan Almon replaced Arthur Zajonc as General Secretary of the Anthroposophical Society in America and stepped off the General Council as well.
– MEMBERSHIP – 1979, 1,693 members. 1989, 2,674. 2002, 4,397. By far the largest impact on membership growth was the Rudolf Steiner Archive & e.Lib which by 2002 had 10,000 visitors per day.

– Doctors are prescribing ten times more OxyContin than in 1997. (*THE ATLANTIC*, 2014)

> **2002 – LOHAS**
> Lifestyle Of Health And Sustainability (LOHAS) market segment identified as 30% of the U.S. population.

– Congress passes the HOMELAND SECURITY ACT, creates Transportation Security Administration (TSA) and Robert Mueller III, Director of the FBI changes agency mission from "prosecution to prevention."

– U.S. invades Afghanistan.

– U.S. is re-elected to the U.N. Commission on Human Rights.

MED – CAMPHILL – Heartbeet Life Sharing Community founded in Vermont.

– Telcom giant WorldCom files for Chapter 11 bankruptcy, the largest filing in history.

– Houston Grand Jury indicts former Enron CFO Andrew Fastow on 78 counts.

– Arthur Zajonc, former General Secretary of the Anthroposophical Society in America, was the Scientific Coordinator for the dialogue with the Dalai Llama on The Nature of Matter, The Nature of Life.

2003

– *International Right Living Award* – The "Alternative Nobel Peace Prize" given to Ibrahim Abouleish, SEKEM Anthroposophical Community, Egypt.

– TIME MAGAZINE cover story on Intentional Communities includes Community Supported Agriculture.

– U.S. invades Iraq on false claim of Weapons of Mass Destruction (WMDs). "Between 6 and 10 million people around the world protest. Baghdad falls. No WMDs are found.

AG – LOS ANGELES TIMES reports: One-third of California wine growers move toward "sustainability" put 160,000 acres in transition to organic and Biodynamic.

– *DEFAMATION IN MOTHERING MAGAZINE WEB SITE* – critics from PLANS attempt to use chat room to defame Rudolf Steiner, Anthroposophy and Waldorf education. *AKnights* counters the move by contacting *Mothering* editors and pointing out Mothering's *Terms Of Service (TOS)* forbid such actions by PLANS. Defamatory posts are removed.
https://go.elib.com/2bLFp

> **WINES**
> **"GOING NEW AGED"**
> **LOS ANGELES TIMES**
>
> "... reducing the use of chemicals, 600 growers put 160,000 acres on the road to becoming sustainable."
>
> Cory Brown, Oct 1, 2003
> www.LATimes.com

– Jean Yeager, Administrative Director, publishes *"REAL CRITICISM WELCOME"* report describing for the Society members the nature of internet defamation.
https://fireborrnecom.files.wordpress.com/2022/11/2004-real-criticism-welcome-rev-011204.pdf

– **ASiA** Joan Almon, General Secretary,, announces Anti-Defamation campaign, "Sounding The Call."
SOUNDING THE CALL – This document is published in "AKNIGHTS" COLLECTION.
https://firebornecom.files.wordpress.com/2022/02/011204-stc-overview.pdf

– PLANS Attorney files declaration with the Federal Court stating that he has been suffering from significant mental illness for the past two years and been unable to function. PLANS agrees to keep him as their attorney. Then, quickly, they seek other representation to conclude the litigation.
https://firebornecom.files.wordpress.com/2022/11/2004-011404-kendall-declaration-of-insanity.pdf

Front Page - Sacramento BEE, 1997

– *U.S. Critics* – PLANS newest attorney files a motion for a summary judgment and asks the Court to declare that *"Anthroposophy Is A Religion."* To counter this, ON BEHALF OF DEFENDANTS, DOUGLAS SLOAN, PROFESSOR OF HISTORY AND EDUCATION AT TEACHERS COLLEGE, MAKES A DECLARATION, BASED ON RESEARCH, ABOUT THE ACTUAL NATURE OF ANTHROPOSOPHY AND THE ANTHROPOSOPHICAL SOCIETY.
https://go.elib.com/dILEF

– Airline industry given $15 billion "soothing" economic concessions for 9/11.

– Insurance industry given $10 billion "soothing" economic concessions for 9/11.

– *AKnights* – Robert Mays and Sune Nordwall create *WALDORF ANSWERS WEB SITE* to have **comprehensive responses to the disinformation** put out by critics.

www.waldorfanswers.org This site receives 30,000 visits per year. Visit this site to read all FIRST AMENDMENT COURT FILINGS.

2004
– *"International Right Living Award"* – Alternative Nobel Peace Prize given to Nicanor Perlas, Anthroposophical Leader in the Philippines.

ASiA – Anthroposophical Society in America files "Friend of the Court" *Amicus Curiae* **brief in PLANS vs. SCUSD, Twin Ridges First Amendment Federal Lawsuit.** >>>>
AMICUS CURIAE BRIEF INCLUDED IN THE APPENDIX
https://go.elib.com/qgUUt

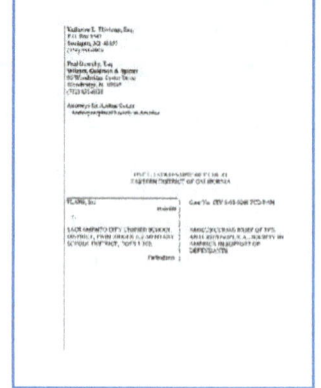

AG **-Biodynamic – Manhattan Wine Tasting.** *"Many of the 500 guests at a Manhattan tasting sponsored by 74 biodynamic and organic producers in June departed with a simple impression: worldwide the Biodynamic movement resembles a small insurgency. In the wine trade, sympathizers, even skeptics feel a tug of enthusiasm."*
The Wine News Magazine, Howard G. Goldberg, August / September 2004

Community Supported Agriculture (CSA) Farming and Gardening were inspired from Steiner's Agricultural and Social ideals in 1985, and by 2004 there are 1,700 such enterprises rebuilding community through food and shared economics.

AKnights alert the *NY Times* to a defamatory book review campaign. All are removed.
THE FLICKERING MIND Published 2004

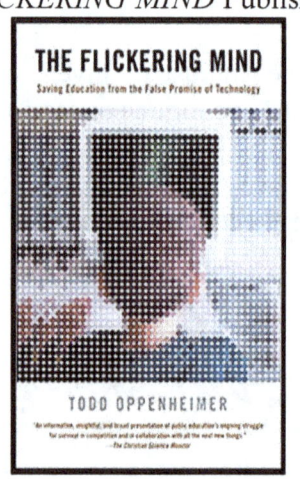

– Facebook launched by Mark Zuckerberg.

ABOUT AMAZON and NY TIMES The *"FLICKERING MIND"* attack is a clear example of the "Culture War" that rages on the internet and media to this day. Here are the exchanges between the anti-defamation group "AKnights," the Anthroposophical Society Administrator Jean Yeager and AMAZON'S LEGAL AND PUBLISHING DIVISIONS. Exchange included in "AKnights" Collection.

Federal Lawsuit decided in 30-minutes. PLANS fails to prove Anthroposophy is a religion for Establishment Clause purposes. PLANS appeals and loses vs. SCUSD, Twin Ridges Public School Districts.

– CORNUCOPIA, an organic agriculture "watchdog" advocacy organization is formed to monitor and counter trade abuses and governmental failures.

– Massachusetts becomes first state to recognize same-sex marriage. Eleven other states pass voter amendments to state constitutions banning same-sex marriages. These states also pass George W. Bush's constitutional ban on gay marriage by referendum.

– Despite having lost the First Amendment court case, PLANS continues its disinformation campaign and writes Benicia Unified School District. This is countered by AKnights.
https://fireborncom.files.wordpress.com/2022/10/020404beniciausd.pdf

NOTES:

1987 Summer – Journal for Biodynamics, Number 163, Page 58-64

Into The Heart's Land, Henry Barnes, Steiner Books, 2013

"*The Emergence Of A Global Threefold Society And The Future Task of the Michaelic Movement*, Jesaiah Ben-Aharon, an essay in THE FUTURE IS NOW: Anthroposophy At The New Millennium, Temple Lodge, 1999

The Anti-Defamation League's The Religious Right – The Assault on Tolerance & Pluralism in America, by Alan M. & Gail Gans & Mark Caplan & Melvin Salberg & David H. Strassle Schwartz | Jan 1, 1994, pg. 291

Chicken Little, Tomato Sauce and Agriculture, Joan Dye Gussow, 1991

The Ecology of Commerce, Paul Hawkin, pg. 116)

Age Of Folly: America Abandons Its Democracy, Lampham's Quarterly, 2019

DEMETER https://www.demeter-usa.org/about-demeter/demeter-history.asp

Chokehold: Policing Black Men, Paul Butler, 2017

Bowling Alone, Robert D. Putnam, Simon & Schuster, 2000

Waldorf Answers – https://www.waldorfanswers.org/

Rudolf Steiner Library, https://rudolfsteinerlibrary.org/

LINKS / END NOTES

END NOTE (1) – PAGE 104 – **1985 CIA COCAINE SMUGGLING**,
https://firebornecom.files.wordpress.com/2022/02/1985-cia-cocaine-smuggling.pdf

1985 CIA COCAINE SMUGGLING

"Most people assume the War on Drugs was launched in response to the crisis caused by crack cocaine in inner-city neighborhoods. This view holds that the racial disparities in drug convictions and sentences, as well as the rapid explosion of the prison population, reflect nothing more than the government's zealous – but benign – efforts to address rampant drug crime in poor, minority neighborhoods. This view, while understandable given the sensational media coverage in the 1980s and 1990s is simply wrong ...

The Reagan administration hired staff to publicize the emergence of crack cocaine in 1985 as part of a strategic effort to build public and legislative for the war (on drugs). The media campaign was an extraordinary success. Almost overnight, the media was saturated with images of black "crack whores," "crack dealers," and "crack babies" – images that seemed to confirm the worst negative racial stereotypes about impoverished inner-city residents. The media bonanza surrounding the "new demon drug" helped catapult the War on Drugs to an actual war.

The timing of the crack crisis [with the Iran-Contra guns and money to Nicaragua] helped fuel conspiracy theories and general speculation in poor black communities that the War on Drugs was part of a genocidal plan by the government to destroy black people in the United States. From the outset, stories circulated on the street that crack and other drugs were being brought into black neighborhoods by the CIA. …

While the conspiracy theories were initially dismissed as farfetched, and downright loony, word on the street turned out to be right at least to a point. The CIA admitted in 1998 [fourteen years later] that guerilla armies it actively supported in Nicaragua were smuggling illegal drugs into the United States – drugs that were making their way onto the streets of inner city black neighborhoods in the form of crack cocaine. The CIA also admitted that, in the midst of the War on Drugs, it blocked law enforcement efforts to investigate illegal drug networks that were helping to fund its covert war in Nicaragua ...

In fact, the War on Drugs began at a time when illegal drug use was on the decline. During the same time period, however, a war was declared, causing arrests and convictions for drug offenses to skyrocket, especially among people of color.

The impact of the war on drugs has been astounding. In less than 30 years, the U.S. penal population exploded from around 300,000 to more than 2 million, with drug convictions accounting for the majority of the increase.

The New Jim Crow, Michelle Alexander, Pp. 5-6

END NOTE (2) – PAGE 110 – **1992 REPORT FROM THE URBAN WALDORF REPORT,** Ann Pratt – **AWSNA NEWSLETTER, SPRING/SUMMER 1992, PGS. 17-18**
https://firebornecom.files.wordpress.com/2022/02/1992-awsna-milwaukee.pdf

Report from the Urban Waldorf Program Milwaukee, WI

The news from our venture is good. We continue to experience challenges in all aspects, but what entirely new adventure into uncharted territory does not? The words: "miracles are happening here" arise almost daily.

We have had many visitors from the Waldorf world for which we are deeply grateful. This continued support has been extremely helpful and has provided us with a healthy and reassuring perspective about ourselves. In this report we will deal with some of these thoughts and with those from individuals from our circle of colleagues here who have been working for many years in this kind of setting.

From our Waldorf friends, we receive encouraging praise for the way we have been able to incorporate the Waldorf curriculum with children who have had no previous experience with the rhythm of the day, working in main lesson books, circle work, painting and all the myriad things we take for granted. As Cheryl Colbert gave her fifth grade class report in our faculty meeting, it was evident to everyone including Henry Barnes who was present at the time, that many of these children are experiencing and enjoying school for the first time. Their self-respect and sense of self-worth has greatly increased. They look at their books from the first block and are amazed at how improved their work is. They love to write compositions now, especially with the fountain pens they have recently received. Cheryl spoke of how earlier they had been totally convinced that they could not possibly fill a whole page. Now they write two and three pages and love doing it! These specific incidents could be recounted for all our classes. Space does not allow for it all.

Perhaps the next most appropriate place to continue is with the fact that a proposal was written by parents of our school to the Milwaukee School Board asking for more space in order to continue the present 5th grade into 6th grade, and to be able to incorporate all aspects of the a Waldorf program through grade eight. This positive appraisal speaks loudly of parent response to our work. There have been a few miracles in each class socially, involving children who had had extremely negative experiences previously and came to us this fall expecting the same. Much to their surprise this did not happen. Real care and concern by the teachers has reversed many such situations and the children have become cooperative and eager learners.

This Parent Teacher Organization proposal contained other elements such as our need to be in our own building in order to fully implement the curriculum. We need added space for a very popular subject, namely eurythmy, as the original idea of using the cafeteria is too complex combined with the schedule of feeding 700 children their lunches. This comes about because there are two schools in this building and sharing of the library, gym, music room, and cafeteria spaces with the other school in our building is a complicated topic. The Multicultural-Multilingual School has children the same ages as ours with an equal population of about 350 children. Busing and playground spaces are also shared, but educational policy on how to deal with problem situations that arise, is not shared. Our parents have expressed concerns and there is a PTO council who helps us work within these confines. These on-going concerns are just some of the many logistical adjustments that have to be made daily.

One of our parents who has a child in kindergarten and who has been a Social worker for many years in this city, had these remarks to make at the occasion of a public hearing of this proposal. "The students I presently service are adolescents who have now entered the system as adjudicated delinquents – many who will move into adult corrections. These at-risk students have the following characteristics: early truant behavior, early lack of nurturance, early lack of continuity of care-takers – of having multiple care-takers, deficits in sensory-motor development, lack of understanding of personal boundaries and lack of accountability for one's own behavior. These are some of the same areas that Waldorf addresses and provides for in a positive manner from the onset and meets within the curriculum and methods of teaching ... Waldorf offers the continuity of the same class teacher with the same students for an extended number of years. Many of the 4th and 5th graders presently at Waldorf came with many such problems and failures in the traditional setting. They have shown vast improvements. What do we have to offer them when they leave? ... We propose that increasing the Waldorf Program will decrease the need for alternative treatments in their adolescent years." Sandra Fair, Social Worker Supervisor, Project EXCEL, Milwaukee, WI.

The following remarks come from one of our teachers who has been teaching children in the city for 17 years. She has experienced on different occasions children learning to trust teachers and to have the courage to risk telling the truth. She said that in the other situations she has been in, following through to positive conclusions was just not possible. One child in third grade, risked admitting that he had stolen something from the Book Fair. We quote: "I validated to him that he had done the right thing and we set about returning it and correcting the situation. His concern was about further punishment. After further conversation it became clear that he was able to admit the theft because of the acceptance by the adult of what it takes to do that, and a willingness to work with him to right the situation. This shift has totally changed our classroom work as well, for our interaction is built on trust that we have met and worked through a problem. On another occasion when a child misbehaved, he was untruthful about this disruptive behavior. The courage to face up to his actions and a desire for things to resolve in an honest manner came about through that fact that he was received with acceptance. He was overwhelmed when he was thanked for his honesty and again the relationship to our work in the classroom was completely transformed for the better. These events represent many days of struggle and miracles did not happen over night, but new foundations were gained and can be built upon." Beverly Machalk/ Music teacher.

We close with a statement from our school psychologist who has daily contact with children in our school. "I have been a school psychologist in this system for 12 years and have worked in many different schools. I feel therefore, that I am in a position to evaluate and assess what goes on in the schools in terms of children's growth and development. What I see happening in Waldorf this year is extremely encouraging for me as an educational psychologist. The basic philosophy of the school, that is educating each child wholistically, provides a supportive and healing structure wherein many of our children, who are angry and needy emotionally, can grow and mature. I have walked into the Waldorf kindergarten classes and have been amazed at the calmness, warmth and radiance of those five and six year-olds. I have watched some of our fifth, fourth and third graders become more focused and more enthusiastic about school. Many of the children are beginning to feel better about themselves. What is it about a Waldorf setting that seems to be able to bring this about? Apart from its dedicated and committed staff, I feel that the significant strength of the program lies in this: When a Waldorf teacher sees a child in class, his/her concern is not so much on how much the child knows or how far behind this child is, but rather, "How can I help this child grow and develop?" The implicit message that each child seems to feel is, "I am worthwhile and sacred!" How can we risk not letting more of our children experience this feeling throughout their school years and carry it through a lifetime?" Josuane Duckworth, School Psychologist.

Although this article is long, it is hoped that a picture has been portrayed that lets you know that this is difficult to do, but thought of in human terms, is well worth every ounce of struggle and effort. We have two classes who are receiving regular public school curriculum because two teachers were not able to sustain their classes and have left. We have had complaints from one of the classes that they miss the Norse stories and the circle work and want to have them back. We need more experienced Waldorf teachers to join our effort next fall. Will some of you come?

Ann Pratt

END NOTE (3) – PAGE 110 – 1992 PAT ROBERTSON ARTICLE PREDICTS BLOODY RELIGIOUS BATTLE BUT SAYS THAT CHRISTIANS WILL BE VICTORIOUS

https://firebornecom.files.wordpress.com/2022/02/3.5.4-1992-pat-robertson-culture-war.pdf

1992 PAT ROBERTSON CULTURE WAR

"NO VICTORY COMES WITHOUT BATTLE"

"If Christian people work together, they can succeed during this decade and winning back control of the institutions that have been taken from them over the past 70 years. If Christian people work together, they can succeed during this decade and winning back control of the institutions that have been taken from them over the past 70 years. Expect confrontations that will be not only on pleasant times physically bloodied ... This decade will not be for the faint of heart, but the resolute. Institutions will be plunged into wrenching change. We will be living through one of the most mulch was. With human history. When it is over, I am convinced God's people will emerge notorious. But no victory ever comes without a battle."

October/November 1992 edition of the newsletter *"Pat Robertsons Perspective"* cataclysmic language for an end of the world attack.

The Anti-Defamation League's The Religious Right – The Assault on Tolerance & Pluralism in America, by Alan M. & Gail Gans & Mark Caplan & Melvin Salberg & David H. Strassle Schwartz | Jan 1, 1994, pg. 291

END NOTE (4) – PAGE 111 – ANTHROPOSOPHICAL SOCIETY APPROACH TO LEADERSHIP – NOT MUCH MORE COULD BE CHANGED

https://firebornecom.files.wordpress.com/2022/02/02-1994-general-council-leadership.pdf

1994 Anthroposophical Society Leadership Group

One of the other innovative things which Arthur Zajonc initiated when he became General Secretary of the at the Anthroposophical Society in 1994-1995 was to create a leadership group. Traditionally, each national group (called a "branch") had a unitary leader. Arthur was a full-time PhD teaching physics at Amherst College and had other responsibilities as well.

Arthur selected two other individuals to work with him as a leadership team for the Society.

Mark Finser, head of the Rudolf Steiner Foundation, which later became Rudolf Steiner Social Finance, a financial and banking group which originated in upstate New York and then moved to San Francisco.

The second person on the leadership group was Joan Almon, a leader of the Waldorf Early Childhood movement.

These three became the administrative group of the General Counsel (or Board of Directors) for the Anthroposophical Society America. This was a radically different departure from the single General Secretary form of organization which had existed since the 1920s. This was a moment where not much more could be changed. The Builders Group initiated a strategic planning group which recommended the hiring of an Administrative Director; the gift of the headquarters building in Ann Arbor which necessitated a move from Chicago; certainly did create a very different culture and organizational gesture.

END NOTE (5) – PAGE 114 – 1996 FORMING THE THIRD REALM

This is an important excerpt from the 30+ page HISTORY OF THE CAO*which is included in the APPENDIX.

The CAO is a committee of the Society and it has changed the nature of the Society.

The relationship of the National Anthroposophical Society and Initiatives arising out of Anthroposophy. A series of meetings which lead to the forming of the Council of Anthroposophical Organizations (CAO).

https://firebornecom.files.wordpress.com/2022/10/1996-forming-the-third-realm.pdf

---

Meeting of Anthroposophic Associations and Large Institutions
New York City, January 23, 1996

Present: Joan Almon, David Alsop, Chuck Beedy, Judith Brockway, Gayle Davis, Mark Finser, Torin Finser, Peter Hinderberger, Michael Howard, Cornelius Pietzner, Chris Schaeffer, Ann Scharff

Mark opened and closed the meeting with the following passage from *The Influence of Spiritual Beings on Man* (lectures of 1911, page 156):

> "The individuals voluntarily allow their feelings to stream together, and this again causes the forming of something which goes beyond the merely emancipated man. An emancipated human being possesses his individual soul, which is never lost when it has once been attained. But when men find themselves together in voluntary associations, they group themselves around centers. The feelings streaming in this way to a center once more give beings the opportunity of working as a kind of group soul, though in quite a different sense from the early group souls. All the earlier group souls were beings who made man unfree. These new beings, however, are compatible with man's complete freedom and individuality. Indeed, in a certain respect we may say that they support their existence on human harmony; it will lie in the souls of men themselves whether or not they give as many as possible of such higher souls the opportunity of descending to man. The more that men are divided, the fewer lofty souls will descend into the human sphere. The more that associations are formed where feelings of fellowship are developed with complete freedom, the more lofty beings will descend, and the more rapidly the earthly planet will be spiritualized."

Those present introduced themselves and shared something of their personal longings and intentions in life, and how these brought them to Anthroposophy. Mark then spoke of the threefold imagination of the Society, arising from the Christmas Foundation Meeting:

- The life of spirit – the School of Spiritual Science
- The life of soul – the membership of the Society, and the working through of human karma
- The bodily process of incarnating – at the time of the Christmas Foundation meeting this was called the *Bauverein*, and it included initiatives such as Ita Wegman's clinic and Marie Steiner's Press, the administration of the Society, and the Goetheanum building association.

In the latter realm Rudolf Steiner left membership very open. He said, for example, that one Waldorf school might want to join and another not. One finds this in the "Conference of Teachers," Feb. 5, 1924. (See attached.) Joan then spoke of the work that is being done with the Collegium, the Branches, and now with the Associations and large institutions. She also spoke of the eventual need for an active center for the Society. The Chicago Branch, which rents office space to the Society, intends to sell its building, and this may take place soon. The Society needs to make decisions as to where

1

it wants to be, what size facility it needs, and whether the library will move. It may need another interim facility, but it needs to work towards a long term home. Such a home could include all administration for the Society, membership work, a center for research and other activities of the School of Spiritual Science, including the library to support such research. Ideally some of the associations working with anthroposophical institutions would also be located near such a center facilitating communication between the Sections and the institutions working closely with Sections. Advanced courses and seminars could be accommodated in such a center. It was pointed out that a center can begin modestly by meeting the needs at hand, and then grow as the needs develop.

Some of the blockages of the Society were discussed both historically and now. Joan pointed out that the split in the Society had a strong impact on the third realm of the Society, where the initiatives were to find a relationship to the Society. The Clinic and the Press were part of the Society at this level, but the split between Ita Wegman and Marie Steiner made the continuation of this relationship impossible. The absence of the associations and initiatives from the life of the Society has had a weakening effect. To overcome it means to some extent one needs to go back and understand the past, and bring sufficient healing so that pain and blockage from the past do not persist as contemporary problems. We do not want to dwell on the past, however, but find new ways to cultivate the relationship to the Society to the initiatives and associations.

A number of questions or contributions were made concerning the Society and the life of the institutions or associations. Some of the comments focussed on a heady aspect of the Society which calls for more heart forces as a balance (and more will forces) and a Christianizing of the intellect which has grown very cold. There also tends to be judgmental atmosphere in the Society or a sectarian atmosphere, which contemporary Americans find very difficult upon meeting it. Another aspect mentioned was the need for a better understanding of research as a central activity of the Society. Also the threefold aspect of the Society was looked at in terms of understanding the principles or laws at work in each of the three spheres. A different principle is at work in each.

Mark explained that the hope for the major conference with the Vorstand and Section leaders (August 4-10, 1997) is that the Society will be ready for large steps - a turning inside out, and that the conference will provide an opportunity to focus on this. At present the plan is to have a few days of intensive work for members of the School followed by a much more public conference which would reach out to all Michaelic souls, not just to Society members. Ideally, the Society would have experienced renewal at all levels by that time, so that a transformed Society can be experienced, prepared to meet the end of the century and to be of service to humanity.

Over lunch, the current life of the associations and institutions was presented. Only a few aspects can be offered here, primarily those affecting many groups as presented by the Associations.

Camphill offered a composite picture of its seven initiatives in North America including total number of community participants, composite budgets, combined assets, etc. Comments followed on what it would be like to have similar composite pictures of the of doctors and the rights of doctors and patients are major areas of concern. There is also a very close relationship between the physicians and the Medical Section. PAAM is the external aspect, the Fellowship of Physicians in the inner aspect with a close relationship to the Section. In some ways the world of medicine is growing more open to valid alternative therapies, but in other ways the situation is growing more difficult because of the shift towards HMOs. The Rudolf Steiner Foundation has been investigating the possibility of establishing an insurance fund that would cover anthroposophic therapies.

After lunch we took up the question of what would it be like to form a council of Anthroposophic Associations. What would its purposes be? How could the Associations serve one another and what would be their relationship to the Anthroposophic Society? What do they have to offer to the Society and what does the Society have to offer to them? A draft of suggestions which are being made by a Strategic Planning Group of the Society was read out and distributed. The detailed suggestions took some by surprise.

We then broke into two groups. Mark's group looked at the ways in the which Associations and institutions could serve the Society and vice versa. Joan's group looked at a number of issues including the impact of the institution's forms on the Society and vice versa. Also the question of whether such a council could serve as an economic body arose, i.e. helping the groups to help each other in the event of tightening financial situations in the future. A closing remark of the group pertained to the importance of bringing the heart forces strongly into any council of Anthroposophic Associations.

As the two groups reformed some of the comments or concerns were as follows: In the past it would have been far more difficult for an institution to affiliate with the Society. Today, one feels a new openness at work in the Society, and it is easier to imagine such an affiliation. At the same time, there is still some sectarianism present and this can create problems for the institutions to affiliate. The training centers and others face the world and need to do so with a strong degree of openness while cultivating Anthroposophy in a deep and penetrating way. Even the word "Society" has a formal, almost fraternity like feeling that reflects something more closed off. Chuck Beedy pointed out that the Biodynamic Association has a particular challenge in affiliating with the Society because half of its Board does not belong to the Society.

There seemed to be a general interest in exploring the possibility of forming a council, and it was proposed that a subgroup form to carry this impulse further. Groups should contact Mark by March 4 with suggestions on who should be on such a subgroup. If no names are forthcoming, the Initiative Group will appoint a planning group.

Joan asked the Associations if they would consider mailing out a Newssheet portraying Anthroposophy in action to their members and friends with their regular mailings of Newsletters. This would be a two sided sheet, attractively done sharing news of the movement from within North America and around the world. She asked whether Jean Yeager, who is assisting with this venture, could call each Association to discuss this in more detail. Jean will follow up with such calls.

Joan Almon
2/13/96

Draft

ORGANIZATION OF NATIONAL ANTHROPOSOPHICAL SOCIETY IN RELATIONSHIP TO ANTHROPOSOPHICAL INITIATIVES

The organization of a National Anthroposophical Society that truly embraces and represents the scope of the Anthroposophical movement would require a new relationship between the society and the so called Anthroposophical Initiatives arising out of Anthroposophy, i.e., Waldorf Schools, Camphill, Bio-dynamic, Adult Education. This relationship would be characterized by a deeper understanding of the society as it was founded at Christmas 1923-24 and the implications of that occasion for anyone working out of Anthroposophy. At that time Rudolf Steiner conceived of a society that intended to unite the esoteric and exoteric aspects in a single organization. Only thus would such a society become a worthy and able vehicle for Anthroposophy in all its aspects.

The various Educational, Agricultural, artistic, medical/therapeutic and social endeavors attempt to work directly out of Anthroposophical insight and knowledge. Their activity depends not on study alone but also as the experience of Anthroposophy as it comes to expression in a particular profession. This experience represents a deep perception of and commitment to the reality of Anthroposophy and as such provides the basis for a relationship to the National Society on an Institutional level.

All of us working in our various organizations are connected as individual society, class and section members. Apart from this alignment, however, the organizations themselves, as expressions of Anthroposophical will, are connected to the society and also to each other. Making these connections more visible and effective is one part of the plan to create a truly representative society.

A key to this aspect is the recognition of the reciprocal nature of the relationship between the society and the daughter movements. Simply put they need each other. To the extent that they can find diverse and effective forms of association they will naturally benefit.

To this end it is suggested that a Council of Anthroposophical Associations (CAA) be formed as an organ of the Society. This would consist of 10-12 individuals representing the major associations (AWSNA, Bio-Dynamics, Medical and Camphill) and larger initiatives (Sunbridge, Steiner College, Antioch Program, and Fellowship Community). The group would probably need to meet 3 or 4 times a year. It is hoped that funding would come from the associations and initiatives. The council would seek ways to help initiatives and vice versa.

1. **HOW THE SOCIETY CAN HELP INITIATIVES**

    a.) <u>Cross fertilization of movements</u> -- There is some cross fertilization between the movement already. In a sense such fertilization always takes place in the sphere of the society in that we meet on the common basis of Anthroposophy. CAA could provide leadership and guidance in this area.

b.) Promote Wider Public Exposure - All organizations are involved with the public. The CAA could provide a point of awareness for public interface that could naturally be beneficial for all. It could promote, coordinate and initiate various public interactions and involvement with other organizations.

c.) Promote awareness of common esoteric/social task -- Anthroposophy is meant to become the guiding principle in the formation of civilization. The movements are on the cutting edge of this reality and have a common bond in this fact.

d.) Identify common and individual needs -- Such identification could form the basis for specific forms of Association between movements.

e.) Promote cohesion between movements -- The CAA could provide a place for experiencing the common bond in Anthroposophy implied in the commitment to work out of Anthroposophy.

2. HOW INITIATIVES CAN HELP SOCIETY

a.) Promote Subject Group Concept -- Organizations formalize their link to the Society by becoming subject group.

b.) Promote Society Membership -- Work towards the understanding that individuals committed to the purpose of the organization need to be members of the Society to fully understand and fulfill their commitment.

c.) Make connection to Society more visible in literature and development -- This is a matter of self image to the extent that the organization identifies with the society it will naturally promote that connection.

d.) Provide financial support by paying dues and supporting the CAA

Initially this work would be carried by a chair working with an IG member plus some secretarial help. Other expenses would be room and board and travel. Eventually this should grow into a strong aspect of the Society and would need a staff person. It was suggested that all funds for this work come from the associations, etc. At first this may seem like an excessive burden in terms of time and money, but if it is correct that the initiatives cannot go much further in their development without the Society playing it's part, then such expense should be regarded as a necessary investment.

ACTION PLAN:

1. Discuss CAA concept at January 23 meeting and determine feasibility. Ask for 3 volunteers to coordinate formation.

2. Discuss CAA concept in various settings AWSNA, Camphill, Sunbridge, etc. and respond to three coordinators with suggestion for Council membership and tasks by March 1.

3. Three coordinators with initiative group review suggestions, form Council and prepare and schedule the first meeting by April 1.

4. First meeting of Council to appoint chair, form appropriate committees and schedule meetings over 12 month period by May 1.

In closing it's important to emphasize that the scope of the CAA work would depend on the imagination of the individual council members and the willingness of the organization out of which they come to support the concept altogether. Individual members would not represent organizations so much as they would sit together with others in a Society organ that attempts to be a point of consciousness for the totality of the Anthroposophical institutional movement. Initially, the CAA would probably have modest impact on the life of the organizations, but in the course of time and through faithful effort it could develop into a significant and effective element in the life and work of Anthroposophy.

Inspirational
relational soul
material

Anthroposophy @ work

END NOTE (6) – PAGE 114 – "RUDOLF STEINER'S EFFORTS TO ENCOURAGE CULTURAL DIVERSITY" By Detlef Hardorp
https://www.waldorflibrary.org/images/stories/Journal_Articles/RB2207.pdf

Rudolf Steiner's Efforts to Encourage Cultural Diversity, Detlef Hardorp
Detlef Hardorp is a German Waldorf science teacher who has visited and taught in North America, especially through the Rudolf Steiner (Summer) Institute. The article will appear in "News from the Goetheanum" for July/August, 1997

Rudolf Steiner spoke out on occasion against cultural homogenization. Indeed, he energetically advocated that which he alone considered "healing," namely, a multicultural society in which the autonomy of each culture is not violated.

In this regard Rudolf Steiner even took concrete political action. With the help of leaflet campaigns and by soliciting signatures from prominent people, he opposed State suppression of minorities. In lieu of a centralized state he called for three autonomous entities: 1) an independent and spiritual/ cultural life, particularly also for people of different ethnic origins who live in the same area, 2) a legal system with the same basic rights for all, and 3) an economic life composed of associations among producers, consumers and distributors.

In 1922, after the first world war there were plans to attach Upper Silesia – an ethnically mixed region – to either Poland or Prussia, or to separate the "ethnically cleansed" cultural groups. Rudolf Steiner launched a political effort with the goal of getting the Silesians of both ethnic groups to reject, under protest, being attached to either Poland or Prussia. In his "Call to Save Upper Silesia" he wrote: "The situation in Upper Silesia particularly calls out for such a threefold system. Here two cultures, two cultural individualities – which are intermingled with each other – are fighting for the chance to live in their own way. The most important causes of friction are education and judicial practices. Only by liberating the spiritual/cultural life can these burning questions be resolved, especially in Upper Silesia. Then both cultures, side by side, the German and the Polish, will be able to develop in accord with their inherent forces, without fearing that they will be violated by the other and without a political State taking one or the other side. Each nationality will set up not only its own educational institutions but also its own administrative bodies for cultural matters, so that conflict is ruled out."

Martin Barkhoff sums up Rudolf Steiner's attitude with the following words: "The German State cannot – according to Rudolf Steiner's social impulse – belong to the Germans, but only to all of its residents equally; the State in Poland, Romania, France cannot belong to the Poles, Romanians, French. Rudolf Steiner fought persistently and vigorously for this impulse of a "multi-cultural society in an ethnically mixed state. [...] Thus it is clear that the most brutal resistance to Rudolf Steiner's efforts came from national groups especially. [...]"

"Such groups and militias answered his political activity with terrorist methods which nearly cost him his life and which made it impossible for him to continue speaking publicly in Germany. In the "Völkischer Beobachter" Adolf Hitler referred to the principle of a threefold social order as being one of those "utterly Jewish methods of destroying the normal mental state and spiritual orientation of the people." In fact Rudolf Steiner's intentions did oppose Hitler's, more clearly than for example did the goals of the communists, who consolidated the terror of the Nazis with terror of their own. Rudolf Steiner endeavored instead to remove the emotional basis that would support Hitler's goals."

Steiner prophesied endless bloodshed if preference were given not to the autonomy of the individual but to the nation which suppresses minorities. Right into the present Woodrow Wilson's idea of "self determination of nations" affords dubious power structures and inviolability which are used against the individual ("dissident") and ethnic minorities in the most brutal way. Here we find fertile breeding ground for State-sanctioned racism – which Rudolf Steiner recognized early on and which he vehemently opposed.

"People over the whole earth are dependent on each other"

In order to brand Rudolf Steiner as a racist, excerpts from a lecture to workers (March 3, 1923) have repeatedly been cited (for example in "Welt am Sonntag," March 9, 1997 and "taz," Sept. 28, 1996). However, one notices, if one reads the whole lecture carefully, that where Rudolf Steiner makes any evaluation at all, it is the physical constitution of the white European that comes up worst. "We poor Europeans have our life of thinking in the head. [...] Through this we take in the whole outer world, and we easily become materialists. The Negro does not become a materialist. He remains human inwardly."

Why? Because, in contrast to the European, he does not so easily lose his relationship to his instinctive life, which Rudolf Steiner refers to here as being representative of the "lively development" of "what is connected to the body and its metabolism," and which he clearly values as positive. He also attributes a "lively development" of the bodily aspect to white Americans, and again, he sees it as positive: "It is [in the case of Americans] understood more through the whole human being [in contrast to the "poor Europeans" with their head thinking]. That is an advantage of the Americans over the Europeans." Black people and Americans are already inwardly human where the European still has some developing to do. The European develops it by "creating in spirit."

Directly following his controversial remarks on the various races Rudolf Steiner clarifies his meaning-. "You see, gentlemen, everything I just described to you has to do with what happens in the human body. The soul and spirit are more or less independent of this." That such an attitude is the opposite of racism was obvious to the Central Security Office of the German Reich in 1941: "Anthroposophy contradicts the National Socialist doctrine on race. According to the National Socialist view the laws of racial heredity relate not only to the body, but to the whole human being also to soul and spirit. Like the Christian Church, Anthroposophy recognizes essentially only a doctrine of bodily heredity, claiming that only the body stems from its parents, whilst the spirit and soul enter into it from the spirit world. Based on such a purely external view of race, anthroposophy must necessarily arrive at an international pacifist attitude."

It is true that Rudolf Steiner did not deny that there are differences in the physical makeup of different groups of people. However, he did not draw a racist conclusion from this but spoke instead of the necessity of symbiotic collaboration within a diverse society. As he said in his controversial lecture: "That's the way it is with the human race. People over the whole earth are dependent on each other. They have to help each other. This follows from their qualities."

END NOTE (7) – PAGE 114 – 1997 CHARGES OF RACISM / ANTI-SEMITISM LEVELED AT ANTHROPOSOPHICAL SOCIETY. – ANTI-DEFAMATION LEAGUE CRITERIA:

"Is There A Pattern Of Behavior?" – Anti-Defamation League

This is the age of worldwide media and the Internet and the anthroposophical movement is a worldwide movement. You can't stub your toe in Brussels without it being on the news in San Francisco that evening.

Since 1997, the worldwide Society has been under sustained attack with charges of "racism" or "anti-Semitism" stemming from one or the other of some 16 quotes from Rudolf Steiner which have been lifted from among 89,000 pages of his collected works.

But, what have anthroposophists **done,** really?

In actuality, there have been one or two incidents worldwide which are based in contemporary fact rather than 70 year old quotations. The first incident arose in Holland in 1995 (See 1995-1996

Racism Charges in Holland). Those charges and any others have generated investigations from appropriate governmental agencies. All of these investigations have said one thing: the incident was an isolated. one. There is no system of racism or Antisemitism within Anthroposophy.

The first leadership group of the Anthroposophical Society had members who were Jewish. One of the most obvious examples of how the Anthroposophical Society does not discriminate is the case of Viktor Ullman, a composer who worked in the bookstore at the Goetheanum before he and his family were taken by the Nazis to Theresienstadt Concentration camp. An event honoring Ullman was conducted in 1998 at the Society's offices in Ann Arbor. (See that report on Page 17 of this book.)

Even one of our harshest critic in the U.S. has not accused the American Society of any action of ill will toward anyone. Neither does he accuse Steiner of any specific action, or even of ill will: "... people assume that the idea of racism is that you have ill will toward people. And Steiner did not have ill will towards people of other races. [...]it's the system that has racism at its foundations and that has to be repudiated." (1)

The Society has maintained in the strongest terms that it is not racist and that there is no system of racism within anthroposophy and further that our practices are open and inclusive. (See *1998 – Position Statement on Diversity*). The Anti-Defamation League suggests that one should look for patterns of behavior when one is seeking to form a judgment of an individual or an organization.

We hope that the following detailing of activities is helpful for the individual to draw their own conclusion. – Jean Yeager

1. "Why Waldorf Schools are Unsuitable for Public Funding," Dan Dugan, November 12, 1999, Spring Valley, NY. Transcript of a speech recorded by Educational Insights, 274 Hungry Hollow Road, Spring Valley, NY 10977.

School is teaching witchcraft, critics say

By Edgar Sanchez
Bee Staff Writer

An experiment with the Waldorf teaching method at Oak Ridge Elementary School in Sacramento has come under fire from critics who claim the public school's program is emphasizing witchcraft instead of basic skills.

About 20 angry parents and concerned citizens picketed the Oak Park school Thursday, demanding that it revert to a traditional learning system.

Of the school's 26 teachers, 11 are expected to transfer to other campuses next fall. Some of them have been asked to leave because they don't want to take the Waldorf training and some because they don't agree with the Waldorf philosophy, officials in the Sacramento City Unified School District said.

The pickets petitioned the district to end Waldorf at Oak Ridge, and to fire principal Irma Jue and

Bee photograph/Erhardt Krause
Pickets in front of Sacramento's Oak Ridge Elementary School on Thursday protest an experimental program there that is using the Waldorf teaching method, which was developed in Germany.

Please see WALDORF, page B4

Waldorf: The system focuses on movement, song and storytelling

Continued from page B1

the school's Waldorf resource teacher. Jue was unavailable for comment Thursday.

But district officials defended the Waldorf system and said no one will be dismissed.

Myths, fables and the study of ancient civilizations such as the Aztecs are part of the curriculum, which is why some parents may have reached erroneous conclusions, one district official said.

"Civilizations such as the Aztecs worshiped the sun," but no one is being taught to idolize the bright star, said Sue Norwood, district spokeswoman.

The new teaching method formally was launched at Oak Ridge Elementary in September and all 630 students are getting some aspects of the Waldorf learning system.

The innovative concept in education was developed by philosopher Rudolf Steiner in 1919 in Germany. His creative approach to learning emphasizes movement, craft, song and storytelling.

On the Oak Ridge picket line however, parents bearing the U.S. flag and various anti-Waldorf signs blasted the program's results.

Under Waldorf, "the teaching methods are very slow," said Tina Means, a parent protester. "My son, a third-grader, is going into the fourth grade barely able to read."

Means, 24, said her son has an attention-deficit disorder, "but he was always able to learn" when Oak Ridge had a traditional curriculum.

Picket Terri Jennings said her two older children graduated from Oak Ridge several years ago with a good grasp of basic skills. But current students, including her first-grade daughter, are not absorbing "the basic skills needed for life," Jennings said.

"Instead, they are being taught that the sun is God," she said.

Marjie Espinoza said she walked the picket line to stand up for five nieces and nephews who attend the school. They and their classmates are being taught satanic beliefs and witchcraft, she said.

"One of the teachers who is against Waldorf showed me some lesson plans," Espinoza said. "To me, they were like satanic, witchcraft."

Katherine Lehman, the resource teacher who helped implement the school's Waldorf program, denied that witchcraft or other "pagan" beliefs are being taught.

"I think it's ridiculous," she said. "Anyone can come in and watch what we're doing in our school. ... It's a very rigorous program, academically structured."

Although Oak Ridge is the city's only public school with a Waldorf curriculum, "this program has been going on worldwide for 75 years," she said.

At Oak Ridge, the program is being bankrolled this year by a $253,000 federal grant. Funding in the 1995-96 school year totaled $238,000, much of it used to begin training the school's faculty in the Waldorf approach.

Several pickets said they were "in the dark" as to what was happening at Oak Ridge until PLANS – People for Legal and Non-Sectarian Groups – began distributing leaflets outside the school.

PLANS, based in the Bay Area, claims the Waldorf program is part of a "cult."

District officials said PLANS has used rumors and other tactics in an unsuccessful effort to end Waldorf programs across the state. PLANS officials could not be reached for comment.

The Waldorf program, initiated by a previous school board, has enjoyed some good successes at Oak Ridge, said Jay Schenirer, the board's new president.

"Before we judge the outcome of this, we must make sure that everyone has visited the classrooms and seen what's going on. Then we can talk about it some more," he said.

"But I'm convinced there is a problem if you have some parents who are upset," Schenirer said. "We need to work with them toward a solution."

END NOTE (9) – PAGE 115 – SACRAMENTO BEE EDITORIAL – ATTACK ON OAK RIDGE
https://fireborncom.files.wordpress.com/2022/02/5.4.0-053197sacbeeeditorial-copy-1.pdf

The Sacramento Bee

Locally owned and edited for 140 years
JAMES McCLATCHY, editor, 1857-1883
C.K. McCLATCHY, editor, president, 1883-1936
WALTER P. JONES, editor, 1936-1974
ELEANOR McCLATCHY, president 1936-1978
C.K. McCLATCHY, editor, 1974-1989
GREGORY FAVRE, executive editor
HOWARD WEAVER, editor of the editorial pages
FRANK R.J. WHITTAKER, president and general manager

The attack on Oak Ridge

When basic public schools become magnet schools – that is, when they take on a particular instructional focus, such as the arts or mathematics or bilingual education – the transition is seldom easy. A number of parents choose to send their children to a different school (as they must be allowed to do), and teachers who dislike the extra training involved or the particular pedagogical focus, or who are close to retirement and for whom retraining makes little sense, ask to be transferred elsewhere. These bumps in the road should be expected whenever a school tries to reinvent itself.

In the case of the Sacramento City Unified School District's Oak Ridge Elementary School, which is nearing the end of its first year as a magnet school using Waldorf teaching methods, the reinvention has been especially difficult.

Waldorf methods focus on listening and speaking skills to bolster the development of literacy – an approach that seemed particularly suited to Oak Ridge's student population, 83 percent of which comes from homes where English is not the primary language. Throughout this school year, parents seemed mostly satisfied with the new methods, according to a parent survey conducted by the school in March. During this winter's open enrollment period, when parents had the option of placing their child at another district school, none did so. The year's attendance figures were up and, though district test scores are not yet in, teachers report great strides by their students in reading.

But in recent weeks, at the urging of a Bay Area-based group called People for Legal and Nonsectarian Schools (PLANS) and a few disgruntled teachers, a protest movement has brewed among a number of parents, marked by picketing and a boycott that kept a third of the student body out of school for parts of last week. PLANS suggests that Waldorf methods involve the teaching of witchcraft, and some parents now believe that the school is religiously opposed to computers.

There is no evidence at Oak Ridge to support the claims. The school says computers haven't been installed due to lack of proper wiring. But with a parent population that includes many recent Hmong or Mien immigrants who don't speak English well, PLANS has found fertile ground in which to plant the seed of paranoia.

The district, and the school itself, can be faulted for not laying more careful groundwork. With such a huge population of non-English-speaking parents, it is doubly important to ensure that they understand what's going on in the classroom.

What's important now is to counter the misinformation campaign and, if ultimately necessary, accommodate any parents who remain convinced that Oak Ridge is the wrong place for their children. There are a number of district students now at other schools who might like to enroll in the Waldorf magnet.

Prior to adopting Waldorf teaching methods, Oak Ridge essentially had nowhere to go but up. On districtwide reading and mathematics achievement tests, students in third through sixth grade scored near the bottom of the district's 60 elementary schools – in a district where only a handful of schools score above national averages. All of which is a powerful argument for trying something new to boost student achievement. The Oak Ridge magnet deserves the chance to show it can make a difference.

END NOTE (10) – PAGE 123 – ASiA – ANNUAL REPORT – "AN INITIATIVE SOCIETY" General Secretary Arthur Zajonc quoted one of Rudolf Steiner's most powerful addresses to members. "Throughout our Society the mood should prevail that welcomes genuine initiatives, be they outer actions or equally as decisive inner initiatives." NEWS FOR MEMBERS, AUTUMN 2001, pg. 14
https://firebornecom.files.wordpress.com/2022/10/2000_2001-initiative-society.pdf

Anthroposophical Society in America
Annual Report 2000–2001

An Initiative Society

Those who join the Anthroposophical Society have various things in common, but in his lectures on the karma of the Anthroposophical Society, Rudolf Steiner grants one aspect astonishing emphasis:

> All this makes it necessary for the anthroposophist to pay heed to one condition of his or her karma—a condition that is sure to be present in him to a high degree. All the many possibilities that are there in life, demand from the anthroposophist initiative—inner initiative of soul. We must become aware of this. For the anthroposophist this proverb must hold good. One must say to oneself: "Now that I have become an anthroposophist through my karma, the impulses that have been able to draw me to anthroposophy require me to be attentive and alert. For somehow or somewhere, more or less deeply in my soul, there will emerge the necessity for me to find inner initiative in life, initiative of soul which will enable me to undertake something or to make some judgment or decision out of my own inmost being." Verily this is written in the karma of every single anthroposophist: "Be a person of initiative, and beware lest through hindrances of your own body, or hindrances that otherwise come in your way, you do not find the center of your being, where is in the source of your initiative. Observe that in your life all joy and sorrow, all happiness and pain will depend on the finding or not of your own individual initiative." This should stand written as though in golden letters, constantly before the soul of the anthroposophist. Initiative lies in his or her karma.
>
> (Karmic Relationships, vol. III, lecture of August 4, 1924)

Rudolf Steiner is amazingly emphatic here. The most important characteristic living in anthroposophists is the impulse to inner initiative. A society for such individuals must therefore be experienced as a home and support for the initiatives they carry as part of their karma. The implications of this statement for our imagination of the Anthroposophical Society are profound. Throughout our Society the mood should prevail that welcomes genuine initiatives, be they outer actions or equally decisive inner initiatives.

Rudolf Steiner expected the Executive of the Goetheanum to model this characteristic. He wrote, "The Executive Committee is to be a committee of initiative, it will not be an administrative committee but a committee of initiative, giving the impulse for what should flow through the Anthroposophical Society as living reality." I believe that Rudolf Steiner's remarks for the Executive Committee also hold true for every leadership group within the Society, and indeed for anyone who takes hold of the impulse for initiative.

I feel, therefore, that the Society should act as a fertile field for the unfolding of human life in relationship to initiative. Invariably initiative can successfully unfold only when undertaken with others who work together to bring something new into the world. Genuine initiatives are social in nature. In the pages of this Annual Report you will read about some of our efforts (that is to say efforts by groups of members) in support of youth, the prison outreach program, our support for the meditative life, our sponsorship of research on attention deficit disorders and hyperactivity, our work with members, among others. Each of these endeavors reflects the unfolding of an inner initiative within a group of like-minded individuals.

Nor need (or do) all initiatives of the Society originate within its Council. Indeed most take place in countless locales when a couple of people get together to share their enthusiasm for something new. In other words I believe that we will all benefit by the Society becoming increasingly a place that welcomes responsible initiatives wherever they occur.

Too often the Society has been experienced as a place of "hindrances." If the Society fails to welcome initiative, then individuals of initiative will take them elsewhere, and much of the most important work on behalf of anthroposophy will arise outside of the Society. If this continues, the Society will inevitably be experienced by its members as a static—even dead—organization that preserves the forms and functions of the past but lacks fresh ideas and impulses. In light of these remarks, it is all the more important today to foster a culture that welcomes initiative at every level, from the smallest study group to the international leadership organs of the Society. Then will joy flow through our common work, because we will have found "the center of our being," the place where our unique contribution to world evolution originates.

—*Arthur Zajonc, General Secretary*

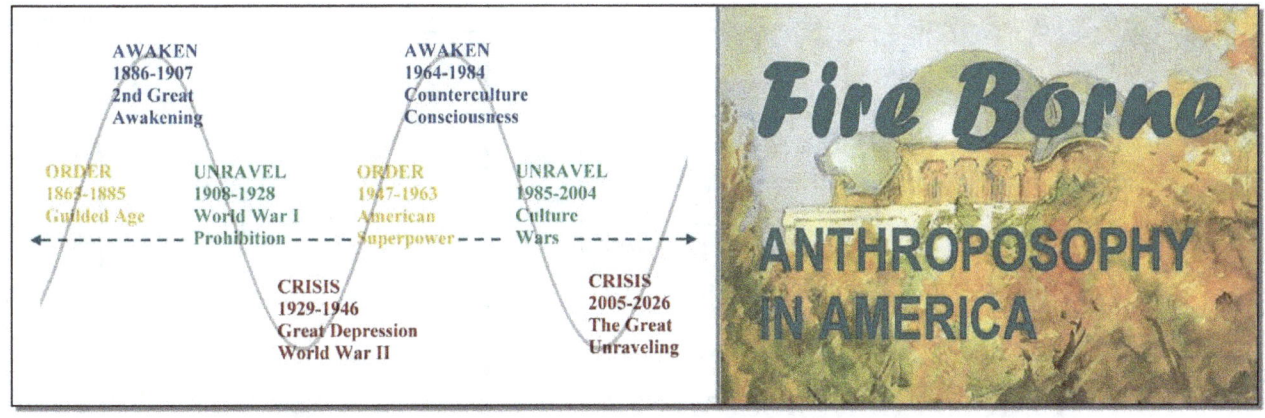

CULTURAL WAVE CHART © 2016 Jean W. Yeager[12]

2005-2026 The Great Unraveling
PHASE: CRISIS

THIS IS A GENERATION IN A CRISIS MODE: **The Moral Landscape is one in which the only thing that seems certain is change. The era starts with a Sub-Prime Mortgage melt-down which tumbles into nationwide bank failures and the Stock Market collapse. A quarter of a million people lose their jobs. Followed by a worldwide pandemic and millions of deaths.**

Abbreviations:	RS Rudolf Steiner	ED Education	MED Medical	ASiA Anthroposophical Society in America
AG Agriculture	SM Spirit Matters	TF Threefold	SCI Science	GAS General Anthroposophical Society

All timeline entries are for U.S. events unless otherwise noted.

2005
– Speculative bubble in housing bursts. World financial markets tumble. U.S. government takes action to save banks.

– 2.2 million credit card offers mailed each month.

TF – "AN EMERGING CULTURE"
SPECIAL EDITION PUBLICATION
By Utne Reader and RSF Social Finance sent to over 200,000 readers describing the work arising out of Rudolf Steiner's insights into economics and Social Threefolding.

– 4,045,000 acres of organic farmland up from 1939 when "Organics" was invented.

---

[12] Dates / phases from THE FOURTH TURNING, William Strauss and Neil Howe, Broadway Books, 1997

128 AWSNA member schools.

END NOTE (1) – **Federal Lawsuit decided in 30-minutes. PLANS fails to prove Anthroposophy is a religion for Establishment Clause purposes. PLANS appeals and loses vs. SCUSD, Twin Ridges Public School Districts.** Will Be Included In Appendix.

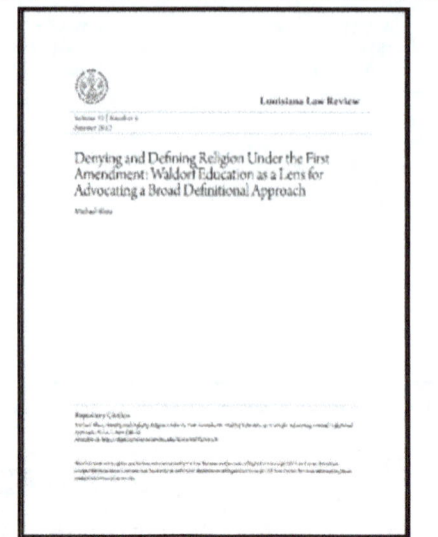

Louisiana Law Review **Commentary: Waldorf Court Case May Have Changed Constitutional Definition of "Religion"**

"… contemporary notions of American religious diversity demand an examination of the legal definition of religion and suggest that controversies like the Waldorf dispute will appear in the future in greater numbers and with greater frequency."

https://digitalcommons.law.lsu.edu/cgi/viewcontent.cgi?article=3075&context=lalrev

LINK TO COURT DOCUMENTS
https://waldorfanswers.org/Lawsuit.html

- IRAQ WAR – *MILITARISM OF U.S. ECONOMY CONTINUES.* Defense Contractors - The Army awarded "no bid contracts" at the rate of $1.5 billion per week, much in the form of cost-plus, often in the form of no audit requirement.

- YouTube launched.

- One in three black men will go to prison during their lifetime according to the U.S. Department of Justice. (*The New Jim Crow*, pg. 265.)

RUDOLF STEINER FOUNDATION REBRANDS AS RSF SOCIAL FINANCE – Adopts "Inspired By The Work of Rudolf Steiner." Becomes among the first in the industry to launch mission-aligned Donor Advised Funds (DAF). With this new format, assets held in a DAF are invested for social and environmental benefit.
RSF QUARTERLY, Spring 2014, "CELEBRATING TRANSFORMATION, www.rsfsocialfinance.org

- ARMY INTRODUCES FUTURE COMBAT SYSTEMS (FCS) – the "technological bridge" for $145 billion: a robotic army of radio controlled cannons, tanks, mortars which would require nothing in the way of food, armor, water, ammunition or sexual companionship.

2006
- "Subprime Mortgage Meltdown" created by increased risk mortgage lending. Derivatives and "Shorting" part of the process.

- U.S. Dept. of Justice reports white youth more likely than black youth to engage in illegal drug sales. (*The New Jim Crow,* pg. 264 (FN 10))

- 2006-2010 Police conduct 52,000 stop and frisks in an eight-block area of Brooklyn. (*Chokehold*, pg 82.)

ED – The Alliance for Public Waldorf Education founded. https://www.publicwaldorf.org/who-we-are

ASiA – June 6 – Jean Yeager retires as Administrative Director of the Anthroposophical Society in America . Marian Leon is named as his replacement.

- Three percent of the American Army are foreign nationals who receive college loans, pensions and can study the art of restaurant management.

- San Diego Archdiocese reached a $198 million settlement with 144 childhood sexual abuse claimants.

- Twitter created by Dorsey, Glass, Stone and Williams.

2007
- Countrywide Financial bankruptcy triggers U.S. Mortgage crisis.

- "Reading the reports from the scene of the country's August melancholy accident in the country's credit markets – the burst in of the home-mortgage bubble, banks sinking into the sand of the home-mortgage bubble, banks sinking into the sand of the sub-prime loans, hedge funds losing 100 percent of their imagined value in a matter of days, Dow Jones Industrial Average dropping 250 points in the space of a half hour…" (*An American Folly*, pg. 239)

- Oct. 15, first baby-boomer files for Social Security.

- U.S. Dept of Health reports African American 12th graders more consistently have lower usage rates than white 12th graders for most drugs, illicit or licit. (*The New Jim Crow*, pg. 264)

- Purdue Pharma executives plead guilty to misleading the public about the risks of addiction to the Oxycodone in a lawsuit brought by the U.S. Dept. of Justice and paid $634.5 million in fines. Three executives also plead guilty to criminal charges. ... Pain was no longer something that had to be endured – it could be easily and quickly treated with pills. (*THE ATLANTIC*, 2014)

- Roman Catholic Archdiocese of Portland agrees to pay $75 million settlement to 177 claimants of sexual molestation.

- The Archdiocese of Seattle agrees to pay $48 million in settlement to more than 160 claimants

2008
- Los Angeles Archdiocese agrees to pay $660 million settlement to 500 alleged victims.

- The first hip-hop concert at Yankee Stadium. Double bill Eminem and Jay-Z.

- Fannie Mae and Freddie Mac, Federal Mortgage underwriting agencies, near collapse.

- IndyMac Bank (CA) fails and starts a wave of bank failures in U.S. By year end, 25 banks fail.

- Lehman Brothers bankruptcy.

- EPA reports 180-185 million pounds of glucophosphate is used in agricultural situations. (*In 20 year time span covered by EPA records of sales and use, glyphosate rose faster and more substantially than any other pesticide. Glyphosate based herbicides have been, by far, the most heavily applied pesticides in the U.S)*

- Ireland, Iceland, Germany, Spain, and others require political solutions.

- House rejects $700 billion bank bailout plan – Dow drops 777 points.

- G20 meets for first time since WWII.

- 240,000 Americans lose their jobs. This is as many as in the 1929 Stock Market crash.

- 4,815,000 acres of organic certified farms in U.S.

- 8 million Millennial food gardeners (age 18-34)

2009
- Barack Obama inaugurated.

- Dow Jones at 12-year low.

- OATH KEEPERS is an anti-government group which claims membership over 5,000 former military and law enforcement personnel.

"It is ironic to think that man might determine his own future by something so seemingly trivial as the choice of an insect spray.

All this has been risked – for what? Future historians may well be amazed by our distorted sense of proportion. How could intelligent beings seek to control a few unwanted species by a method that contaminated the entire environment and brought the threat of disease and death even to their own kind? Yet this is precisely what we have done. We have done it, moreover for reasons that collapse the moment we examine them ...

Rachel Carson, *Silent Spring*, 1965, pg. 29

- Credit card law created to protect consumers. In 9 months before law went into effect, banks raise interest rates on 65% of all cards and slash upper limits on credit card balances.

- TEA PARTY MOVEMENT is an American conservative movement within the Republican Party. Members of the movement have called for a reduction of the national debt of the United States and federal budget deficit by reducing government spending, and for lower taxes.
(https://en.wikipedia.org/wiki/Tea_Party_movement)

RSF SOCIAL FINANCE (2009)
Total Assets: $123,005.000   Investor Funds: $64,785,000
Loan Portfolio: $69,149.000   Client Accounts: 1,228
RSF QUARTERLY, Spring 2014, "CELEBRATING TRANSFORMATION, https://rsfsocialfinance.org/

2010

- ASiA - **HISTORIC BY-LAW CHANGE.** After a year of consultation with attorneys and an extensive written proxy process and the General Council of the Society changed the New York state non-profit corporate form which it had adopted in 1933 when it was first incorporated from "Membership " to "Non-Membership." The "Membership" form meant that, since 1933, the Society had to have 10% of its membership agree in writing or in person with any major change (the sale of 211 Madison Ave., Regionalization of Council membership, or this change of the corporate form.) After this change, major issues (like regionalizing the Board membership, sale of property, investments, etc.) could be enacted by a simple majority vote of the Board of Directors and no member involvement required. **Previously, to get Member "buy-in" meant the Membership had to agree with the proposal. This means that going forward, Members may (or may not) propose changes, but the General Council can dispose (or enact) the changes.** (Will be included in the Administrative Collection.)
https://firebornecom.files.wordpress.com/2022/09/2010-asa-bylaws.pdf

- Tea Party protest events were well funded by tobacco companies, big oil and the Koch brothers. Mainly anti-Washington, anti-Affordable Care Act ("Obamacare"), and anti-TARP, the financial system bailout. (https://en.wikipedia.org/wiki/Tea_Party_protests)

- Copiapó mining accident, also known then as the "Chilean mining accident", began on 5 August 2010, with a cave-in at the San José copper–gold mine, located in the Atacama Desert 45 kilometers north of the regional capital of Copiapó, in northern Chile. 33 miners were trapped from August 5 to October 13. Wikipedia

- Eurozone crisis. Bail outs for countries.

- WikiLeaks makes 466,743 secret U.S. government documents available.

- The Affordable Care Act (health care reform) enacted. Also known as "Obamacare."

3,000 CSA GARDENS UP FROM ONE IN 1985 – 20 YEARS

- "DEEPWATER HORIZON" CATASTROPHE, a British Petroleum (BP) - drilling platform in the Gulf of Mexico is the largest oil industry disaster in history. The ruptured pipe pumps millions of gallons of oil into the gulf for months before it is able to be stopped.
- (https://en.wikipedia.org/wiki/Deepwater_Horizon_oil_spill)

- Monsanto patents glyphosate as an antibiotic for killing bacteria within the human digestive tract. Concerns are expressed about immune system damage.

- Haiti devastated by earthquake.

- Pakistan flooded by cyclonic storm.

- eBook Q1 revenue up 193%

- Police brutality is so widespread, and so predictable, that many small and medium-sized cities purchase insurance policies to pay money to people who have been subject to police abuse. (*Chokehold*, pg. 55)

- Transportation Security Administration (TSA) "pat downs" bring swift public outcry. One "don't touch my junk" video goes viral.

- Instagram launched as an exclusively iPhone app; android version launched a year later.

2011
- U.S. has a national debt crisis. The Standard and Poors (S&P) rating agency downgrades U.S. Sovereign debt rating making the U.S. dollar worth less.

- Occupy Wall Street – thousands of protesters take over Zucotti Park in New York City. Considered by some to counter the "Tea Party Movement."
- (https://en.wikipedia.org/wiki/Occupy_Wall_Street)

- Popular uprising in Libya, Egypt and Syria crushed by military response.

- **ASiA** – The Rudolf Steiner Library of the Anthroposophical Society in America, Chatham/Hudson, NY, was awarded a $1,500 grant from the State of New York for a pilot digitization project and purchase a flat-bed scanner. https://rsl.scoolaid.net/bin/home

- Southern Poverty Law Center estimates 100,000 hard core supporters of Sovereign Citizens Movement (SCM) which applauds the American founding but rejects the existing rule of law. There may be another 200,000 followers. (*Lapham's Quarterly, Spring 2018 pg. 196*)

- Portugal and Greece bailed out second time.

- **CLIMATE CHANGE** Weather related issues: hurricanes creating a tsunami, drought in East Africa prompting a major famine.

- 5,383,000 acres of organic farmland in U.S.

- U.S. has highest rate of incarceration in the world, dwarfing the rates of nearly every developed country and even surpassing those of repressive regimes like Russia, China and Iran. *(The New Jim Crow,* pg. 6)

- Osama Bin Laden killed by a Special Forces raid.

- U.S. Representative Gabrielle Giffords shot in assassination attempt.

2012
- Barack Obama re-elected President.

- Super PACs gave $609 million in this presidential election.

- **TF** – RSF Social Finance CEO, Doug Shaffer, reported new financial innovations in the *"Impact Investing"* newsletter if the STANFORD SOCIAL INNOVATION REVIEW *"Inspiring Leaders Of Social Change:*
    "These philanthropic funds will provide loan guarantees, equity investments, and other types of capital that position social enterprises—for-profits, nonprofits, and hybrids — to obtain additional

equity or debt financing and give them time to develop. We intend to support catalytic enterprises, and we know that not all of them will succeed. The goal is to recycle about two-thirds of money into new financing (we'll consult the lead donors in each fund on the exact target ratio)."

> ## RSF Local Initiatives Fund
>
> RSF (Rudolf Steiner Foundation) Social Finance launched the RSF Local Initiatives Fund, in collaboration with lead donors, to pilot an **integrated capital approach** to financing regional food systems—one that coordinates investments, loans, and grants to provide flexible capital for social entrepreneurs. That project proved to us that providing a tailored mix of different types of capital can help early-stage social enterprises deliver on their missions.
>
> Funders were excited about the results as well, and we are about to launch four new **Integrated Capital Funds**:
> 1. RSF Fair Trade Fund,
> 2. RSF Biodynamics Fund,
> 3. RSF Soil Health Fund, and
> 4. RSF Women's Fund.
>
> https://ssir.org/articles/entry/a_new_path_for_social_enterprises_through_the_valley_of_death#

– Space shuttle Atlantis makes its final mission.

– U.S. withdraws troops from Iraq leading to the "Iraq insurgency" or "Iraq crisis," an irregular war fueled by political and sectarian violence.

– "In 1972, there were fewer than a total of 350,000 people being held in prison compared with more than 2-million today (2012)." (*The New Jim Crow*, pg. 8)

– Glycosophate harm shown to be caused by low doses in GM crops. *(2012 – TOXICITY STUDY by Gilles-Eric Seralini, France, who studied rats fed on diet of NK603 Roundup tolerant GM maize and given water containing Roundup at levels permitted by US law showed severe liver and kidney damage.)*

– Financial melt-down averted because it triggered tax hikes and spending cuts.

– U.S. economy rises – 7.7% unemployment (lowest in 4 years).

– U.S. Supreme Court upholds the Affordable Care Act (dubbed "Obamacare" by Republicans).

– September 11 – Benghazi Libya Consulate attack. Four Americans killed. The role of Secretary of State Hillary Clinton subject of subsequent congressional hearings.

– "Superstorm Sandy" hits the East Coast. This is the second deadliest hurricane in history.

– Mass school shooting, 27 killed – Sandyhook Elementary, Newtown, CT by Alan Lanza.

- Mass school shooting, 3 killed – Clackmas Town Center, OR.

- Mass school shooting, 5 killed, 3 injured – Minneapolis, MN.

- Sikh Temple shooting, 6 killed, 4 injured – Oak Creek, WI.

- Mass school shooting, 12 killed, 58 wounded – Aurora, CO.

- Mass school shooting, 6 killed, Seattle, WA.

- Penn State football scandal started in 2011 but resulted in Penn State not playing football in 2012. Penn State coach Jerry Sandusky indicted and convicted on dozens of counts of child sexual abuse dating back years.

- U.S. Department of Housing and Urban Development (HUD) study finds African Americans face discrimination virtually every time they enter the housing market including travel website Airbnb. (*Chokehold*, pg. 182.)

> **"Operant Conditioning" Military Style Training To Kill"**
> Lt. Col Dave Grossman
> From "ON KILLING"
> *"Violent videogames hardwire young people for shooting at humans. The entertainment industry conditions the young and exactly the same way the military does. Civilian society apes the training and conditioning techniques of the military at its peril."*

2013

Remaking the Food System

Investors and philanthropists must work together to generate more ecologically responsible and locally grown food for more people.

By Don Shaffer CEO RSF Social Finance Sep. 30, 2013, Stanford SOCIAL INNOVATION Review

The food system, and how to fix it or rebuild it, was a hot topic at the recent Social Capital Markets (SOCAP) conference – for good reason. Many of us in the social enterprise sector – investors, entrepreneurs, philanthropists – see the need for an alternative food system that dramatically expands access to fresh food and supports sustainable local food production, and that ultimately helps create more resilient communities. For that to happen, we need to get outside our comfort zones and work together. Collaboration between philanthropists and investors in particular is essential to building an alternative food system.

- Federal Government runs out of money and shuts down – first since the 1990s.

- Gun Control legislation loses steam – no ban on assault weapons is enacted.

- 313 million people live on farms >1% of these claim farming as an occupation.

- Average age of farmers 58.3 years

- George Zimmerman, who was charged with killing Treyvon Martin, is acquitted.

- Detroit, Michigan files for bankruptcy.

- 13 million Millennial food gardeners (up 63% from 2008)

– Urban food gardening rises 29% from 2008 to 9 million households.

– IRS "over-reach" targets non-profits and is penalized for "malpractice".

– 38% more households have incomes >$35,000 compared to 2008. These households are food gardening.

– 2 million more households participated in community gardens than in 2008, an increase of 200% in five years.

– Boston Marathon Bombing.

– Eric Snowden makes more WikiLeaks revelations.

– The Supreme Court finds in favor of gay marriage.

– 16% of state prisoners are doing time for drug offenses.

– It costs taxpayers an average of $25,000 per year to keep an inmate incarcerated.

– Clinton Foundation tax returns show that of $140 million in grants and contributions received, only $8.8 million was given for direct aid and research. The rest was spent for administration including $8.5 million in travel. (*The American Folly*, pg. 326)

– **BLACK LIVES MATTER** a decentralized social/political party organized against incidents of police violence.

2014

AG – Farms For Tomorrow (www.farmsfortomorrow.com), a farm succession website and audio/video podcast forum conducted by Media Arts Cooley Ludke and John Swain, was inspired at the 2014 Biodynamic conference break-out session with John Bloom. The site offers tips and stories about transitions from top farmers and gardeners.

ASiA – The Rudolf Steiner Library of the Society which had its home in "The Carriage House" in Harlemville, NY since 1972, is sold. Founding Director, Fred Paddock had passed away in 2012 so this move to a temporary location at the Stone Church in Philmont, NY *(2017 Anthroposophical Society in America Annual Report Online, pgs. 22-23)*

TF – RSF Social Finance CEO, Doug Shaffer, reported new financial innovations in the *"Impact Investing"* newsletter if the STANFORD SOCIAL INNOVATION REVIEW *"Inspiring Leaders Of Social Change:* "The fact that we're seeing this fresh focus on the uses of capital to achieve social benefits tells us that there is a real opening now for vastly greater collaboration between impact investors (individuals, networks, and firms), foundations (community and private), and community banks. As intermediaries working in social finance, it's up to us to create a finance infrastructure that enables social enterprises—and the communities they serve—to thrive."

Impact Investing

Integrated Capital for Social Enterprises

To build a thriving social enterprise sector, we need to rethink the purpose of capital and employ a new strategic funding approach.

By Don Shaffer | Jul. 17, 2014

To build a thriving social enterprise sector, we need to rethink the purpose of capital and employ an integrated capital strategy. Integrated capital is the coordinated and collaborative use of different forms of capital (equity investments, loans, gifts, loan guarantees, and so on), often from different funders, to support a developing enterprise that's working to solve complex social and environmental problems.

In 2011, our organization, RSF Social Finance, provided a $50,000 program-related investing (PRI) loan for equipment even though Viva Farms had no collateral, because the River Styx Foundation made a 100 percent loan guarantee. In 2012 and 2013, RSF provided gift funding for three AmeriCorps positions and a farm manager to coordinate winter education and farm planning programs. A new $200,000 loan for farm stand improvements and additional equipment will involve $50,000 from the Seattle Impact Investor Fund through a revenue loan agreement; $200,000 from RSF; and a loan guarantee from River Styx.

This support has allowed Viva Farms to train about 250 people and launch 15 farm businesses that produce on more than 70 acres.

As this work illustrates, RSF has the advantage of being able to draw on a diverse mix of both investment and philanthropic funds under one roof to support organizations we see as models for systemic change. We're ideally positioned to serve as a laboratory for the integrated capital approach, and we're taking on that challenge by reorienting our entire funding operation around the concept.

https://ssir.org/articles/entry/integrated_capital_for_social_enterprises 3/4

– President Obama's signature racial justice project, *"My Brother's Keeper"* starts with the huge bi-partisan support and a record number of African American men in the East room of the White House. Also attending were many corporate execs and influencers like Bill O'Reilly and Al Sharpton. The president quipped: "…there are people of good faith who want to get some stuff done."

– Summer Olympics in Rio de Janeiro, Brazil.

- Winter Olympics in Sochi, Japan

- Republicans win Senate in mid-term election.

- House Benghazi special committee asks for emails from Secretary of State Clinton and learns there is no U.S. government email server, only a private server.

- Dr. Dre's collaboration with Apple to market his Beats headphones positioned him to be hip-hop's first billionaire. (*Chokehold*, pg. 245)

- ISIS Terror group – the Islamic State – begins campaign of terror by beheading care workers.

- Robin Williams commits suicide.

- Glyphosate usage booms in US due to genetically modified crops. Usage increases 15-fold.

- Fatal Force used by police: Michael Brown killed in Ferguson, MO, a St. Louis suburb by Darten Wilson.

- Fatal Force: Eric Garner killed in Staten Island by being placed in a chokehold.

- Two NYPD officers were shot to death.

- Grand Jury failed to bring charges against the officer who killed Eric Garner.

- Kendrick Lamar, a critically-acclaimed hip-hop artist appeared on Saturday Night Live and changed his lyrics to express homicidal imaginings about the police. ("There's a history here – of hip-hop artists whose characters spit homicidal lyrics about the police and who, far from being ostracized are embraced by the masses.") (*Chokehold*, pg. 245)

- Ukraine and Crimea battle – Russia takes over Crimea. U.S. institutes major trade and economic sanctions against Russia.

- Sony Corporation hacked by "Guardians of Peace" a Russian internet hacking group.

- U.S. begins to normalize relationships with Cuba.

- Bernie Sanders enters presidential contest as a Democrat rather than as an independent to bring progressive issues. "I'm not Ralph Nader so I run as a Democrat."

- Hillary Clinton gives up 55,000 emails to investigators.

RSF SOCIAL FINANCE (2014 Q1 estimate)

Total Assets: $162,998,000   Investor Funds: $99,704,000
Loan Portfolio: $74,769,000   Client Accounts: 1,836

RSF QUARTERLY, Spring 2014, "CELEBRATING TRANSFORMATION,
https://rsfsocialfinance.org/

2015

GAS – "There is a slow decrease in Society members, from 45,000 worldwide to 44,000 in 2015, mostly due to deaths." *(2015 Annual Report Online,* pg 2 https://anthroposophy.org/learn-more/governance/)

ASiA – Membership 3287. In 2000, membership was 4220.
https://firebornecom.files.wordpress.com/2022/10/ep-membership-1992_2020.pdf

ASiA – Katherine Thivierge joined ASiA as Director of Operations in August 2015.
- Financially, in 2014 it was reported that ASiA was at a "moment of truth" and hoped that cutbacks would not damage capacities. In 2015, the picture improved significantly. *(2015 Anthroposophical Society in America Annual Report Online, pg. 20)*
- Rudolf Steiner Library re-opened in November in a climate-controlled, 2500 square foot, easily accessible new location in Hudson, NY. *(2015 Anthroposophical Society in America Annual Report Online, pg. 14)*
- Two copies of *"Being Human",* the Society's newsletter, were sent free to several thousand Waldorf teachers and parents by the Association of Waldorf Schools of America (AWSNA).
- The Anthroposophical Prison Outreach (APO) program, originally started as a lending library of Rudolf Steiner's books, expanded services to prisoners and provided a correspondence course.

In addition, APO published a study guide written especially for prisoners on Steiner's *"How To Know Higher Worlds."*, one of the "basic" books. >>>>

– Torin Finser, General Secretary, ended his letter in the *2015 Annual Report:*
   "I would like to end this letter with a thought provoking comment made by another departing General Secretary, Hartwig Shiller from Germany**:**
   'Anthroposophy has found its way into the world (our many initiatives), yet the world has not yet found its way into our Society.'"

– In March, Clinton embroiled in server scandal. ("Death March" her staff calls it.)

– Sanders announces he wants a serious debate with Clinton about serious issues and goes after her hard on trade and Iraq. (Keystone XL Pipeline and Trans Pacific Partnership (TPP))

– Republican Donald Trump "cascades" down an escalator in Trump Tower to announce his candidacy. (Trump's key phrases: Mexico immigrants "criminals, rapists", immigration "build a wall", Obamacare "a big lie", Hillary "a corrupt insider", Americans victims of insiders "drain the swamp", and Trump re-used Ronald Reagan's slogan – "Make America Great Again").

- October 13 – Sanders and Clinton debate in Las Vegas.

- October 22 – Benghazi Hearing intensifies.

- Sanders "surge" with very little infrastructure and contributions of $27. "Billionaires can't buy Bernie".

- World Health Organization (WHO) cancer agency IARC classifies glyphosate as "probable carcinogen to humans. (Group 2A).

2016
ASiA – 2016 Membership 3358 up from 3287 in 2015.
https://fireborncom.files.wordpress.com/2022/10/ep-membership-1992_2020.pdf

- Presidential election influenced by fake social media "news" by foreign governments.

- July 21 – Guccifer 2.0 cyberattack emails. This is a Russian military group who weaponizes Wikileaks.

- July 25 – Democratic convention in Philadelphia. Debbie Wasserman-Schultz controversy.

- "Alt Right" label coined by Trump Press Secretary Kellyanne Conway for "anti-immigrant, anti-women" group.

- Super PAC contributions reach $1.1 billion nearly 2x of 2012 contributions.

- 34% of deaths in prisons and jails due to suicide.

- Hillary Clinton's Internal Emails Hacked and released by Wikileaks as well as transcripts of Hillary Clinton's Goldman Sachs speeches. This cyberattack, and its implications were not understood at the time.

- Wikileaks quickly followed by the Access Hollywood video released with Trump's sexual commentary which took the media spotlight. News of the recording broke two days before a debate with Hillary Clinton.

- Trump says, "No proof Russia behind email hack."

- Affordable Care Act insurance premiums go up dramatically.

- University of California San Francisco (UCSF) discovers glyphosate in 93% of urine samples collected across the U.S. as part of Detox Project commissioned by the Organic Consumers Association.

AG "Beginning in 2016, with initial visioning, the BDA (Biodynamic Association), Demeter, and key stakeholders began to talk about how to work together more collaboratively and understand what is living in the biodynamic movement…"*Biodynamics, Spring 2021, pg. 10*
www.biodynamics.com/unification-faq

- Two weeks before the election James Comey announces the FBI has "nothing more to investigate" re: the Clinton / State Department email server.

- November 9, Trump elected President.

2017
- Study shows low dose Roundup causes liver cancer (Michael Antoniou, Kings College, London).

ED – Rudolf Steiner College, Fair Oaks, CA goes out of business and transfers use of assets to Maristem, a program for young adults with ASD on the autism spectrum.

ASiA – The Anthroposophical Society in America transfers the Rudolf Steiner Library to Rudolf Steiner Cultural Foundation (RSCF) which was formed to move forward with the legal, financial and business of the library. *(2017 Anthroposophical Society in America Annual Report Online, pgs. 21-23)*

2018
- SCHOOL SHOOTING – Marshall county High school, Kentucky, Gabriel Ross Parker killed 2 and wounded 18.

- SCHOOL SHOOTING – Marjorie Sherman Douglas High school, Parkland, Florida former student Nicholas Cruz killed 17 and wounded 17.

- SCHOOL SHOOTING– Santa Fe Highschool, Santa Fe, TX, Dimitrios Pagourtzis killed 10 and wounded 13 with a shotgun and .38 revolver. Multiple IEDs, pipe bombs, propane tanks and pressure cookers were found in the parking lot.

> **2018**
> *"Wall Street, Land Of The Lawless"*
> **Ralph Nader –**
>
> "… lawlessness and its many exercise forms of raw power is itself the norm. What it has wrought is the institutionalization of criminality – with overworld and underworld often blurring together – producing inequality of wealth and income …."

AG – "NOTICE: On July 31, 2018, Stellar Certification Services is ceasing to certify organic operations. After this date, Stellar certified operations in the Organic Integrity Database will appear as "[NOP] Under Control of NOP" until they have obtained certification with a new certifier."
https://www.demeter-usa.org/nop/

AG – DEMETER ASSOCIATION has made a partnership with Certified Organic Farmers (CCOF) one of the country's oldest certifying agencies.

> *"Our partnership with Demeter continues as we work with their inspectors to perform dual organic and Biodynamic inspections. Initially we thought we'd only achieve this in 2019, but with hard work and determination, we found opportunities in 2018 and performed a number of these inspections as early as July!" FROM THE CCOF WEBSITE*
> https://www.ccof.org/article/welcome-stellar-and-demeter-usa-operations

- Harvey Weinstein sexual activities prompt his firing and lead to nationwide *"Me Too"* demonstrations.

- Al Franken, resigns Senate seat because of sexual allegations.

- Dec 26 – Partial government shutdown.

- Dec 31 – Nikki Haley resigns as UN Ambassador.

2019

– Jan 4 – Pres Trump considers declaring national emergency to bypass Congress on southern border wall.

– Jan 7 – Trump televised announcement of border security.

– Jan 8 – Trump on Primetime television about 18-day government shutdown.

WALDORF 100 – A Worldwide Centennial Celebration

"The global spread of Steiner/Waldorf education, even into the furthest corners of the earth, has continued until today. Interest in Waldorf teaching approaches is evident in about half of all the world's nations (about 100 countries), independent of language, religious affiliation, or political situation. There are Waldorf kindergartens and schools, and teacher training facilities, on all continents. Parents across the globe are making an extraordinary commitment to support growth and strive towards a future in which humanity is attainable and healthy development and social participation is truly possible. The Waldorf education movement, with about 1,100 schools and over 2,000 kindergartens around the globe, has become the largest free school movement in the world."

(Nana Göbel)
https://www.waldorf-100.org/en/waldorf-education/history/

– Jan 12 – Government shutdown becomes longest in history (22 days).

– Jan 15 – William Barr confirmed Attorney General. Speaker Pelosi sends President Trump letter suggesting he reschedule State of the Union due to unpaid Secret Service due to shut down.

– Jan 17 – BuzzFeed reports Trump directed former attorney Michael Cohen to lie to Congress about Moscow Tower Project. Report alleges Cohen did not reveal this to Mueller investigation. Trump calls for Space Force after missile defense review.

– Jan 21 – Supreme Court supports exclusion of transgender men and women in military service.

– Jan 25 – Mitch McConnell, Chuck Schumer agree to three-week stop-gap spending measure and ends government shut down in 35 days. Trump threatens national emergency if no deal on border wall made in these three weeks.

– Feb 1 – Trump withdraws U.S. from Intermediate Range Nuclear Forces Treaty accusing Russia of non-compliance.

– Feb 5 – Trump's Second State of the Union address. Fundraising dinner raises $2.4 million from 76,000 donors streamed on his Facebook page.

– Mar 24 – Summary of Mueller Report released which finds Trump did not collude with Russians to win 2016 Pres election, AG Barr concludes obstruction of justice inconclusive.

– November 2019 – COVID-19 (coronavirus SARS-CoV-2) VIRUS PANDEMIC starts in Wuhan

China and sweeps Asia.

- **GEORGE FLOYD KILLED by police chokehold and kneeling on his neck. Launches hundreds of nationwide "Black Lives Matter" protests. Spawns "Defund The Police" movement across the country.**

- December 15, Stockholm, Sweden – RIGHT LIVELIHOOD AWARD (RLA) known as the "Alternative Nobel Prize" was awarded to three activists who belong to the global Anthroposophical movement. Dr. Ibrahim Abouleish for his life's work the Egyptian Sekem Initiative as well as to the founder of the Centre for Alternative Development Initiatives (CADI), Nicanor Perlas and his colleague Professor Walden Bello, both Civil Society activists in the Philippines. GLOBAL AWARDS FOR ANTHROPOSOPHICAL ACTIVISTS

- "Anti-Fascist Groups" called "Antifa" are present in some violent protests. Notable in Portland, OR.

RSF – 2019 Rudolf Steiner Social Finance (RSF) Trustees voted to create and fund a new financial organization to support Anthroposophical work named **SPIRIT MATTERS**.

- DEMOCRATIC PRIMARY results in Presidential Candidate Joe Biden and Vice Presidential Candidate Kamala Harris.

- Georgia Senate Runoff election for two U.S. Senate seats is called. The outcome could change the Republican/Democratic majority in the Senate.

AG – Council Of Biodynamic Organizations (CBO) formed.

AG – Demeter and Biodynamic boards merge.

2020
ASiA – 2020 Membership 3763 up from 3545 in 2019.
https://firebornecom.files.wordpress.com/2022/10/ep-membership-1992_2020.pdf

- January 9 – WHO announces mysterious Coronavirus-related pneumonia in Wuhan, China.

- January 20 - CDC (Centers for Disease Control and Prevention) says 3 airports will begin screening for Coronavirus.

- Jan 21 – CDC confirms first U.S. Coronavirus case.

- January 23 – Wuhan under quarantine.

- January 31 – WHO (World Health Organization) issues Global Health emergency. 9,800 cases and 200 deaths worldwide.

- February 2 – COVID-19 sweeps Europe and enters U.S. from East.

- February 3 - President Trump declares Public Health Emergency.

- March 6 – 21 passengers on California cruise ship test positive for Covid-19.

- March 11 – WHO (World Health Organization) declares Covid-19 a Pandemic.

- March 13 – Trump declares COVID-19a national emergency. Bans travel of non-US citizens from Europe.

- March 17 – University of Minnesota begins testing Hydroxychloroquine as a treatment for COVID-19.

- Hospitals are overwhelmed. Clinical trials on hold.

- March 17 – U.S. reports its 100th death from COVID-19. Administration asks Congress to send direct financial relief.

- March 19 – California issues a statewide "Stay At Home" order.

- NO CENTRALIZED U.S. RESPONSE to the pandemic. Each state is left to craft their own strategy.

- Center for Disease Control (CDC) doctors address the nation on daily television shows hosted by President Trump. The recommendations are: wear a mask, socially distance (6-feet), avoid social gatherings, close down restaurants and schools.

- European shortage of Personal Protective Equipment (PPE). Ventilator shortage leads Trump administration to sell U.S. supplies to "highest bidder."

- March 26 – Senate passes Coronavirus Aid Relief and Economic Security Act (CARES Act) providing $2 trillion in aid to hospitals, small businesses and state and local governments.

MED – 100th ANNIVERSARY OF ANTHROPOSOPHIC MEDICINE

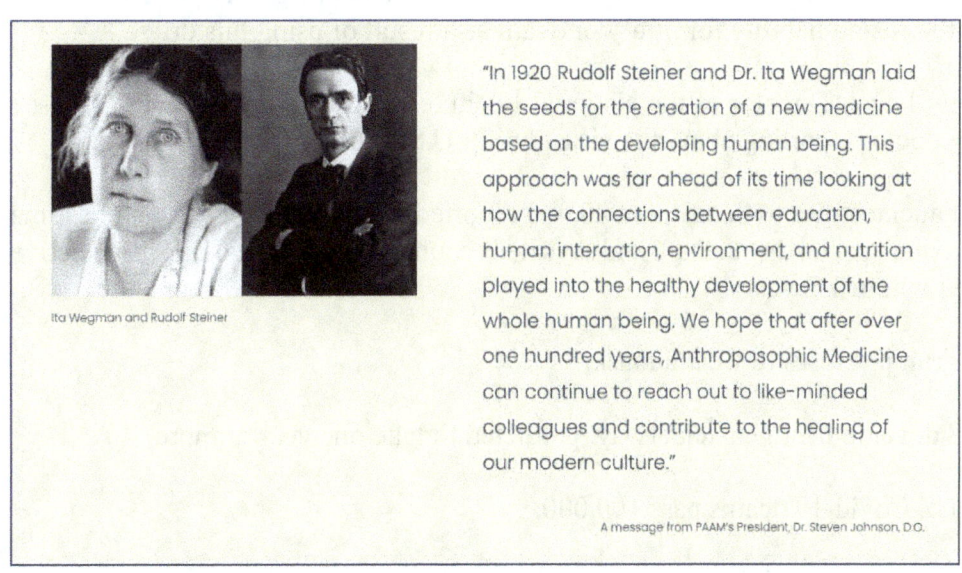

A message from PAAM's President, Dr. Steven Johnson, D.O. (2021)
Physician's Association for Anthroposophical Medicine (PAAM)
https://anthroposophicmedicine.org/about-paam

- U.S. SHORTAGE of Personal Protective Equipment (PPE) in the FEMA Federal government stockpile also means that PPE are sold to the "highest bidder" states.

- March 27 – House approves CARES Act and President Trump signs into law.

- March 30 – FDA Issues Emergency Use Authorization (EUA) use of Hydroxychloroquine sulfate and chloroquine phosphate products – malaria products.

- CDC recommendations cause huge disruption and anger among citizens. Some private school communities (including Waldorf) that had long-standing "personal choice" policies regarding vaccinations, were informed that those policies were eliminated. School communities and parents abruptly had to deal with the change.

- VIRUS DEATH TOLL begins to rise as U.S. becomes the country most severely impacted by the virus.

ASiA – John Bloom, General Secretary. 2020 marks end of John's first four year term. He commented about the "unrecognized gift" in the time of Covid:
> *"By the force of necessity, and against the judgment of some, we began developing a spiritual understanding of technological activity even as we looked forward to a time of again meeting in person. This may be the under recognized gift of 2020. And whatever else the year brought; our US Society continued to grow in membership."*

- April 16 – President Trump entertains idea of reopening the US economy for Easter Sunday. White House issues broad guidelines for how people could return to work, church, restaurants and other venues.

- May 1 – Remdesivir granted Emergency Use Agreement (EUA) by FDA. This means the manufacturer has no liability for injury or death as a result of using this drug.

- Dr. Anthony Fauci, Director of the National Institute of Allergy and Infectious Diseases becomes the leading doctor reporting about the virus during U.S. Press briefings.

- May 12 – Fauci testifies to Senate that 80,000 reported deaths are likely an underestimate. He warns against relaxing "social distancing" and says he is cautiously optimistic that an effective vaccine will be achieved within 1-2 years.

- President Trump refuses to wear a mask.

- VACCINE development gets underway, predicted to take one year or more.

- May 28 – US Covid-19 deaths pass 100,000.

- June 15 – FDA rescinds EUA for Hydroxychloroquine.

- June 30 – Fauci warns new Covid-19 cases could hit 100,000 a day.

- MICHIGAN MILITIA members arrested by FBI for plan and actions to assassinate Governor Whitmer.

- August HIURRICANE LAURA slams into Louisiana Gulf coast.

- September JUSTICE RUTH BADER GINSBURG dies. The Court make-up changes with the appointment of Amy Comey Barrett to replace her.

- October PRESIDENT DONALD TRUMP tests positive for COVID.

- November ELECTIONS – Georgia officials reject Trump's bid to overturn election results. Supreme Court rejects Texas bid to overturn election results in four states. Biden/Harris ticket wins popular vote and Electoral College vote. Supreme Court rejects bid to overturn the election.

- Donald Trump claims voter fraud and irregularities in 5 states. Challenges in courts but provides no evidence. All cases thrown out.

- Press briefings about the virus are dropped but many states have daily state briefings.

- Trump claims the "election was stolen" and calls for supporters to "take the election back."

- US Senate Runoff ballot in Georgia won by the Democratic candidates, OSHOFF and WARNOCK.

MED – Thomas Südhof, a graduate of the Hannover Waldorf School in Germany, recently shared the Nobel Prize in Medicine for his discoveries regarding the regulation of neurotransmitter vesicles in the brain. (https://waldorfanswers.org/)

2021

ASiA – 2021 Membership 3819 up from 3756 in 2020.
https://go.elib.com/9ld65

> *"In the meetings of the Anthroposophical Society a great truth can be experienced. When human beings meet together seeking the spirit with unity of purpose then they will also find their way to each other -- they will find the path from soul to soul."*

SM – SPIRIT MATTERS adds The Anthroposophical Society in America as a supported organization.

- COVID-19 – 500,000 deaths in U.S. / 29 million U.S. vaccinated (12%) https://go.elib.com/FV2iY

- January 6, 2021 – U.S. Capitol violently attacked by rioters seeking to block Electoral College vote for Joe Biden. Five people are killed including a Capitol Policemen beaten to death.

- President Donald Trump is impeached for the Capitol Insurrection. Forty-five (out of fifty) Republicans vote against impeachment.

- January 20 – Joe Biden sworn in as President.

- January – BLACK LIVES MATTER movement (founded 2013) nominated for Nobel Peace Prize.

- April 19 – COVID-19 67,443 new cases per day up from 53,000 4-weeks ago.
https://www.ajmc.com/view/a-timeline-of-covid-19-developments-in-2021

- Russia which has been in Crimea/Ukraine since 2014 – very quickly builds up military forces. Ukrainian President calls upon western European nations for defense. Ukraine is not a NATO member but defensive weapons flow in from NATO which escalates the conflict into full-scale battles.

– September 27 – COVID-19 117,000 cases/day – 64% vaccinated. (NYTimes).

– October – World Health Organization (WHO) endorses first vaccine against Malaria.

– October 28 – Facebook changes its name to "Meta Platforms".

– November – Atlanta Braves win World Series.

– November 8 – US borders re-opened to citizens from 33 countries barred by COVID-19 restrictions.

– November 13 – Climate change agreement reached in United Nations.

– December – Tornadoes rip through South and Midwest.

> **October 2021**
> **The Rudolf Steiner Archive & e.Lib**
> ... was founded by James (Jim) Stewart in 1980 to make Steiner's published works available on the world wide web. The e.Lib/Archive averaged 60,000 visitors per day from users around the world. After almost 42 years, Stewart donated the entire Archive (documents, equipment, and databases) to be carried on by Dr. Christopher Wietrzykowski as Executive director, now renamed Steiner Online Library.

2022
January 1 – AG END NOTE (2) - BIODYNAMIC DEMETER ALLIANCE FORMED unifying the Biodynamic Association and Demeter USA. *"The goal was to create an organization that could serve as a national network to offer leadership in the United States in helping to solve the multiple layers of crisis we find ourselves collectively facing."* **Sheila Foster named first Executive Director.**
https://firebornecom.files.wordpress.com/2022/10/2022_06_02-gmail-biodynamic-demeter-alliance-welcomes-first-executive-director.pdf

– January 21, 2022 – COVID-19 760,000 new cases/day – triple the number of Jan. 2021. 147,000 in hospital with COVID-19. 1,700 deaths/day.(12) THE WEEK, January 21, 2022

– February 2 – Russian court sentences opposition politician Alexi Nevalny to 3 ½ years in prison.

– February 7 – Tom Brady leads Tampa Bay Buccaneers to Super Bowl win.

– February 15 – Deep freeze power outage in Texas kills more than 200 people.

– February 18 – NASA "Rover" lands on Mars.

SM – SPIRIT MATTERS adds The Waldorf School Association as a supported organization.

– March – container ship runs aground in the Suez Canal blocking billions of dollars of trade for six days.

– March 11 - $1.9 trillion COVID-19 stimulus package signed into law.

– April – Minneapolis jury finds ex-cop Derek Chauvin guilty in George Floyd murder case.

– May – Space-X successful flight.

– May 7 – Cyberattack cuts off key gasoline supply.

– June 2 – Netanyahu voted out in Israel election.
– On Friday, June 24, 2022, the US Supreme Court overturned Roe v. Wade, the landmark piece of legislation that made access to an abortion a federal right in the United States.

– June 28 – Partial collapse of condominium in Surfside, FL kills 98.

– July – Twenty-third Olympic Games in Tokyo.

– July 22 Sixth COVID-19 wave rolled across the country. "Only 64% of Americans are vaccinated." THE WEEK

– July 29 – Federal employee COVID-19 vaccine mandate.

– August – The US withdraws from Afghanistan after a two-decade war. Taliban takes over.

BECOMING THE SPIRIT OF DETROIT
FOLLOW THIS LINK TO Read About **ELDERBERRIES MORAL IMAGINATION AND COMMUNITY DESIGN**
https://go.elib.com/dQXWe

– August 5 – The latest Omicron BA.5 COVID-19 subvariant drove new U.S. infections up to 140,000 new reported cases and the real number is likely closer to 1-million so said THE WEEK magazine August 5. No one has a plan, said the Baltimore SUN in an editorial, "What we're seeing is a wave of mindless 'indifference' to the virus, enabled by a strange new passivity from government and health officials." (pg. 6)

– August 10 – Andrew Cuomo resigns as governor of New York due to sexual impropriety allegations.

ASiA – September 9 – **MAKING WAY FOR NEW LEADERSHIP** John Bloom steps away from the General Secretary position after eight years. General Council Board Chair Helen-Ann Ireland, Board Chair announced by email that two key members of the Society's Leadership Team (LT) have "stepped aside." Katherine Thivierge, Administrative Director; Deb Abrams-Dematte, Development Director will depart. In a separate communication, John Beck, Communications Director resigned. This comes just before a nominating committee will begin the process of finding the next General Secretary starting at the October Annual General Meeting.
https://go.elib.com/1AHxm

– September 14 – Facebook whistleblower brings forth files but company plays it down.

– September – Texas enacts anti-abortion law.

– September 22 – COVID-19 booster shots cleared by FDA.

– President Biden finally "calls out the elephant in the room," said CNN.com reporter Frida Ghitis. "Biden's broadsides are divisive and damaging," said Bret Stephens in the *New York Times*. "I happen to agree that Trump poses 'a unique threat to democracy.' But conflating 'MAGA Republicans' with any conservative who opposes abortion rights and gay marriage, he's chosen to 'treat tens of millions of Americans as the enemy within.'" THE WEEK, September 23, 2022, pg. 16

ASiA – MAJOR CHANGE IN THE ANTHROPOSOPHICAL SOCIETY GENERAL SECRETARY ROLE – LINK TO THE NOMINATING COMMITTEE INTRODUCTION

The ASiA is transitioning from a General Secretary position, compensated through an honorarium/stipend, to a General Secretary/Country Representative as a full-time (right-livelihood) position. The intention is to allow the individual chosen to be financially able to take up the enormous collaborative leadership tasks on behalf of the Anthroposophical Society in America. This will open up the position to candidates who might not otherwise be able to consider this important work.

This change is significant. The role of General Secretary is not merely a position to fill but a representative for the spiritual work that is being cultivated in America. The General Secretary is an equal member of the Leadership Team, who through spiritual striving and focused will, are weaving a worthy vessel for the Good Spirit of our Society.

https://go.elib.com/siidb

END NOTE (3) ASiA – MAJOR CHANGE IN GENERAL SECRETARY NOMINATING PROCESS – AMENDED AND RESTATED SEPTEMBER 2023
LINK TO COMPLETE PROCESS
https://go.elib.com/FLUTz

<snip> *(8) After a reasonable period of not less than six (6) weeks, the Nominating Committee will present its recommendation of three to four candidates to the Executive Council of the General Anthroposophical Society. The candidates deemed acceptable by the Executive Council of the General Anthroposophical Society will then be submitted to the General Council for selection of the next General Secretary. If the General Council does not find that a suitable candidate has been presented, it may request that a new slate of candidates be developed by the Nominating Committee.*

ASiA 2022 – OCTOBER ANTHROPOSOPHICAL SOCIETY IN AMERICA ANNUAL GENERAL MEETING.

Took place in Washington DC. Attendees visit the Capital, walk the Mall and see historical sights.

This is the centennial of the crisis which surrounded the Anthroposophical Society in 1923. Leading up to the Annual General Meeting of the Anthroposophical Society in America:

"This is the moment in which we stand. No doubt, the last two years have been exhausting; and, we are challenged now to cultivate new resolve. There is much renewal to be found within—the sources and practices of anthroposophy, and where there is good manifesting in the world." John Bloom, Feb 12, 2022

- John Bloom, General Secretary. 2020 marks end of John's second four-year term.
- The General Secretary position has been re-imagined.
- Nominating committee takes up the task of finding the next G.S.

2022 ANNUAL REPORT PUBLISHED – Membership up 337 new members to 4,156 members, UP FROM 3819 (2021) — a 9% increase from 2020. (SOURCE: 2021 annual report, pg.28) (https://indd.adobe.com/view/76ee1f78-f807-4530-9d01-31e41455aecf)

Historical documents show that in 2002 membership was 4,397. See the membership report 1992-2020 to see how membership has fluctuated. In 1979, records show membership was 1,693. https://fireborrnecom.files.wordpress.com/2022/10/ep-membership-1992_2020.pdf

FOLLOWING A GOOD STAR

Rudolf Steiner was very clear that he wanted an Anthroposophical Society which would do spiritually inspired work in practical spheres: education, medicine, farming, and others. In his words of farewell when he laid the Foundation Stone Steiner said,

> "… bear out with you into the world your warm hearts in whose soil you have laid the Foundation Stone for the Anthroposophical Society, bear out with you your warm hearts in order to do work in the world that is strong in healing…. if we show ourselves to be worthy, then a good star will shine over that which is willed from here. My dear friends, follow this good star. We shall see whither the gods shall lead us through the light of this star."

As we approach the 100th anniversary of the Foundation Stone meeting some feel that it is important to take a look back – with some objectivity - and see what our warm hearts have done in the world. Would Rudolf Steiner say that we have shown ourselves to be worthy? Have we a good star shining over that which we willed? Is the Society strong and healing? How'd we do?

NOTES:

Into The Heart's Land, Henry Barnes, Steiner Books, 2013

Chokehold: Policing Black Men, Paul Butler, 2017

Age Of Folly: America Abandons Its Democracy, Lampham's Quarterly, 2019

New Passages, Gail Sheehy (Sheehy)

The New Jim Crow: Incarceration In The Age of color Blindness, Michelle Alexander, 2010

Rudolf Steiner Library, Hudson, NY. https://rudolfsteinerlibrary.org/

END NOTES / LINKS:

END NOTE (1) – PAGE 146 – **ASiA 2005 FEDERAL LAWSUIT DECIDED IN 30-MINUTES**. PLANS fails to prove Anthroposophy is a religion for Establishment Clause purposes. PLANS appeals and loses vs. SCUSD, Twin Ridges Public School Districts. Will Be Included In Appendix.

END NOTE (2) – PAGE 165 – **BDA BIODYNAMIC DEMETER ALLIANCE FORMED** Unifying the Biodynamic Association and Demeter USA. *"The goal was to create an organization that could serve as a national network to offer leadership in the United States in helping to solve the multiple layers of crisis we find ourselves collectively facing."*
https://go.elib.com/sFilp
Sheila Foster named first Executive Director.

END NOTE (3) – PAGE 167 – **MAJOR CHANGE IN GENERAL SECRETARY NOMINATING PROCESS – AMENDED AND RESTATED SEPTEMBER 2023.** Included In Administrative Collection.
https://go.elib.com/sAAUA

APPENDIX
HISTORICAL DOCUMENTS FROM THE FIRST AMENDMENT LAWSUIT

2004 – Anthroposophical Society in America files "Friend of the Court" *Amicus Curiae* brief in PLANS vs. SCUSD, Twin Ridges First Amendment Federal Lawsuit.

https://firebornecom.files.wordpress.com/2022/02/briefamicus0407091.pdf

Katherine L. Thivierge, Esq.
P.O. Box 1547
Southgate, MI 48195
(734) 558-4909

Fred Dennehy, Esq.
Wilentz, Goldman & Spitzer
90 Woodbridge Center Drive
Woodbridge, NJ 07095
(732) 855-6158

Attorneys for Amicus Curiae
 Anthroposophical Society in America

UNITED STATES DISTRICT COURT
EASTERN DISTRICT OF CALIFORNIA

PLANS, Inc.) Plaintiff) v.)) SACRAMENTO CITY UNIFIED SCHOOL) DISTRICT, TWIN RIDGES ELEMENTARY) SCHOOL DISTRICT, DOES 1-100,)) Defendants.)	Case No. CIV S-98-0266 FCD PAN AMICUS CURIAE BRIEF OF THE ANTHROPOSOPHICAL SOCIETY IN AMERICA IN SUPPORT OF DEFENDANTS

TABLE OF CONTENTS

Table of Authorities iii

Statement of Interest 1

Statement of Facts 2

Legal Argument 2

Conclusion 15

TABLE OF AUTHORITIES

CASES

Abington School District v. Schempp, 374 US 203, 83 S.Ct. 1560, 10 L.Ed.2d 844 (1963).........9
Africa v. Pennsylvania, 662 F2d 1025, 1032 (3d Cir. 1981), cert. denied 456 U.S. 908, 102 S.Ct. 1756, 72 L.Ed 2d 165 (1982)... 3, 11, 12
Alvarado v. City of San Jose, 94 F.3d 123 (9th Cir. 1996) 3, 10, 11
Ashcroft v. Mattis, 431 U.S. 171, 52 L.Ed. 2d 219, 97 S.Ct. 1739 (1977).........................6
Edwards v. Aguillard, 482 U.S. 578, 107 S.Ct. 2573, 96 L.Ed.2d 510 (1987).....................9
Friedman v. Southern California Permanente Medical Group, 102 Cal App. 4th 39 (2002) 11
Hall v. Beals, 396 U.S. 45, 24 L.Ed. 2d 214, 90 S.Ct. 200 (1969).................................6
LaAbva Silver Min. Co. v. United States, 175 U.S. 423, 44 L.Ed.223, 20 S.Ct. 168 (1899).........6
Malnak v. Yogi, 440 F. Supp. 1284, CD N.J. 1977)... 3, 4
Malnak v. Yogi, 592 F.2d 197 (3d Cir. 1979)..................................... 3, 4, 11, 12, 13, 14
Maryland Casualty Co. v. Pacific & Oil Co., 312 U.S. 270, 85 L.Ed., 826, 61 S.Ct. 510 (1941)..6
Nashville, Chattanguan St. Louis Railway vs. V. Wallis, 288 U.S. 249 (1933), 77 L.Ed. 730, 53 S.Ct. 345 (1933)...6
Oklahoma District Council of Assemblies of God v. New Hope Assembly of God Church, Inc., 548 P. 2d 1029, 1976 Okla. 46 (1979)...10
Peloza v. Capistrano Unified School Dist., 37 F.3d 517 (9th Cir. 1994) 9
Sierra Club v. Morton, 405 U.S. 727, 31 L.Ed. 2d 636, 92 S.Ct. 1361 (1972);.....................6
Torasco v. Watkins, 367 U.S. 488, 6 L.Ed. 2d 982, 81 S.Ct. 1680 (1961)...........................9
United States Bank of Oregon v. Independent Insurance Agents of America, 508 U.S. 439, 124 L.E. 2d 402, 113 S.Ct. 2173 (1993)...6
United States v. Allen, 760 F.2d 447, 450-51 (2d Cir. 1985)....................................10

OTHER AUTHORITIES

Owen Barfield, Romanticism Comes of Age, 76-77 (Wesleyan University Press, 1967) 12
Rudolf Steiner, "The Mission of Spiritual Science and of its Building at Dornach," Approaches to Anthroposophy, 18-19 (Rudolf Steiner Press, 1992; also quoted in Gunther Wachsmuth, Life and Work of Rudolf Steiner, 100-101 (Whittier Books, Inc, 1955)................................ 14
Rudolf Steiner, "Was soll die Geisteswissenschaft? Eine Erwiderung auf 'Was wollen die Theosophen?", Philosophie und Anthroposophie: Gesammelte Aufsätze, 441 (Rudolf Steiner Verlag, 1984) 13
Rudolf Steiner, Fruits of Anthroposophy 64, 72-73 (Rudolf Steiner Press 1986)................. 11, 13
Rudolf Steiner, Spiritual Science: A Brief Review of its Aims and of the Attacks of its Opponents (John M. Watkins, London, 1914)... 14
Statutes of the Anthroposophical Society, #4 .... 11, 14
Statutes of the Anthroposophical Society, #9 10
Tribe, American Constitutional Law 827-28 (West Law, 1978)......................................10

STATEMENT OF INTEREST

The Anthroposophical Society in America, Inc., (the "Society") is a separate legal entity from Defendant public school districts and the charter and magnet Waldorf-method public schools at issue. Moreover, it is a separate and distinct entity from the various private Waldorf schools, the Association of Waldorf Schools of North America (AWSNA) and Waldorf teacher training academies, such as Rudolf Steiner College and others in the United States. Hence, the Society has no party interest in these proceedings.

However, the Society is the legal representative of anthroposophy[1] in this country and is charged with a responsibility for the reputation of anthroposophy and its public face. The Society believes that a decision by this Court that adopts the plaintiff's position, that the use of Waldorf method educational practices in defendant public schools advance anthroposophy and that anthroposophy is a religion, would profoundly mischaracterize anthroposophy and cast the relationship of anthroposophy with Waldorf education, independent Waldorf teacher training academies, and several hundred independent entities which characterize themselves as Anthroposophical in a false light. Therefore, we request the Court's leave to put before it the character of anthroposophy as well as the salient features of the Society for consideration in this matter.

---

[1] Anthroposophy (from the Greek "anthropos", meaning human, and "sophia", meaning wisdom) is a method of spiritual scientific inquiry developed by Rudolf Steiner (1861-1925). Steiner demonstrated the results of his research in more than 40 books and 6,000 lectures on wide ranging subjects including the application of his research into practical, everyday life such as the education of children (Waldorf Education), agriculture (Biodynamics), medicine, therapeutics, pharmaceuticals, the fine arts, the performing arts, finance, and others. The anthroposophical movement is a confederacy of independently organized, financed and operated initiatives whose only commonality is the methodology of anthroposophy.

STATEMENT OF FACTS

The Society, which was incorporated in 1933 in the State of New York, offers this *amicus curiae* brief to the Court in its capacity as the official and legal representative of anthroposophy in the United States.

In the case at bar the Plaintiff PLANS alleges, *inter alia*, that the California charter and magnet Waldorf-method schools in question advance "the religious doctrines of anthroposophy" and that their doing so is offensive to the constitutional prohibitions against the establishment of religion. Complaint for Declaratory and Injunctive Relief, Paragraphs 8 and 11. Central to the plaintiff's argument is the allegation that "anthroposophy" rises to the legal definition of a "religion" for Establishment Clause purposes. The Society disputes this characterization and offers the Court this *amicus* brief to substantiate the Defendant School Districts' position that the Court should not answer in the affirmative the question "Is Anthroposophy a religion?".

LEGAL ARGUMENT

PLAINTIFF CANNOT PROVE THAT ANTHROPOSOPHY IS A RELIGION.

A. A DETERMINATION OF THE DEFINITION OF ANTHROPOSOPHY, NECESSARY FOR A JUDICIAL DETERMINATION THAT ANTHROPOSOPHY IS A RELIGION, IS NOT AN APPROPRIATE UNDERTAKING FOR THIS COURT.

Plaintiff is endeavoring to prove, in support of its argument that the use of certain Waldorf methods by public charter and magnet schools in the defendant school districts violates the Establishment Clause of the United States and California Constitutions, that "anthroposophy" is a "religion," and that the religion of anthroposophy is promulgated in the schools in question.

In order to prove these propositions, plaintiff must prove what anthroposophy is, and must demonstrate that the methods used in the defendant Public Schools are intended to establish or advance the practice of anthroposophy. The first question to be addressed by the parties, according to this Court's directive of April 11, 2001, is "whether Anthroposophy is a system of belief and worship of a superhuman controlling power under a code of ethics and philosophy requiring obedience therefore." April 11, 2001 Tr. 4, 5 to 7.

Alvarado v. City of San Jose, 94 F.3d 1223 (9th Cir. 1996) sets forth the standard test for a determination of what constitutes a "religion" for Establishment Clause purposes. Alvarado relies heavily on the concurring opinion of Judge Adams in the Third Circuit decision of Malnak v. Yogi, 592 F.2d 197 (3d Cir. 1979) ("Malnak II"), which affirmed Malnak v. Yogi, 440 F. Supp. 1284, CD N.J. 1977) ("Malnak I").

> First, a religion addresses fundamental and ultimate questions having to do with deep and imponderable matters. Second, a religion is comprehensive in nature; it consists of a belief-system as opposed to an isolated teaching. Third, a religion often can be recognized by the presence of certain formal and external signs.
>
> Alvarado, supra, at 1229, quoting Africa v. Pennsylvania, 662 F2d 1025, 1032 (3d Cir. 1981), cert. denied 456 U.S. 908, 102 S.Ct. 1756, 72 L.Ed 2d 165 (1982), quoting Malnak II at 207-210.

The Malnak cases addressed the question of whether a public high school course taught with the intent of inculcating a specific practice of transcendental meditation constituted the advancement of or establishment of a "religion". In Malnak I and Malnak II, the meaning of "transcendental meditation" for the purpose of legal analysis was not an issue for the Court. A definitive understanding of transcendental meditation as used in the school in question was unambiguously set forth in a textbook that was taught to the students in the class. The fact that the very ideas under scrutiny were laid out in a textbook which was part of a specific educational practice intended to teach a specific meditation practice relieved the Court from the burden of formulating its own definition of "transcendental meditation." The textbook further relieved the Malnak Court from making a ruling as to what beliefs, methodologies and practices ought to be considered to be a part of "transcendental meditation" and what beliefs, methodologies and practices should be considered extraneous to "transcendental meditation." The Malnak Court, in short, was not faced with the immense burden of defining "transcendental meditation."

Courts, for good reason, have been reluctant to make abstract determinations involving the legitimacy of representations made about the beliefs of private organizations. Here, the task plaintiff seeks to thrust upon the Court—to render a judgment as to whether "anthroposophy" is a religion under the Establishment Clause—is made immeasurably more difficult than the task undertaken by the New Jersey District Court and the Third Circuit because, unlike the concept of "transcendental meditation" in Malnak I and Malnak II, there is here no specific textbook of "anthroposophy" assigned to students or teachers or any definition of "anthroposophy" agreed upon by all parties.[2] But plaintiff here, as a first step in resolving its lawsuit, is demanding that this Court undertake to define what "anthroposophy" is as well as to determine whether this "anthroposophy" is a religion under the Establishment Clause.

In order to do what plaintiff demands, this Court would have to first determine that there is a single, univocal set of beliefs or practices which it can confidently isolate from others and definitively label "anthroposophy." This Court would have to segregate from the thousands of writings, loosely described as "anthroposophical," those which it deems to represent "anthroposophy" and those which it deems do not.[3] Then the court would have to compare this

---

[2] There is no textbook of "anthroposophy" here (unlike the situation in Malnak) because "anthroposophy" is not taught in the defendant schools.

[3] The Court would also have to interpret and paraphrase a vast set of writings which have been characterized by their authors as esoteric and nondogmatic, the contents of which have been emphatically represented by those authors not

anthroposophy with what is being presented by the plaintiff. This is precisely the sort of quixotic enterprise that a steady stream of case law for decades has warned the courts against.

Thus, the question of whether "anthroposophy is a religion" under the Establishment Clause would (1) require an ancillary ruling as to what constitutes "anthroposophy" and what does not, and (2) demand a determination of what is the proper status and interpretation of any documents that are alleged to be "anthroposophical." The procedure would constitute a colossal exercise in judicial inefficiency.

The determination of whether an entity called "anthroposophy" (whatever that is determined to be) constitutes a "religion" under the Establishment Clause would divert this case from what it should be about—a consideration of whether specific pedagogical methodologies are in fact exclusively "Waldorf", whether "Waldorf-methods" are inextricably linked with "anthroposophy", whether teachers in the defendant schools intended to use specific pedagogical devices for the students in those schools and whether those pedagogical devices violate the Establishment Clause of the Federal or State Constitutions. The determination of an abstract question about "anthroposophy", in isolation, is the functional equivalent of a complaint for a declaratory judgment seeking an advisory opinion as to whether "anthroposophy" constitutes a "religion," and is properly analogized to such a case.

Courts have consistently dismissed actions filed as declaratory judgment suits on the grounds that the question sought to be determined is not a "case or controversy" under Article III of the United States Constitution, which limits the jurisdiction of the federal courts by requiring that such courts only address matters of actual cases or controversies. Actual cases or

---

to constitute ordinary, exoteric "information." In order to characterize such fundamental writings of "spiritual research" as "beliefs," the Court would have to make a determination that those authors were either misrepresenting their own work or that they were in error about the belief content of their own work.

controversies on matters presenting a real, not a hypothetical controversy, involve concrete and current, not uncertain or contingent, events. Nashville, Chattanguan St. Louis Railway v. V. Wallis, 288 U.S. 249, 77 L.Ed. 730, 53 S.Ct. 345 (1933); LaAbva Silver Min. Co. v. United States, 175 U.S. 423, 44 L.Ed.223, 20 S.Ct. 168 (1899). It is well settled that the Court "is without power to grant declaratory relief unless [an actual controversy] exists." Maryland Casualty Co. v. Pacific & Oil Co., 312 U.S. 270, 272, 85 L.Ed. 826, 61 S.Ct. 510 (1941). The plaintiff must prove the current existence of the dispute that justifies an adjudication of the parties' rights based on current pertinent facts in order to establish a case or controversy warranting declaratory judgment. Ashcroft v. Mattis, 431 U.S. 171, 52 L.Ed. 2d 219, 97 S.Ct. 1739 (1977). Absent such proof, any judgment rendered by the Court would be an advisory opinion, which federal courts are constitutionally forbidden to issue. United States Bank of Oregon v. Independent Insurance Agents of America, 508 U.S. 439, 446, 124 L.E. 2d 402, 113 S.Ct. 2173 (1993); Sierra Club v. Morton, 405 U.S. 727, 31 L.Ed. 2d 636, 92 S.Ct. 1361 (1972); Hall v. Beals, 396 U.S. 45, 48, 24 L.Ed. 2d 214, 90 S.Ct. 200 (1969). The enormously broad question of what anthroposophy "is"—whether it is a method or a system of beliefs and worship—is simply not necessary for a judicial determination of whether there has been a violation of the Establishment Clause in the schools here. Whether the character of what was imparted was religion or not may be relevant; but the definition and ontological status of something as diverse, difficult and removed from any school setting as is the entire subject of "anthroposophy," is simply beyond the proper scope of inquiry.

Anthroposophy is not on trial here. The only question arguably at issue in this litigation is the constitutional status of what is being taught in the defendant school districts. Any pronouncements by this Court on the definition of anthroposophy, the proper interpretation of anthroposophy, whether particular anthroposophical writings constitute methodologies or "teachings or beliefs of any kind"—<u>without specific reference to specific practices shown to have been conducted at specific schools</u>—would be hypothetical, advisory and beyond the proper interest of the Court.

Civil courts traditionally have been held to lack jurisdiction to determine the issue of compliance by a religious group with the rules, philosophies and precepts of larger religious groups with which they are affiliated. Resolution of the "is anthroposophy a religion" question would entail precisely this sort of determination. It would force the Court to choose among competing definitions and varieties of anthroposophy, i.e., differences between casual readers of anthroposophical publications, longtime students and others.

If the Court chooses to treat anthroposophy as a religion, then anthroposophy is entitled to the protections of the First Amendment, which prohibits the exercise of jurisdiction by the civil courts to decide which are in fact the <u>true</u> "rules," "philosophy" and "precepts" of the given "religion." Simple judicial efficiency dictates that the question of whether anthroposophy is a religion must be determined—if at all—only after the question of what (if any) purported "anthroposophical" tenets are allegedly being practiced in the schools in question.

Plaintiff's representatives, have stated their intention to introduce more than 100 "documents" into evidence to which they hope to define or reinvent "anthroposophy" for the Court. While the Society has no wish for the Court to engage in the kind of circus of hypotheses, interpretations and innuendoes that plaintiff is apparently eager to stage, it is profoundly interested that such "evidence" be seen in light of the views of the entity best situated to put it in accurate perspective.

It is respectfully submitted that the kind of philosophical farrago that plaintiff seeks to perpetrate on the participants is not the kind of business that the Court should be about. Determination of the essential issue in this case—whether Waldorf methods intentionally advance religion in the defendant school districts and by what means the plaintiff measures that advance—would lead to the clear, precise and mercifully efficient procedure proper for a determination of the case.

B. ASSUMING, ARGUENDO, THAT THE COURT WERE TO UNDERTAKE TO POSIT A DEFINITION OF "ANTHROPOSOPHY", THE COURT SHOULD NOT MAKE THE DETERMINATION THAT "ANTHROPOSOPHY" IS A RELIGION FOR PURPOSES OF THE ESTABLISHMENT CLAUSE.

Assuming the Court were to formulate a definition of anthroposophy, plaintiff by summary judgment and/or summary adjudication motion has asked the Court to determine it is a religion under the Establishment Clause. Such a determination would have staggering practical implications for the federal courts. If the Court in this case were to make a determination as to whether "anthroposophy" constitutes a religion for the Establishment Clause, would it not also be necessary for a similarly situated court to undertake to determine the religious status of Montessori education, given the existence of a lawsuit alleging that the operation of Montessori pedagogical methods in a school violated the Establishment Clause? The mere showing that an educator's (such as Maria Montessori, John Dewey or Rudolf Steiner) <u>pedagogical</u> views have been influential in the curriculum of a given school and that those educators (Montessori, Dewey or Steiner) elsewhere expressed spiritual or philosophical views cannot be grounds for examining the "religious" status of the educator's views under the Establishment Clause. This issue is already settled concerning John Dewey, one of the most influential pedagogical pioneers of public education and one of the signers of the founding document for the so-called "religion" of Secular Humanism, *The Humanist Manifesto I* in 1933.

In Torasco v. Watkins, 367 U.S. 488, 6 L.Ed. 2d 982, 81 S.Ct. 1680 (1961), the U.S. Supreme Court considered the constitutionality of a required oath under the First Amendment. Without focusing upon the Free Exercise or Establishment Clauses, the Court in footnote included "secular humanism" as a non-theistic "religion." Id. at 495, n. 11.

In Peloza v. Capistrano Unified School Dist., 37 F.3d 517 (9th Cir. 1994), a high school biology teacher tried to balance the teaching of evolutionism with creationism based on the claim that Secular Humanism (and its core belief, evolutionism) is a religion. The Ninth Circuit emphatically rejected the claim that secular humanism (and evolutionism) may be considered to be a "religion" under the Establishment Clause:

> We reject this claim because neither the Supreme Court, nor this circuit, has ever held that evolutionism or secular humanism are "religions" for Establishment Clause purposes. Indeed, both the dictionary definition of religion and the clear weight of caselaw are to the contrary. The Supreme Court has held unequivocally that while the belief in a divine creator of the universe is a religious belief, the scientific theory that higher forms of life evolved from lower forms is not. Edwards v. Aguillard, 482 U.S. 578, 107 S.Ct. 2573, 96 L.Ed.2d 510 (1987).

In the Supreme Court decision Abington School District v. Schempp, 374 US 203, 83 S.Ct. 1560, 10 L.Ed.2d 844 (1963); Justice Clark stated:

> "[T]he State may not establish a 'religion of secularism' in the sense of affirmatively opposing or showing hostility to religion, thus 'preferring those who believe in no religion over those who do believe.'"

It may well be that an educational pioneer's personal beliefs, such as John Dewey's in "Secular Humanism" is potentially protected for Free Exercise, but not prohibited, under Establishment Clause principles. The Second Circuit has held that while evolutionism or secular humanism may be "religions" for purposes of the Free Exercise Clause, "anything 'arguably non-religious' should not be considered religious in applying the establishment clause." <u>United States v. Allen</u>, 760 F.2d 447, 450-51 (2d Cir. 1985), quoting Tribe, <u>American Constitutional Law</u> 827-28 (1978).

Thus, the personal spiritual, moral or religious belief of a pedagogical innovator does not "infuse" that person's pedagogical methodology with religion simply because of the fact that that innovator had personal spiritual, moral or religious beliefs. One must look to the specific practices in order to determine the issue.

C. THE ANTHROPOSOPHICAL MOVEMENT AND THE ANTHROPO-SOPHICAL SOCIETY ARE NOT "RELIGIOUS" WITHIN THE MEANING OF ALVARADO.

The Society has contended from its inception that anthroposophy is not a univocal system of dogmas or beliefs, <u>but a language of inquiry</u>, <u>a scientific method</u> that embraces the sometimes diverse insights of its participants. A court must be precluded from choosing among such diverse insights and defining, categorizing or interpreting anthroposophy in any one way. <u>See Oklahoma District Council of Assemblies of God v. New Hope Assembly of God Church, Inc.</u>, 548 P. 2d 1029, 1976 Okla. 46 (1979).

The Statutes of the Society[4] state emphatically that anthroposophy is <u>not</u> a religion. <u>It has no dogma.</u> The Statutes of the Society state: "A dogmatic stand in any field whatsoever is to be excluded from the Anthroposophical Society." <u>Statutes of the Anthroposophical Society</u>, #9.

The Society does not propound a system of beliefs. It views anthroposophy as a cognitive methodology, a path to knowledge:

> The findings made in spiritual science arise from thought processes that have been enlivened and re-formed and because of this also have an enlivening effect on

---

[4] The statutes are the founding principles and organizational document of the worldwide Society (Swiss equivalent to by-laws) and are specifically incorporated into the By-laws of the Anthroposophical Society in America, Inc.

human souls when taken in to those souls and tested for their truth… [T]he essential aim of spiritual science … is to enter with one's mind into the sphere of free thought activity.

Rudolf Steiner, Fruits of Anthroposophy 64, 72-73 (Rudolf Steiner Press 1986).

The Society does not engage in religion, insist upon religion or interfere with religious practice. It consciously and emphatically stands apart from religion. Many members of the Society engage in traditional religions; many do not. Some practice non-theistic spirituality; many other members are connected to no religious practice. The Society honors each member's own religion and the moral injunctions of that religion. The Statutes of the Society state that "Anyone can become a member, without regard to nationality, social standing, religion or scientific or artistic conviction… The Anthroposophical Society rejects any kind of sectarian activity." The Statutes of the Anthroposophical Society, #4.

Nor is anthroposophy a religion for Establishment Clause purposes. As stated in Section A above, Alvarado v. City of San Jose, 94 F. 3d 123, relies heavily upon the detailed concurring opinion of Judge Adams Malnak v. Yogi, 592 F. 2d 197 (3rd Cir. 1979) ("Malnak II"). There Judge Adams articulated a test incorporating "indicia" or "factors," to consider in determining whether a group could be considered a religion for Establishment Cause purposes. Those indicia are:

> First, a religion addresses fundamental and ultimate questions having to do with deep and imponderable matters. Second, a religion is comprehensive in nature; it consists of a belief-system as opposed to an isolated teaching. Third, a religion often can be recognized by the presence of certain formal and external signs.
>
> Alvarado v. City of San Jose, at 1229, quoting Africa v. Pennsylvania, 662 F2d 1025, 1032 (3d Cir. 1981), cert. denied 456 U.S. 908, 102 S.Ct. 1756, 72 L.Ed 2d 165 (1982).[5]

---

[5] See also Friedman v. Southern California Permanente Medical Group, 102 Cal App. 4th 39 (2002), which similarly relies on Africa, and Malnak II.

The "formal and external signs" listed by the court include: "formal services, ceremonial functions, the existence of clergy, structure and organization, efforts at propagation, observance of holidays and other similar manifestations associated with a traditional religion." Africa, 662 F. 2d at 1035-36.

Addressing the first factor outlined in Malnak II, many anthroposophical publications discuss "fundamental and ultimate questions having to do with deep and imponderable matters." However, Anthroposophy discusses findings based on philosophical questioning and research. The Anthroposophical Society in America, Inc., does not propound specific beliefs or dogma about these ultimate questions nor are there "sacred" texts. Rather, the Society encourages personal inquiry or research. The scientific methodology—the mode of inquiry—which characterizes anthroposophy should not be confused with the published results of Rudolf Steiner's personal research which, while arguably embracing "ultimate" questions, were never intended to be anything but a presentation of his findings for anyone interested in testing them.[6]

---

[6] It is easy to understand Steiner's extreme reluctance to have his lectures recorded; and it is easier still to realise why, in his lectures and books, he kept on repeating, almost to exasperation, such phrases as "what is contained in", "what is reflected by", and so forth -- if we only recollect that, of all men, he spoke from the Consciousness Soul to the Consciousness Soul. 'Think these thoughts without believing them", he once said; and in nearly all his utterances he employed the mode, not of discursive argument, but of pure assertion -- though he could syllogise as well as anyone if he chose to, as he showed in *The Philosophy of Freedom*. And this reluctance, and these phrases and habits of his, and the essential nature of anthroposophy, place -- so it seems to me -- rather a heavy responsibility upon its adherents. I cannot think it is unduly paradoxical to say that it is really a kind of betrayal of the founder of anthroposophy to believe what he said. He poured out his assertions because he trusted his hearers *not* to believe. Belief is something which can only be applied to systems of abstract ideas. To become an anthroposophist is not to believe, it is to decide to use the words of Rudolf Steiner (and any others which may become available) for the purpose of raising oneself, if possible, to a kind of thinking which is itself beyond words, which *precedes* them, in the sense that ideas, words, sentences, propositions, are only subsequently *drawn out of it*. This is that concrete* thinking which is the *source* of all such ideas and propositions, the source of all meaning whatsoever. And it can only take the form of logical ideas and propositions and grammatical sentences, at the expense of much of its original truth. For to be logical is to make one little part of your meaning precise by excluding all the other parts. To be an anthroposophist, then, is to seek to unite oneself, not with any groups of words, but with this concrete thinking, whose existence can only be finally *proved* by experience.

Owen Barfield, Romanticism Comes of Age, 76-77 (Wesleyan University Press, 1967)

*The word 'concrete' may here be taken as meaning 'neither objective nor subjective'.

They are certainly not "binding" for members of the Anthroposophical Society. Anthroposophy does not authoritatively address the fundamental questions comprising the first test of <u>Malnak II</u>.

Without question, Anthroposophy does not meet the second <u>Malnak</u> test for religion under the Establishment Clause. It is manifestly not a "belief-system" of any kind. Rudolf Steiner could not have said so more emphatically. The Statutes of the Society make it crystal clear. The Society admits members of totally different religions and belief-systems. On January 11, 1916 in Liesal, near Basel in Switzerland, Rudolf Steiner said the following:

> Now it is often asked how spiritual science or anthroposophy stands in relation to the religious life of man. By reason of the whole character of anthroposophy, it will not intervene in any religious creed, in the sphere of any sort of religious life. Spiritual Science never can entertain the wish to create a religion... One cannot, therefore, call spiritual science, as such, a religious faith. It neither aims at creating a religious faith nor in any way at changing a person in relation to his religious beliefs. In spite of this, it seems as if people were worrying themselves about the religion of the Anthroposophists. In truth, however, it is not possible to speak in this way, because, within the Anthroposophical Society, every kind of religion is represented, and there is nothing to prevent anyone from practicing his religious faith as fully, comprehensively, and intensively as he wishes.

Rudolf Steiner, "The Mission of Spiritual Science and of Its Building at Dornach," <u>Approaches to Anthroposophy</u> (lecture of 11 January 1916), pp. 18-19 (Rudolf Steiner Press, 1992). Also quoted in: Günther Wachsmuth, <u>The Life and Work of Rudolf Steiner</u>, pp. 100-101 (Whittier Books, Inc., 1955).

Still later, Steiner was emphatic that anthroposophy was not only <u>not</u> a religion, but that it should have no sectarian tendencies whatsoever. He stated:

> It is a perversion of the truth to ascribe sectarian tendencies to Anthroposophy, for it certainly has no such intentions. It is a perversion of the truth to believe that it wants to be a new religious foundation. It does not want to do any such thing.

Steiner, <u>The Fruits of Anthroposophy</u>, 70 (Anthroposophic Press, 1986).

> [Anthroposophy] does not consider itself a new religious confession; it is as far away as possible from the founding of a religion or the development of a sect of

any kind. It wishes to be a true and proper continuation of the natural scientific way of thinking...

Rudolf Steiner, p. 7, <u>Spiritual Science: A Brief Review of Its Aims and of the Attacks of Its Opponents</u> (London: John M. Watkins, 1914).

Nor does the third <u>Malnak</u> factor apply to anthroposophy. The Society is not characterized by the formal and external signs of religion. The Society has no priests. It has no formal services. It offers no sacraments. It prescribes no practices. Anthroposophy does not claim to lead to "salvation." The Anthroposophical Society is not organized as a church and it accepts and honors the most wholly diverse faiths of its members, as is outlined in the Statutes:

Anyone can become a member, <u>without regard to</u> nationality, social standing, religion, or scientific or artistic conviction...

<u>The Statutes of the Anthroposophical Society #4</u> (emphasis added).

For the preceding reasons, anthroposophy, even if it were subject to judicial definition, is not a "religion" under the operative Establishment Clause tests.

CONCLUSION

As early as April 11, 2001, the Court asked "[w]hether Anthroposophy is a system of belief and worship of a superhuman controlling power under a code of ethics and philosophy requiring obedience thereto." April 11, 2001 Tr. 4, 5 to 7. Based upon the above facts and arguments, it is respectfully submitted that the question should be answered in the negative.

Respectfully submitted,

_____
Katherine L. Thivierge
Attorney for Amicus Curiae
   The Anthroposophical Society in America
P.O. Box 1547
Southgate, MI 48195
(734) 558-4909

_____
Fred Dennehy
Attorney for Amicus Curiae
   The Anthroposophical Society in America
Wilentz, Goldman & Spitzer
90 Woodbridge Center Drive
Woodbridge, NJ 07095
(732) 855-6158

Dated: July 13, 2004.